CABLE GUYS

Cable Guys

Television and Masculinities in the Twenty-First Century

Amanda D. Lotz

NEW YORK UNIVERSITY PRESS

New York and London

NEW YORK UNIVERSITY PRESS
New York and London
www.nyupress.org

References to Internet websites (URLs) were accurate at the time of writing.
Neither the author nor New York University Press is responsible for URLs that
may have expired or changed since the manuscript was prepared.

Library of Congress Cataloging-in-Publication Data
Lotz, Amanda D., 1974-
Cable guys : television and masculinities in the 21st century / Amanda D. Lotz.
p. cm.
Includes bibliographical references and index.
ISBN 978-1-4798-0074-2 (hardback) -- ISBN 978-1-4798-0048-3 (paper)
1. Masculinity on television. 2. Men on television. 3. Cable television--Social aspects--United
States. 4. Television broadcasting--Social aspects--United States. I. Title.
PN1992.8.M38L68   2014
791.45'65211--dc23   2013042414

New York University Press books are printed on acid-free paper, and their binding materials
are chosen for strength and durability. We strive to use environmentally responsible
suppliers and materials to the greatest extent possible in publishing our books.

Manufactured in the United States of America

10 9 8 7 6 5 4 3 2 1

Also available as an ebook

To Robert, Nick, Wes, and Sayre, who have taught me much and offered even more to think about.

In solidarity with the men, particularly those of my generation, who have discarded the patriarchal legacies they were offered. Though your struggles are rarely acknowledged, they are an important contribution to changing gender norms for all.

CONTENTS

ACKNOWLEDGMENTS

By some measures, I've been writing this book for nearly a decade, as I've known for at least that long that I wanted to make some sense of the changing stories about men offered by contemporary television. Discovering the form, organization, and arguments that became this book was a long and sometimes frustrating process. I'm deeply satisfied by the form it has finally taken and am tremendously thankful to the many who have helped it find its way.

An array of undergraduate and graduate students helped track down information, pinpointed relevant episodes of long-running series, and aided in a variety of often unglamorous tasks such as fact checking, bibliography proofing, and indexing. Many thanks to Jimmy Draper, Jennifer Fogel, Kitior Ngu, Elliot Panek, Amanda Turner, Loren Fanroy, and McKinley Owens for their detailed work and contributions and to the University of Michigan Undergraduate Research Opportunity Program and Department of Communication Studies Pohs Fund for helping me remunerate them. I offer gratitude as well to my fine colleagues in the University of Michigan Department of Communication Studies. Many sat through multiple colloquium iterations of this work as I tried to find my central arguments and offered helpful suggestions and questions that led me to yet new considerations.

Special thanks to Kelly Kessler and Brenda Weber, who read early drafts and offered suggestions and encouragement useful in shoring up the foundation of the book. Thanks as well to Anna Froula and David Greven, who, along with Brenda, shared SCMS and ASA conference panels on masculinity, as well as ideas and discussion. This work would also have been impossible without the resources of the Donald Hall Collection in the Department of Screen Arts and Cultures, led by the extraordinary Phil Hallman.

I also appreciate several audiences that engaged the work in a variety of preliminary forms and those who invited me to offer the talks. The opportunity to speak one's work and face questions always opens up new ways of thinking. My thanks to audiences at the University of Kansas (Bärbel Göbel), Muhlenberg University (Jeff Pooley), the University of Wisconsin-Madison (Jonathan Gray), DePauw University (Jonathan Nichols-Pethick), the University of Copenhagen (Eva Novrup Redvall), and Tallinn University Baltic Film and Media School (Hagi Šein).

I owe a great debt and offer deep gratitude to Ron Becker, who read the first proposal for this project in 2009 and offered engaged and challenging criticism that sent me back to reconceive the project. His reviews and feedback throughout the process offered engaged comment and needed critique and exemplify the ideal possibilities of scholarly review. Thanks as well to editorial assistants Ciara McLaughlin and Alicia Nadkarni and the team at NYU Press for a top-rate author experience. Special thanks to editor Eric Zinner for his patience as I worked to find my voice in a new area and especially for the encouragement to "roar" once I found my place in the conversation. My thanks as well to my intellectual compatriot Sharon Ross, who always manages to know when her intervention is needed. Her generous listening and encouragement came at just the right time and continue to echo in my head in moments of uncertainty.

Last, but never least important, is Wes, the partner who helps me juggle the balls—at least this project required watching shows you found more interesting. You make it easy to forget about the persistence of patriarchal masculinity. And thanks to Calla and Sayre for their patience and for giving me entirely new lenses through which to consider gender.

Introduction

Depending on what channel you tuned to on a Monday night in January 2010, US television offered very different versions of masculinity. Broadcast stalwart CBS alone provided a menagerie of contradictions. Its prime-time program lineup began with *How I Met Your Mother* (2005–2014), a comedy that depicted six urban professionals negotiating their twenties' transition from college to marriage and family life—the 2000s take on *Friends*. The series offered a solid ensemble of characters, but Neil Patrick Harris, in the role of Barney Stinson, often stole the show. Barney was renowned for his sexual conquests and love of finely tailored suits, but was more a caricature of a suave and debonair ladies' man than a sincere manifestation. The series contrasted Barney with male friends Ted (Josh Radnor)—who narrated the series, telling his children the ongoing story of his search for his wife—and Marshall (Jason Segal), the contentedly coupled man of the group. Harris's over-the-top depiction of Stinson was imbued with added contradictory meaning given the audience's probable extratextual knowledge of Harris as an out gay man, and the series' storylines and laugh-track organization made clear that Barney's masculinity was not to be emulated or idealized. Rare moments exposed Barney's playboy masculinity as performance to the audience, although his surface identity was rarely revealed as false to his friends. This allowed Barney to operate as a mechanism for voicing an embodiment of masculinity that the series often mocked; Barney's promiscuity, objectification of women, and performance of a masculinity unreformed by feminism was laughed at in comparison with Ted's and Marshall's pursuits of heterosexual partnership and respectful treatment of women.

But at 9:00 on that Monday night in 2010, CBS offered a very different gender script. The extremely popular *Two and a Half Men* (2003–)

depicted two brothers raising their son/nephew. At the time, Charlie Sheen dominated this top-rated series in the role of Charlie Harper, a quintessential playboy made rich from his success writing advertising jingles. Charlie lived alone in a plush Malibu beach house until his nebbish brother, Alan (Jon Cryer), and nephew, Jake (Angus T. Jones), move in after Alan and his wife divorce. Hilarity ensues as Charlie offers the wrong life lessons to Jake, despite the fact that the show decidedly supports Charlie's skirt-chasing masculinity over Alan's caricatured depiction as effeminate, with many jokes being based on the suggestion that Alan is gay. Charlie's portrayal too was imbued with extratextual meaning even in 2010—a year before Sheen's public meltdown and firing from the show—as a result of his notoriety before the series as an alleged patron of Hollywood madam Heidi Fleiss, publicly acrimonious divorce from actress Denise Richards, and arrests for domestic abuse, substance abuse, and other bad acts involving drugs and prostitutes. Unlike in *How I Met Your Mother*, Charlie's womanizing and the other boorish characteristics of patriarchal masculinity he displays are never revealed as performance, and the text commonly sides with Charlie to support, rather than critique, his masculinity. Despite similar characterizations, *How I Met Your Mother* and *Two and a Half Men* offered very different assessments of the twenty-first-century cad.[1]

The study in contrasting masculinities offered on CBS was then followed by *The Big Bang Theory* (2007–), a comedy from the same creative team behind *Two and a Half Men* that lampoons the social awkwardness of four geeky but brilliant young PhD physicists and the attractive, blonde aspiring actress who lives next door. The four men all embody the same science-nerd masculinity, and most of the series' humor is based on laughing at them. The series does not feature a contrasting masculinity—as exists between Charlie and Alan—which encourages audiences to view the characters less as caricatured outsiders than as men performing masculinities particular to their subculture.

The contradictory comedies of CBS were far from the only stories on offer in 2010. Opposite *How I Met Your Mother*, FOX aired the medical drama *House, MD* (2004–12), built around the spectacular diagnostic skills of its damaged and eponymous lead. Dr. Gregory House was too complicated to be a traditional leading man. Tortured, both physically and psychically, he was not a man to identify with, nor was he offered as a desirable partner. His diagnostic skills may have positioned him as a hero, but his inability to relate with people and tendency even to show cruelty toward suffering patients made him seem a misanthrope. Season after season chronicled the mind games and abuse he heaped on coworkers and friends; and though some kernel of care may have lain at his core, unless a character was dying of a rare and mysterious disease, a relationship with House always seemed far more trouble than it was worth.

The 9:00 hour then offered the contrasts of two modern hero narratives, FOX's 24 (2001–10) and NBC's *Heroes* (2006–10). The eight seasons of 24 elevated Jack Bauer to the status of a worldwide cultural icon, known even to those who never watched the series.[2] The long-suffering of Bauer as an agent of the US Counter Terrorism Unit (CTU) who sacrifices all aspects of his personal life in service to country might be viewed as the progeny of the 1980s action film hero, as his capacity for suffering and improbable endurance readily recalled Bruce Willis's John McClane from the *Die Hard* franchises. Yet although Bauer consistently and improbably prevailed, he was a reluctant and put-upon hero who lacked the bravado and much of the swagger—although not the self-assuredness—of blockbuster heroes past. Bauer was not depicted as emotionally removed and could be overcome and tearful in response to the situations he endured and their consequences for others. Despite right-wing pundits' hero worship of Bauer, others argued that each act of torture made him less heroic, a reading affirmed by the series conclusion, in which Bauer was expelled from the country as a nonromanticized outlaw.[3]

Summarizing *Heroes'* take on masculinity is made impossible by its broad ensemble cast that unpredictably shifted sides and drew heavily from a comic book aesthetic with epic tales of good and evil. At a minimum—and consistent with its 2010 lead-in, *Chuck*—the series deviated from the notion of the exceptionalism of unerring heroes such as Superman in its original construction of characters who were "ordinary" people who came to know they had powers. The male characters of *Heroes* and 24 were thus afforded the most improbable opportunities to save the world, consistent with patriarchal, savior masculinities common to the most popular versions of superheroes.

A final entry of note to the Monday night schedule had just debuted, TNT's *Men of a Certain Age* (2009–11), which starred Ray Romano as one of three friends facing middle age. As was the case with his long-running, popular domestic situation comedy, *Everybody Loves Raymond* (1996–2005), Romano co-created this series, which explored the anxieties of three men who had been friends since childhood as they realized that the life ahead of them was fleeting and struggled with the outcome of the way they had handled their lives. Here, perhaps owing largely to the age of the characters, audiences were offered men who lacked the certitude that the world was their idiomatic oyster. The three friends didn't yet know what they wanted from life, and most certainly didn't know how to achieve it.

Of course, hundreds of other shows were also available on television in these few hours on this one night, yet few others offered original scripted narratives. With a flip of the channel to cable's USA, audiences could find *WWE Monday RAW Wrestling*, while male-targeted Spike offered its mixed-martial-arts series *UFC Unleashed*, and ESPN scheduled the more traditional sports programming of college basketball. On one level these sports contests provided little deviation from the depictions of masculinity characteristic of sports television, which for the previous sixty years had emphasized men's physical prowess and the importance of winning. However, by the early 2000s, I suspect close analysis of the narratives and storylines imposed on the contests through commentary and promotion might reveal that a broader range of priorities and concerns for the male athletes is emerging and becoming part of common sports discourse.

Certainly by 2010, it was archaic to think only of what was "on" television at a particular hour. DVRs were nearing a reach of 50 percent of the population and allowed easy reordering and rescheduling of viewing, while computers and mobile screen devices enabled selective downloading and streaming of programs, films, and amateur videos that further multiplied the possible masculinities "television" offered. And were I to consider other nights or other hours of the day, I could easily fill this book with yet other cursory summaries of the men and masculinities produced for the television screen.

The point is that an arbitrarily chosen Monday night in January 2010 offers only a chance and partial snapshot to illustrate the range of stories about men and embodiments of masculinity available on television, and few of these stories about men introduced thus far even receive further mention here. At the beginning of the twenty-first century, it was impossible to assert any singular argument about "men on television"—and in truth, television had always offered a range of men and masculinities. Even in the 1950s era of fathers who knew best and assorted cowboys and lawmen, the breadth of television's fictional offerings made it difficult to sustain any general claim about its male characters—to say nothing of the real men, such as news anchors, sports figures, and politicians, who also figure prominently in television programming.

Of the vast range of foci a book about men and television could offer, *Cable Guys: Television and Masculinities in the Twenty-First Century* explores the stories told about men in a multiplicity of scripted series—nearly exclusively on cable—that delved into the psyches and inner lives of their male characters. These series depict male characters' feelings and relationships in stories that probe the trials and complexities of contemporary manhood in a manner previously uncommon—if not entirely lacking—for this storytelling medium. *Cable Guys* consequently explores emergent and varied depictions of men—particularly of straight white men—negotiating contemporary gender roles and embodiments of masculinity in their one-on-one friendships with other men in *Boston Legal, Scrubs, Psych,* and *Nip/Tuck*; in the homosocial enclave of the male group as depicted in *Entourage, Rescue Me, The League,* and *Men of a Certain Age*; and the struggle to know how to and to be "a man" in series that address the whole life of male characters— what I term "male-centered serials"—such as *The Sopranos, The Shield, Californication, Rescue Me, Breaking Bad, Hung, Dexter, Sons of Anarchy,* and *Men of a Certain Age*. This book's analysis seeks to understand an array of questions about the construction of masculinity in these shows, including the following: What characteristics do these series that meditate on the contemporary condition of being a man attribute to "good" men? What is at stake in storytelling that reveals men to be unsatisfied with and uncertain about contemporary life? How might same-sex friendships and intimacy with other men now be subtly, but meaningfully, supported in popular television? Why does misogynistic and homophobic talk dominate depictions of men's interactions in all-male spaces that are simultaneously clearly changed by feminism? And generally, how might audiences make sense of emergent gender dynamics relative to the contradictions of a cultural medium that remains full of characters that offer up old patriarchal norms? *Cable Guys* contextualizes this analysis amidst a matrix of broader narrative trends, industrial shifts, and social and cultural adjustments that enable the particular storytelling of these series.

Despite the intentionality that might be signaled by its title, this book is not deliberately focused on cable series. I did not choose early-twenty-first-century original cable series as my object of analysis and then endeavor to analyze the negotiation of masculinity evident in such series. Rather, the origins of the project date to the early 2000s as my casual viewing of such cable series as *The Shield, Rescue Me,* and *Nip/Tuck,* as well as the network series *Boston Legal* and *Scrubs,* left me with a sense that there was "something going on" with the male characters and depictions of masculinity across the series. These shows were followed by several more that also seemed to speak explicitly to the condition of contemporary men, and, after nearly a decade of contemplation, this book identifies connections and disjunctures among the characterizations and narrative tropes and analyzes why they emerge and what challenges contemporary male characters face.

When I began to organize the series that most explicitly and deeply attended to male characters' struggles with identity, I found they nearly exclusively appeared on cable channels. As I address further in chapter 1, the institutional specificity of cable is important to explaining why so many series with conflicted, morally ambiguous male characters emerged. Cable channels are funded by both commercial advertising dollars and viewer subscription payments that enable narrowcasting strategies such as developing unconventional protagonists and exploring ideas somewhat outside the mainstream. Although I examine such industrial factors in chapter 1, this book is foremost about the stories and characters US television offered about men struggling to find their place in the early twenty-first century, not television's varied industrial contexts. Chapters 2 and 3 explore the male-centered serial, which, to date, is a form that has only succeeded on cable. Chapter 4 assesses male characters' interactions in the homosocial enclave—a narrative context that also, to date, can only be found in cable series. Chapter 5 examines the depiction of male friendship, and in this case, two of the most significant depictions of the intimacy and relationship maintenance characteristic of such friendships originated from broadcast networks. This chapter consequently bridges broadcast and cable storytelling because the topical focus demands it. Other chapters would have considered broadcast shows as well if similar exemplars existed. There are many other books one could write about men on television in the early twenty-first century; the framing provided by my title and the particular acknowledgment of the preponderance of cable channels as the originators of these series are meant to specify that by several measures, this book is more precisely about "cable" than "television" broadly.

What Do We Know about Men on Television?

It is revealing that so little has been written about men on television. Men have embodied such an undeniable presence and composed a significant percentage of the actors upon the small screen—be they real or fictional—since the dawn of this central cultural medium and yet rarely have been considered as a particularly gendered group. In some ways a parallel exists with the situation of men in history that Michael Kimmel notes in his cultural history, *Manhood in America*.[4] Kimmel opens his book by noting that "American men have no history" because although the dominant and widely known version of American history is full of men, it never considers the key figures *as men*.[5] Similarly to Kimmel's assertion, then, we can claim that we have no history of men, masculinity, and manhood on television—or at best, a very limited one—despite the fact that male characters have been central in all aspects of the sixty-some years of US television history. It is the peculiar situation that nearly all assessments of gender and television have examined the place and nature of women, femininity, and feminism on television while we have no typologies of archetypes or thematic analyses of stories about men or masculinities.

For much of television studies' brief history, this attention to women made considerable sense given prevailing frameworks for understanding the significance of gender representation in the media. Analyses of women on television largely emerged out of concern about women's historical absence in central roles and the lack of diversity in their portrayals. Exhaustive surveys of characters revealed that women were underrepresented on television relative to their composition of the general populace and that those onscreen tended to be relegated to roles as wives, love interests, or sex objects.[6] In many cases, this analysis was linked with the feminist project of illustrating how television contributed to the social construction of beliefs about gender roles and abilities, and given the considerable gender-based inequity onscreen and off, attention to the situation of men seemed less pressing. As a result, far less research has considered representations of men on television and the norms or changes in the stories the medium has told about being a man.

Transitioning the frameworks used for analyzing women on television is not as simple as changing the focus of which characters or series one examines. Analyzing men and masculinity also requires a different theoretical framework, as the task of the analysis is not a matter of identifying underrepresentation or problematic stereotypes in the manner that has dominated considerations of female characters. The historic diversity of stories about and depictions of straight white men has seemed to prevent the development of "stereotypes" that have plagued depictions of women and has lessened the perceived need to interrogate straight white men's depictions and the stories predominantly told about their lives.[7] Any single story about a straight white man has seemed insignificant relative to the many others circulating simultaneously, so no one worried that the populace would begin to assume all men were babbling incompetents when Darrin bumbled through episodes of *Bewitched*, that all men were bigoted louts because of Archie Bunker, or even that all men were conflicted yet homicidal thugs in the wake of Tony Soprano. Further, given men's dominance in society, concern about their representation lacked the activist motivation compelling the study of women that tied women's subordinated place in society to the way they appeared—or didn't appear—in popular media.

So why explore men now? First, it was arguably shortsighted to ignore analysis of men and changing patterns in the dominant masculinities offered by television to the degree that has occurred. Images of and stories about straight white men have been just as important in fostering perceptions of gender roles, but they have done their work by prioritizing some attributes of masculinity—supported some ways of being a man—more than others. Although men's roles might not have been limited to the narrow opportunities available to women for much of television history, characteristics consistent with a preferred masculinity have pervaded—always specific to the era of production—that might generally be described as the attributes consistent with what is meant when a male is told to "be a man." In the past, traits such as the stoicism and controlled emotionality of not being moved to tears, of proving oneself capable of physical feats, and of aggressive leadership in the workplace and home have been common. Men's roles have been more varied than women's, but television storytelling has nevertheless performed significant ideological work by consistently supporting some behaviors, traits, and beliefs among the male characters it constructs as heroic or admirable, while denigrating others. So although television series may have displayed a range of men and masculinities, they also circumscribed a "preferred" or "best" masculinity through attributes that were consistently idealized.

The lack of comprehensive attention to men in any era of television's sixty-some-year history makes the task of beginning difficult because there are so few historical benchmarks or established histories or typologies against which newer developments can be gauged. Perhaps few have considered the history of male portrayal because so many characteristics seemed unexceptional due to their consistency with expectations and because no activist movement has pushed a societal reexamination of men's gender identity in the manner that occurred for women as a component of second-wave feminism. Male characters performed their identity in expected ways that were perceived as "natural" and drew little attention, indicating the strength of these constructs. Indeed, television's network-era operational norms of seeking broad, heterogeneous audiences of men and women, young and old, led to representations that were fairly mundane and unlikely to shock or challenge audience expectations of gender roles.

One notable aspect of men's depictions has been the manner through which narratives have defined them primarily as workers in public spaces *or* through roles as fathers or husbands—even though most male characters have been afforded access to both spaces. A key distinction between the general characterizations of men versus women has been that shows in which men functioned primarily as fathers (*Father Knows Best, The Cosby Show*) also allowed for them to leave the domestic sphere and have professional duties that were part of their central identity—even if actually performing these duties was rarely given significant screen time. So in addition to being fathers and husbands, with few exceptions, television's men also have been workers.[8] Similarly, the performance of professional duties has primarily defined the roles of another set of male characters, as for much of television history, stories about doctors, lawyers, and detectives were necessarily stories about male doctors, lawyers, and detectives. Such shows may have noted the familial status of these men but rarely have incorporated family life or issues into storytelling in a regular or consistent manner.

This split probably occurs primarily for reasons of storytelling convention rather than any concerted effort to fragment men's identity. I belabor this point here because a gradual breakdown in this separate-spheres approach occurs in many dramatic depictions of men beginning in the 1980s and becomes common enough to characterize a subgenre by the twenty-first century. Whether allowing a male character an inner life that is revealed through first-person voice-over—as in series such as *Magnum, P.I., Dexter,* or *Hung*—or gradually connecting men's private and professional lives even when the narrative primarily depicts only one of these spheres—as in *Hill Street Blues* or *ER*—such cases in which the whole lives of men contribute to characterization can be seen as antecedents to the narratives that emphasize the multifaceted approach to male characters that occurs in the male-centered serial in the early 2000s. Though these series offer intricately drawn and complex protagonists, their narrative framing does not propose them as "role models" or as men who have figured out the challenges of contemporary life. The series and their characters provide not so much a blueprint of how to be a man in contemporary society as a constellation of case studies exposing, but not resolving, the challenges faced.

The scholarly inattention to men on television is oddly somewhat particular to the study of television. The field of film studies features a fairly extensive range of scholarship attending to changing patterns of men's portrayals and masculinities. While these accounts are fascinating, the specificity of film as a medium very different from television in its storytelling norms (a two-hour contained story as opposed to television's prevailing use of continuing characters over years of narrative), industrial characteristics (the economic model of film was built on audiences paying for a one-time engagement with the story while television relies on advertisers that seek a mass audience on an ongoing basis), and reception environment (one chooses to go out and see films as opposed to television's flow into the home) prevent these studies of men on film to tell us much about men on television. Further, gender studies and sociology have developed extensive theories of masculinity and have been more equitable in extending beyond the study of women. Although theories developed in these fields provide a crucial starting point—such as breaking open the simple binary of masculinity and femininity to provide a language of masculinities—it is the case that the world of television does not mirror the "real world" and that the tools useful for exploring how societies police gender performance aren't always the most helpful for analyzing fictional narratives. Sociological concepts about men aid assessments of men and masculinity on television, but it is clearly the case that the particularities of television's dominant cultural, industrial, and textual features require focused and specific examination.

Why *Cable Guys*?

One of the motivations that instigated my 2006 book *Redesigning Women: Television after the Network Era* was frustration with how increasingly outdated frameworks for understanding the political significance of emerging gender representations were inspiring mis-, or at least incomplete, readings of shows and characters that indicated a rupture from previous norms. Tools established to make sense of a milieu lacking central female protagonists disregarded key contextual adjustments—such as the gradual incorporation of aspects of second-wave feminism into many aspects of public and private life—and were inadequate in a society profoundly different from that of the late 1960s. For example, it seemed that some aspects of gender scripts had changed enough to make the old models outdated, or that there was something more to *Ally McBeal* than the length of her skirts, her visions of dancing babies, and her longing for lost love that had led to scorn and dismissal from those applying conventional feminist analytics. Given generational and sociohistorical transitions apparent by the mid-1990s, it seemed that this series and its stories might be trying to voice and engage with adjustments in gender politics rather than be the same old effort to contain women through domesticity and conventional femininity, as was frequently asserted.

I'm struck with a similar impulse in reflecting on how stories about men, their lives, and their relationships have become increasingly complicated in the fictional narratives of the last decade. Indeed, this evolution in depictions of male identities has not received the kind of attention levied on the arrival of the sexy, career-driven singles of *Sex and the City* and *Ally McBeal* or the physically empowered tough women of *Buffy the Vampire Slayer* or *Xena: Warrior Princess*. Assessments of men in popular culture, and particularly television, haven't been plentiful in the last decade. Most of the discussion of men on television merely acknowledges new trends in depiction—whether they be the sensitivity and everymanness of broadcast characters or the dastardly antiheroism of cable protagonists, as I detail in chapter 2. Such trend pieces have offered little deeper engagement with the cultural and industrial features contributing to these shifts or analysis of what their consequences might be for the cultures consuming them.[9]

While these curiosities might motivate any scholar, I suspect the motivations of a female feminist scholar embarking on an analysis of men and masculinity also deserve some explanation. In addition to curiosity about shifting depictions and stories on my television screen, for well over a decade I've also had the sense that "something is going on" with men of the post–Baby Boomer generation, who, like me, were born into a world already responding to the critiques and activism of second-wave feminism. Yet nothing I've read has adequately captured the perplexing negotiations I've observed. For example, on a sunny Tuesday morning just after the end of winter semester classes, I took a weekday to enjoy the arrival of spring with my toddler. We found ourselves in the sandpit at the neighborhood park, and shared it that day with two sisters—one a bit older, the other a bit younger than my nearly two-year-old son—who were being watched over by their father. He was about my age and was similarly clad in the parental uniform of exercise pants and a fleece jacket. With some curiosity I unobtrusively watched him interact with his daughters. Dads providing childcare aren't uncommon in my neighborhood—overrun as it is with academics and medical professionals with odd hours that allow for unconventional childcare arrangements—but something in his demeanor, his willingness to go all in to the tea party of sandcakes his oldest was engaging him with, grabbed my attention for its play with gender roles. It reminded me of the many male friends with whom I share a history back to our teen years who have similarly transformed into engaged and involved dads; they've seemingly eradicated much of the juvenile, but also sexist, perspectives they once presented, and also have become men very different from their fathers. Then his phone rang. Immediately, his body language and intonation shifted as he became a much more conventional "guy." Was it a brother? It was definitely another man. An entirely different performance overtook his speech and demeanor as he strolled away from the sandpit, yet, suggesting that all was not reversed, he proceeded to discuss attending a baby shower, whether he and his wife would get a sitter, and the etiquette of gift giving for second babies. When the call ended he shifted back to the self I had first observed.

Watching this made me reflect on how the gender-based complaints I might register regarding balancing work and family—such as the exhausting demands, the still-tricky negotiations of relationships that cross the working mom/stay-at-home mom divide, and the ever-ratcheting demands to be the Best Mom Ever while maintaining pre-mom employment productivity—have been well documented by others and are problems *with* a name. My male peers, in contrast, must feel out to sea with no land or comrades in sight. Esteemed gender historian Stephanie Coontz has gone so far as to propose the term and reality of a "masculine mystique" as an important component of contemporary gender issues.[10]

This wasn't the first time I'd been left thinking about the contradictory messages offered to men these days. The uncertain embodiment of contemporary manhood appears in many places. For years now I've wondered, even worried, about the men in my classes. In general, they seem to decrease in number each year, perhaps being eaten by the ball caps pulled ever lower on their foreheads. As a hopefully enlightened feminist scholar, I try to stay attuned to the gender dynamics of my classroom—but what I've commonly found was not at all what I was prepared for or expected. Consistent with the *Atlantic* cover story in the summer of 2010 that declared "The End of Men" and touted that women had become the majority of the workforce, that the majority of managers were women, and that three women earned college degrees

for every two men, the young women in my classes consistently dominate their male peers in all measures of performance—tests, papers,
class participation, attendance.[11] I haven't been able to explain why, but
it has seemed that most—although certainly not all—of the young men
have no idea why they find themselves seated in a college classroom
or what they are meant to do there. Though I must acknowledge that
despite evidence of female advancement in sectors of the academy like
mine, men still dominate in many of the most prestigious and financially well-rewarded fields, including engineering, business, and com-
puter science.

I brought my pondering about classroom gender dynamics home at
night as I negotiated the beginning of a heterosexual cohabitation in
the late 1990s and thought a lot about what it meant to become a "wife"
and eventually a "mother." There were also conversations about what it
meant to be the husband of a feminist and how being a dad has changed
since our parents started out, although the grounds for these talks were
more uncertain and role models and gender scripts seemed more lacking. Both in charting our early years of marriage and still in facing parenthood, my husband and I have often felt adrift and without models.
Although we had little to quibble with in regard to our own upbringing, neither of us was raised in households in which both parents had
full-time careers, which seemed quite a game changer and has proved
the source of our most contentious dilemmas. While a wide range of
feminist scholarship and perspectives has offered insight into the challenges of being a mom and professor, my husband and his compatriots
seem to be divining paths without a map or a trail guide. As the mother
of both a son and a daughter, I feel somewhat more prepared to help my
daughter find her way among culturally imposed gender norms than
my son; at least for her the threats and perils are known and named.

So these are some of the many occurrences, ponderings, and situations that have left me thinking about men for the last decade. Watching
night after night and television season after season, I filed stories and
images away throughout the early 2000s and began trying to sort them
out late in the decade. I struggled for a long time to make sense of this
project, to force some sort of rational ordering upon it. Men had always
been prevalent, and the possible objects of analysis only increased with
a growing array of new cable channels offering more and more shows,

which made it difficult to identify a defensible set of criteria for select-ing specific shows to analyze. This book could be about one hundred different shows, could emphasize several other themes or situations, and could explore many other aspects of men's representation. I deem the shows considered here worthy of study because of the preponder-ance of themes and topics that develop across a multiplicity of series and, in some cases, because of their deviation from past norms. I don't assert that the stories and men discussed here are more important than others; they are just the pieces of the puzzle of televised masculinity I ultimately chose to put together, and I hope others will do the same with the many left out.

In addition to the wealth of subject matter, there are several other challenging aspects to writing a book about men on television, the fore-most of which is that there are so few others. On one hand, this is a good thing—the subject is wide open; but the lack of established litera-ture added to the struggle of determining the book's scope. It wasn't just the depiction of men on television in the last decade that was ripe for analysis; I could have picked pretty much any moment in the last sixty years. I don't mean to suggest that there isn't any work on the subject. There is a wide range of very good essays, articles, and chapters, many of which take a fairly specific focus by looking at a particular show, but there is not a body of work or an established paradigm from which to easily expand.[12] *Cable Guys* may not be *the* book about men, mascu-linity, and television—if such an endeavor is even possible—but it pro-vides frameworks and analytic strategies aimed at organizing analysis and theory building in this area, which has been under-considered by television studies and gender studies alike.

Organizing *Cable Guys*

Cable Guys draws upon a theoretical approach to media that combines perspectives characteristic of communication, film, and cultural studies but is most firmly rooted in a distinctive, nascent scholarly area com-monly identified as television or media studies. The deliberately con-textualized analysis and argumentation identify broad trends in the fictional storytelling of a particular time and considers these trends as cultural discourses that importantly reflect and contribute to the norms of masculinity perceived by those who engage them. Such an approach blends insights regarding television's industrial system of production and broader cultural environment to situate its analysis of texts. It explores trends in and changing norms of storytelling about male characters and makes arguments regarding the cultural significance of those adjustments. Although gender politics and men are its topical focus, the book is about television and *televised* men. Thus, at the same time that it comments about representations of male characters, it does so with an interest in locating its analyses amidst other arguments about television, its industrial processes, and its storytelling mechanisms. It uses some insights drawn from masculinity studies but foregrounds the dynamics of television's industrial processes to such a degree that it may offer little contribution to the theorization of identity for real men in return.

The next chapter offers a more thorough introduction to the key ideas and context of this book by explaining choices of analytical boundaries and terminology. It situates the key intellectual perspectives and prepares subsequent analyses by reviewing aspects of broader sociocultural conditions, the industrial environment of the post-network-era surge in original scripted cable series, and the representational trends of gender in the 1980s and 1990s that prepare the creation and circulation of the stories considered here.

Chapters 2 and 3 function as companion chapters focused on exploring various aspects of the male-centered serial. This form emerges in the 2000s and describes the narrative organization of many of the series that probe the interior negotiations men face in embodying contemporary masculinity and gender scripts. This narrative subgenre includes programs such as *The Sopranos*, *The Shield*, and *Rescue Me* and is a storytelling form that allows a multidimensional portrayal of men by presenting the breadth of their daily existence in both public working lives and private family lives in contrast to emphasizing one or the other, as has been the tendency of television series. This story form offers unparalleled depth of characterization that is sometimes augmented with narrative techniques such as first-person voice-over to provide further insight into characters' inner lives. The appearance of male-centered serials in the early 2000s allowed the presentation of a fuller range of male experience in television storytelling and created a venue for subtly nuanced and evolving characters that added considerable complexity to any proposition about the state of men and masculinity on television. Chapter 2 explains the distinctiveness of this narrative form, the attributes of the male-centered serial, and its storytelling characteristics. It also offers a broad examination of a number of male-centered serials and explores thematic commonalities among them. Chapter 3 continues the focus on male-centered serials in a more detailed examination of the frequency with which the male protagonists of these shows attempt to solve their central problematic through illegal means and considers what this narrative trend suggests about men's anxieties regarding their status in society.

In contrast to the previous two chapters' focus on individual male protagonists, chapter 4 explores groups of men and their interactions within a homosocial enclave. The homosocial enclave does not just happen to exclude women but is a place of deliberate refuge among men who share long relationships or are united by the expediency of survival—in the case considered here, among firefighters—so that the narrative context explores a group of men intimately familiar with each other, either as friends since school days or as part of the brotherhood of the fire station. Examining the homosocial enclave presented in contemporary shows reveals how men police the boundaries of acceptable masculinities within these spaces as well as exposes their strategies for negotiating between a desire for homosocial interaction and anxiety regarding homosexual desire, particularly in relation to shifting cultural acknowledgment and acceptance of gay identity in recent decades.

Chapter 5 then moves from the fraternal environment of the firehouse or a gang of friends to portrayals of men engaging in intimate nonsexual relationships with other men. These series depict men expressing concerns and anxieties and otherwise baring themselves in intimate friendships. The narratives of many of the series considered here emphasize telling a story about a dyadic friendship even if the broader narrative focuses on episodic legal, medical, or detective plots to provide something for the characters to relate through. Analysis in this chapter explores how these series use a variety of narrative techniques to diffuse the potential gay panic created by the intimacy of the friendships, and how in some cases, dyadic hetero intimacy disrupts heteronomativity.

In his 2012 updated edition of *Manhood in America*, Kimmel, who typically downplays assertions of "male crisis," writes of "Masculinity in the Age of Obama" that "[t]he very foundations on which masculinity has historically rested have eroded; the entire edifice seems capable of collapse at any moment."[13] The foundation of masculinities in American culture has largely been patriarchy, a system of privilege that has long advantaged men, and certain types of men specifically. Much like the culture-at-large that has been negotiating between that patriarchal past and the challenges introduced by feminism, the series, stories, and characters considered here have not announced themselves as warriors in a revolution for the future of manhood. Most have appeared on television screens with little fanfare in series ostensibly about many other things than what it is to be a straight white man in twenty-first-century America. These series have nevertheless offered extensive deliberation on this subject, alongside their tales of outlaw motorcycle clubs, firefighting, meth making, and plastic surgery.

1

Understanding Men on Television

There is no easy starting place for assessing men and masculinity on US television at the beginning of the twenty-first century. The past of this object of analysis is too expansive for simple summary and the limited existing research is too brief and haphazard to build a comprehensive picture of even general typologies from secondary sources. Although men were the central characters and figures in both fictional and news programming for much of the medium's history, it was not until gender issues became a central part of social deliberations and the roles of men began adjusting in response to various "new women" in the 1970s that much attention was paid to men as "men on television."

This study is delimited in a number of ways that require clarification and explanation, as the construction of topical and thematic boundaries and choices of exclusion are deliberate and always meaningful. The first delimitation is one of chronology, described most simply here as the beginning of the twenty-first century. As the following discussion explores, that era was characterized primarily by the emergence of television storytelling that began—technically in the late 1990s—to offer up conflicted and complicated male protagonists struggling in some way with the issue of how to be a man at this time. But two related concepts require further explanation beyond the chronological distinction of the twenty-first century. These series were part of a specific cultural milieu, but as I make clear, it is sociocultural events that began some thirty years prior that provide the particularly salient aspects of this milieu and require the extended explanation of "post-second-wave" as a descriptor of the sociocultural context most relevant here. The industrial context of US television in the twenty-first century is also crucial to grounding the institutional dynamics specific to cable relative to the long history of broadcast television at this particular time.

Another delimitation involves explaining the key theoretical terms and understandings guiding my analysis. Dismantling the binary opposition of feminine and masculine in order to create a language that speaks of various masculinities has been one of the great advances of gender theory in the last quarter-century. The somewhat endless possible modifiers for masculinities that result, however, require exceptional deliberation and precision in establishing key terms, especially when many lack shared use. My insistence upon speaking of "hegemonic masculinity" as *specific to each series* rather than consistent across texts or within US culture requires explanation, which is offered amidst a brief summary of the theoretical tradition of hegemonic masculinity in gender studies and media scholarship. I also locate my critical foundations and enumerate other key vocabulary in this subsection. I do use the term "patriarchal masculinities" in the first subsection; for now, this term should be understood as referring to behaviors or attributes that reinforce men's dominant gender status in the culture.

Finally, I briefly establish the relevant television storytelling context for the series discussed here through an exploration of the aspects of television masculinity most common in the era immediately preceding this study. Scholarship about men and masculinity on television from the 1980s through the 2000s frequently attended to a gender construct termed the "new man" that arguably represented a preliminary phase of post-second-wave negotiation of masculinity on television. Many of the men and their struggles with masculinity examined in this book extend the project of the new man's challenge to patriarchal norms by illustrating a next stage of negotiation between patriarchy and feminism in the construction of culturally sanctioned masculinities. The male characters of the 1980s and 1990s bore the imprint of a patriarchal culture in the initial throes of incorporating feminism into its structuring cultural ideology, while the series and masculinities considered here indicate more extensive—although far from complete—effects of feminism.

The expanded influence of feminism can be seen most notably in the differences between what the narratives blame for men's struggles in different historical contexts. Though some may presume that the depiction of contentious lives and identity crises for straight white men illustrates a response to lost privilege and an endeavor to reclaim it, the analysis that follows indicates a far more complicated construction of the causes of these men's problems.[1] Although the protagonists in the male-centered serial appear perpetually flummoxed about how to be "men" in contemporary society, they do not blame, contest, or indict the feminist endeavors that created the changes in norms that lead to their uncertainty. In moments when frustration and anger with their circumstances become explicit, they most commonly blame their fathers—those who embody patriarchy—for leaving an unsustainable legacy. Like the new men who preceded them, the male characters considered here embody masculinities increasingly influenced by feminist ideals regardless of whether they are protagonists in the male-centered serials, those shown interacting in homosocial enclaves, or those depicted sharing intimate heterosexual friendships. The consistency with which the series show characters struggling over particular aspects of masculinity—as well as the aspects of patriarchal masculinities not indicted or struggled over—informs assessments of the state of cultural discourses that construct socially preferred masculinities at this time.

Why the Beginning of the Twenty-First Century?

The negotiation of emergent masculinities apparent in cable drama in the early 2000s cannot be clearly traced to a single cause but can be linked to a confluence of industrial, sociocultural, and textual forces explored below. Perplexingly, it is not the case that something in particular happens at the transition to the twenty-first century—there is no catalytic moment or event—but rather, gradual adjustments in all of these areas over the preceding decades contribute to creating a context in the early twenty-first century in which contestation of aspects of patriarchal masculinity and uncertainty about culturally preferred masculinities occurs. Journalists increasingly attended to evidence of shifting gender norms in US society throughout the early 2000s so that the depiction of fictional characters considered here existed alongside sometimes anxious discourse about men and male gender roles on the covers of popular books and newsstand fare. The *Atlantic*'s Hanna Rosin claimed the "End of Men" in a widely discussed cover story that she expanded into a like-titled book published in September 2012, while a *Newsweek* cover story, a book, a television show, and an advertising campaign featured titles demanding that American men "Man Up."[2]

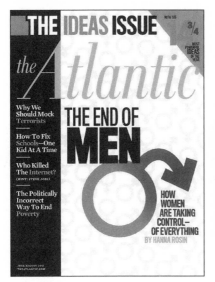
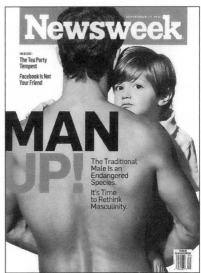

Figures 1.1 and 1.2. Popular journalism addressing and constructing anxiety about mid-2000s masculinities.

Though much of this attention could be dismissed as merely the latest instance of the perennial concern about men's roles that emerges whenever some deviation from patriarchal masculinities arises and that is often described as evidence of "men in crisis," there were also hints of sociocultural changes in men's roles that suggested something more than a superficial phenomenon at stake.

Speculation on gender crisis often exists as a pendulum within popular culture, swinging back and forth with considerable regularity, and, as these cases suggest, the focus was on men in the early twenty-first century. Even public intellectuals such as esteemed gender historian Michael Kimmel explored the consequences of pressure to be a "guy" in *Guyland: The Perilous World Where Boys Become Men*, while Leonard Sax, who studies gender differences in the brain, published *Boys Adrift*, both in 2009.[3] Each offers a social-scientific perspective—of a sociologist and psychiatrist, respectively—on concerns about the situation among young, mostly white, and otherwise privileged men in books aimed at a popular audience. Their framing of the situation in terms of "panic" seemed meant to incite the moral concern optimal for book sales, and each attends most superficially to media while neither considers television at all. In *Manning Up: How the Rise of Women Has Turned Men into Boys*, Kay Hymowitz explores the phenomenon of the Millennial generation extending adolescence through their twenties, though despite the title, it seems more a distinctly classed generational phenomenon than a gender crisis.[4] Sociologist Eric Klinenberg's more recent study of the rise of single living in *Going Solo: The Extraordinary Rise and Surprising Appeal of Living Alone* explores the changing life patterns and living arrangements of young and older Americans without the alarmist agenda and offers much more extensive context for the phenomenon Kimmel and Hymowitz identify.[5]

Rather than relying on casual evidence of a new male crisis characteristic of journalistic and "academic-lite" assessments of changing gender scripts, I locate the origins of the complicated negotiations of masculinities and manhood in the series considered here in second-wave feminism and its outcomes. I very deliberately do not use the frame of "postfeminism"—a term I now find too fraught with contradictory meanings to be useful—and also dismiss the assertion that these gender relations are characteristic of "third-wave feminism."[6] The challenge to patriarchal masculinities evident in many aspects of the series is more clearly an outcome of second-wave activism—albeit long in fruition—than a result of more nascent feminist generations or their endeavors, which makes "post-second-wave" my preferred terminology.

Why "Post-Second-Wave" Masculinities?

Changes in gender relations occurring in the late twentieth century—particularly those related to securing equal opportunity of access to public realms such as education and employment—are typically considered as an outcome of feminism and as gains in the rights of women. However, the changed social and cultural spheres wrought by second-wave feminism have had enormous, if under-considered, implications for men as well. Too often, simplistic journalistic assessments of gender politics—particularly those of conservative punditry—suggest that the gains feminism has delivered for women correlate with lost rights or freedoms for men.[7] But social justice is hardly a zero-sum condition, and the revised gender scripts that have been produced by second-wave feminism, the gay rights movement, and related adjustments in cultural norms—such as economic shifts eliminating the "family wage" for men and necessitating two-income households to achieve middle-class status—have introduced complicated changes in the gender scripts available to men as well. Understanding why particular masculinities emerge in early 2000s cable series—some of which openly contest many aspects of patriarchal masculinities—requires assessing these series in relation to the sociopolitical changes of the last twenty-five to thirty-five years. I identify this time span as "post-second-wave" for a variety of reasons, but acknowledge some apprehension about this identifier.[8]

As it is used here, "post-second-wave" encompasses both the explicit activist endeavors that began affording women greater rights and the way that activism became constitutive of the social milieu that acculturated American men and women born after the late 1960s. It is not strictly a chronological marker, intended to suggest "a time after" the era of midcentury feminist activism known as the "second wave" in the United States, a period commonly identified as roughly the late 1960s through the 1982 failure of the Equal Rights Amendment. Rather, I use "post-second-wave" as a more conceptual designation to acknowledge the accomplishments of second-wave feminism in significantly adjusting dominant ideology and gender scripts. Indeed, much evidence of activist gains required a quarter of a century to come to fruition and appeared only after a period of retrenchment widely referred to as "backlash": a term Susan Faludi used to identify a prevalent theme in popular media in the 1980s and early 1990s through which women's problems were consistently presented as created by second-wave feminism's efforts toward women's liberation.[9]

The contestation of patriarchal masculinities I consider owes far more to the activist work and consciousness raising begun during second-wave feminism than to anything else. Policy changes providing greater equality of opportunity for women in the workforce may have been enacted in the 1970s, but the wide-ranging and deep adjustments in cultural formations and gender scripts that they enabled required significant time to manifest. The benefits of these adjustments were first substantially enjoyed by women, who—like me—were children at that time, and who, along with male peers, grew up with contested gender politics but also a nascent gender order fundamentally different from that of our mothers and fathers. Consequently, it requires decades to really observe the social transformation of professional ranks and corresponding shifts in families and dominant social scripts for women and men, and similarly as long to observe changes in cultural forms.[10]

To be clear, in acknowledging the success of second-wave feminism, I do not mean to suggest that it ended patriarchy or that feminism's work is now done. Much evidence makes clear that Western societies remain characterized by patriarchal dominance, but it is also evident that the work of second-wave feminists notably and significantly changed these societies, in particular, by opening many public spaces to women and adjusting prevailing notions of their roles. Though using the modifier "post-second-wave" to distinguish the emergent masculinities explored here may suggest more exclusively causal importance of the second-wave women's movement than I really intend, no other term offers more precise identification, and the explicit link to feminism is significant to the perspective of the project.[11]

Gender scholars or cultural historians have yet to name or identify a shared term for describing gender politics and relations after the period of "backlash," yet an important transition in the central fault lines of gender politics and dominant cultural debates occurred near the end of the century. The nexus of increased attention to international policy in the wake of the 2001 terrorist attacks and the subsequent "Great Recession" shifted the US political focus and inadvertently revised the representational context of popular culture. This new era has been categorized, uncertainly, as "postracial" and "postfeminist"—both, unquestionably, complicated and disputed concepts, typically deployed without explanation of their intended connotation. Yet, their prevalence probably stems from the conceptual purchase they possess for acknowledging the notable difference between the issues central to American cultural debates in the 2000s and those of the preceding two decades.[12] Discourses about the menace of "welfare moms" and the domestic destruction wrought by "working women" that were preponderant in cultural politics during the 1980s and early 1990s were replaced by a turn away from these cultural debates in the early twenty-first century to political questions of "weapons of mass destruction," "enemy combatants," and the wars in Afghanistan and Iraq. The economic crisis delivered by an under-regulated banking industry, followed by a return to examination of and debate about economic policies ranging from health care to the unionization of government workers to all manner of deficit-cutting and austerity measures, monopolized the cultural agenda, bringing uncommon popular attention to class and wealth distribution—though notably, issues of gay rights and marriage persisted and even dominated the cultural agenda at times, particularly in the late 1990s through the early 2000s.

As some of the contentious cultural debates of the 1980s and 1990s moved out of focus, revisions in dominant ideology occurred and incorporated *aspects* of their contested feminist and antiracist politics. The cultural politics of the 1990s were dominated by a seemingly continuous debate over so-called political correctness that melded with interrogation of crises that intersected aspects of gender and race, including the Rodney King beating, police acquittal, and LA riots, Anita Hill's charges of sexual harassment during Clarence Thomas's Supreme Court nomination, and Nicole Simpson's murder and the subsequent trial and acquittal of O. J. Simpson. During the turn to world politics and economic policy following 2001, certain forms of multiculturalism that were openly contested in the deliberation over these news stories throughout the 1990s became increasingly hegemonic, as did women's place in the workforce, the criminalization of domestic violence, and the inappropriateness of hostile workplaces.[13] Other initiatives—such as those related to immigration policy—remained contested, while still others—such as accessibility to affordable childcare—fell off the sociopolitical agenda or were decreasingly perceived as feminist issues, as was the case with universal healthcare.

It remains the work of a cultural historian to flesh out this process of adjusting cultural norms and ideology with more nuance and to pose terminology that identifies this postbacklash era. The absence of such work leaves me with "post-second-wave"—a term not meant to exclusively signal cultural adjustments that can be linked to second-wave feminist activism but nevertheless a descriptor of the cultural milieu created in the aftermath of its most extensive policy endeavors. Indeed, because cultural change is complicated and slowly realized, a nexus of intersecting social developments, including the shift to post-Fordist economic practices and the rise of neoliberalism, simultaneously also shape the milieu in a way that makes it difficult to sustain assertions of a singular or particular cause. The cultural forces most salient to the negotiation of patriarchal masculinities I consider can be linked explicitly with feminism, but though I privilege feminism's role in reshaping cultural norms in this analysis, it clearly cannot be extricated from other developments.

"Post-second-wave," then, does not merely indicate developments that can be tied directly to second-wave feminist activism but also describes a generation—or period of acculturation—marked by the contestation of patriarchy and revision of common gender scripts, among other things including high rates of divorce and the emergence of the AIDS epidemic. Admittedly, generation is a tricky and analytically contested construct, most commonly distinguished by demographers on the basis of trends in birthrate. In acknowledging the salience of generation here I highlight how acculturation with or after second-wave feminism is a defining component of post-Boomer generational identity, as the Baby Boom generation was the last one to be acculturated with pre-second-wave gender ideologies. Aspects of generational identity consequently become an important consideration because of the degree to which those in the post–Baby Boom generations—those born after 1965—came of age in a culture negotiating gender politics very differently from those born previously. Generational identity is certainly relevant, but must be understood as a blunt categorization. Some members of the Boomer cohort identified inequity, imagined different power relations, and actively endeavored to enact broad social change. Some among those born since the mid-1960s came of age during the time characterized as "backlash" and consequently adopted limited adjustments in gender scripts relative to those who grew up after these gains became less contested.

Generational identity proves relevant not only in terms of the audiences for television series but also in terms of characters, as nearly all of the characters considered here are of post-Boomer generations, and the series consequently tell stories of characters presumably acculturated in a different milieu than their predecessors.[14] Unlike characters of Boomer generations that have dominated television storytelling until recently, audiences could expect post-Boomer characters to embody attitudes toward social scripts in a manner consistent with the generation's experience. For example, storylines suggesting that women might not belong in the workforce, which were readily evident up through the late 1980s, have disappeared, replaced by characters that grew up with Title IX and other legal remedies that opened up previously impossible and contested opportunities. A post-second-wave outlook—by which I mean a perspective in which many of the gains in access to the public sphere are assumed as "natural"—consequently became the status quo among both male and female characters of the cohorts termed "Generation X" (born 1965–1982) and "Millennials" (born 1982–2001). The shift in characters' generational identity reflects the rising of post-Boomer generations into the core target of commercial television networks as Boomers aged beyond the brackets that advertisers have historically emphasized. Generational identity is therefore simultaneously a social, textual, and industrial phenomenon.

Another contextual factor that affects gender scripts encompasses political and cultural changes related to queer politics and gay identity. The gay rights activism that emerged relatively coterminously with second-wave feminism also might reasonably explain notable shifts in gender scripts for gay and straight men. As I address more extensively later in the chapter, the significant sociopolitical shifts in the recognition and acceptance of gay masculinities is paradoxically absent from the stories of the male-centered serial and complexly present in stories about the homosocial enclave and intimate male friendships. Where many other aspects of television have come to consistently represent gay male identities, many of the shows examined here illustrate an uncommon paucity and nearly utter absence of gay characters so that gay identity functions as a structuring absence in several of the series. Insights of queer theory become more useful in exploring the series discussed in the last two chapters, which make textually explicit the challenge of negotiating among homosociality and homosexuality.

I thus alight upon "post-second-wave" as an imperfect, yet the most apt, descriptor of the context examined here. As the discussion below details, the shifting sociological dynamics in gender politics at this time provided television outlets seeking certain types of audiences—the young, affluent, and liberal in particular—with an incentive to deviate from patriarchal masculinities.[15] The competitive dynamics of cable allowed more narrow audience targeting as well as the open disregard of audiences uncomfortable with male protagonists unconventional in their gender performance and moral ambiguity. Struggling to emerge as more than an also-ran, cable sought characters and narratives that could generate cultural discussion and that posed an alternative to those of broadcast fare. Of all the character types and themes that might generate such attention, deeply textured, straight white male protagonists engaged in identity crises provide a vehicle simultaneously unconventional and well within the confines of cultural acceptability.

The Twenty-First-Century Television Industry

The shifting masculinities considered here emerge near the end of the twenty-year period of industrial change for US television that I term the "multi-channel transition."[16] From the mid-1980s through the mid-2000s, the US television industry gradually adjusted to a number of alterations in its technological, economic, and distribution norms that allowed piecemeal modification of typical institutional practices. These changing industrial practices likewise led to shifts in the programming available on television as a new competitive environment enabled the commercial viability of types of stories and narrative foci that would have been uncompetitive in the network era. By the end of this transition, the industrial norms of US television had been substantially changed from a competitive environment in which viewers faced a limited choice of content and network control of viewing to one of multitudinous offerings with notable and expanding ability to control when and where to view content. These changes pushed the industry to the verge of radical adjustment as a result of sustained challenges to key features of its economic model.

The most relevant aspects of the broad array of industrial changes that presage the narratives in question are those related to the development of commercially viable original narrative series on cable television. This began during the 1980s and 1990s as the number of television programming outlets increased exponentially to create a much broader range of content and significantly fragment the viewing audience, which enabled channels to target more specific viewer tastes and preferences. By 1999, evidence of the end of a "broadcast" norm for television as a mass audience aggregator was preponderant. The once "Big Three" networks had doubled to six, yet gathered only 58 percent of those watching television during prime time—one benchmark for tracing the steady shift toward greater aggregate viewing of cable channels. The new competitors became the destination for audiences seeking to fulfill a desire for more specifically targeted tastes or sensibilities than those offered by the broadcast networks, whose economic and programming model relied upon attracting a mass audience.

Significantly, while the sum total of some hundred-plus cable channels drew away a substantial number of broadcast viewers, any single cable channel gathered at most a few million, which makes it difficult to assert that cable was "replacing" broadcast. The niche-focused cable channels relied on a different economic model than the broadcast networks and were supported through dual revenue streams of subscription fees paid by cable service providers as well as advertising, while broadcasters (at least through 2010) were mainly supported through advertising alone.[17] The competition for audiences forced the broadcasters to adjust their programming to attempt the narrower appeal that made cable a more relevant, and thus compelling, option for some viewers. However, the broadcast economic model does not reward niche appeals, which contributed to the growing gulf between the nature of some cable and broadcast fare.[18]

One consequence of this robust array of channel choice was an increased need for extensive marketing and promotion as channels could no longer expect viewers to just happen upon content or even their channel; by this point, "channel surfing" through available offerings could take longer than most programs. Channels needed to find a way to stand out among the increasingly vast competition, and the most successful channels accomplished this through clear channel branding supported by programming that reiterated the brand. Following the somewhat surprising success of the Lifetime cable channel in commanding the largest cable audience in prime time for twenty-six months in 2001–2003, many others took note of and replicated its strategy. At this time, Lifetime branded itself as "Television for Women," and thus identified its target as a segment of the audience (women)—one long perceived as too narrow for commercial viability.[19] The fragmentation of the television audience—encouraged by growing channel options—and Lifetime's ability to clearly announce what viewers could expect to find on its channel led to its considerable early-century success, while more generally branded competitors failed to develop a clear identity or consistent audience. Others quickly adopted Lifetime's strategy and began narrowing their brand by promoting a particular identity through channel tags, promotional efforts, and endeavors to create programming that reinforced the brand message.

Relatively resource poor at launch, most cable channels begin their existence with program schedules filled with Hollywood and original films; low-cost, original, nonnarrative series (series that do not require writers or actors, often categorized as reality or factual television); and "off-network" series that were previously aired on and developed for US broadcast networks. Only a few develop programming beyond this. The heavy reliance on off-network series and Hollywood theatricals inhibits a channel's efforts to develop a specific brand identity because the content available for purchase is limited by what others have developed— often for a broad audience—and this tends not to precisely match the more narrow brand common to cable channels. Developing original narrative series became a crucial step in connecting brand identity with programming as a few channels sought to compete more directly with broadcast networks and command greater advertising revenue. Yet, original scripted programming is expensive and thus risky, and many efforts throughout the mid- to late 1990s failed.[20]

Premium cable channel HBO identified a successful strategy beginning in the late 1990s that contributed to changing viewer expectations of original cable series. The cultural buzz about the series *Sex and the City* (1998–2004) and *The Sopranos* (1999–2007) led to a reimagining of the storytelling possibilities of cable, if not all US television. HBO established Sunday as the one night of the week when it would feature new episodes of original series and grew its programming to maintain this offering year round. Such a programming strategy hardly made it a competitor with broadcast networks, whose economics demanded an evening full of programming, seven nights a week. But the strategy of offering content thematically and visually distinct from broadcast and basic cable and building to a consistent year-round appointment provided a road map subsequently followed by basic cable channels such as FX, USA, and TNT in the early 2000s and AMC later in the decade.[21]

This somewhat extensive explanation of shifting competitive strategies among broadcast and cable channels is necessary because the emergent depictions of manhood and masculinities explored here overwhelmingly originate from cable channels. The development of cable channels as originators of scripted programming bears considerable responsibility for enabling these series to offer characters that contradict previously hegemonic patriarchal masculinities, and it is cable's ability to derive commercial success by narrowcasting to smaller and specific audience niches that allowed these unconventional characters.[22] Cable channels are the predominant outlet for the stories and characters considered here, and the fairly consistent failure of series focused on men's lives or unconventional masculinities on broadcast channels such as *What about Brian* (ABC, 2006–2007), *Big Shots* (ABC, 2007–2008), *October Road* (2007–2008), *Eli Stone* (ABC, 2008–2009), and *The Philanthropist* (NBC, 2009) further suggests a meaningful industrial component to this storytelling adjustment.

The transition of the US television industry out of its network-era norms produced a range of programming adjustments beyond those explored here and arguably had the consequence of enabling a proliferation of diametrically opposed depictions of men and constructions of masculinity. The fragmentation of the television audience allowed channels to target those eager for complex and sophisticated depictions of men's contemporary struggles—as evidenced by the series this book examines—but it also enabled the creation of programming targeting audiences desiring unreconstructed, patriarchal masculinities, such as those offered by *Howard Stern* (USA, 1994–2005), *The Man Show* (USA, 1999–2004), the first iteration of Spike ("the first cable network for men," 2003–2006), *Jersey Shore* (MTV, 2009–2012), and many of the reality shows that dominated television schedules at the transition to the twenty-first century that relied on traditional gender stereotypes (*The Real Housewives* franchise; *Teen Mom*; various celebrity dating programs). Still others targeted gay masculinities through both the representation of gay characters and a variety of lifestyle programming that may not have appeared to straight audiences as gay friendly but avoided reinforcing heteronormativity in a manner that made them more welcoming to gay audiences. Talk shows hosts such as Rush Limbaugh and Bill O'Reilly offered yet another masculinity, one Kimmel identifies—perhaps erroneously—as prevalent in the era, though certainly loud and blustering.[23] Attitudes toward women spouted by pundits on

Fox News, the self-absorbed and catty women featured in much MTV fare and the *Real Housewives* franchise, and the traditional femininity offered by talk formats starkly contrasted with the post-second-wave gender environments of many cable dramas, indicating the difficulty of making coherent claims about gender on television.

The series examined here originated on general-interest cable channels—not those particularly targeted to men—and feature balanced mixed-sex viewing audiences.[24] Developing programs about complicated male characters was part of a strategy to increase male viewership—which always has been less substantial than that of female counterparts and showed signs of further losses at the time—but notably, these series were not presented as "Television for Men" and this breadth of intended audience also contributes to explaining why these shows develop stories and characters that challenge patriarchal masculinities.[25] Notably, cable was a more likely viewing destination for many men than broadcast programming. In a statement indicating advertisers' recognition of the importance of cable for reaching male viewers, media planner Brad Adgate noted, "Outside of the Fox animation Sunday night block, I wouldn't use broadcast prime to reach young males. . . . It seems like it would be more effective to target using cable networks like History, FX, Comedy Central, Discovery, AMC and Spike, among others."[26]

Although this review of institutional adjustments is necessarily cursory, it should be clear that the shifting competitive economics of the television industry did not cause the emergence or contestation of a particular masculinity. Rather, these industrial changes introduced a new competitive environment in which depicting the negotiation of male identity and gender politics became feasible. Relatedly, it is also important to acknowledge how the context of these shows—and the assumptions I make about their role in culture—differ from those of the network era. On one hand, the fact that cable channels do not have to try to craft universally appealing male characters contributes significantly to enabling their deployment of emergent masculinities. Yet, it is also the case that the deviations from the patriarchal masculinities dominant in the past are not being viewed by the mass audiences of the network era—which arguably reduces their cultural significance.

This conundrum exists as an unresolved dilemma in much scholarship about post-network-era television, as the field remains without a compelling theoretical frame, such as Horace Newcomb and Paul Hirsch's "cultural forum," which explained the relationship of television storytelling and its cultures of production and reception in the network era. Fragmentation of the television audience into ever more narrowly targeted outlets and the variation in its norms—the fact that audiences of successful broadcast shows range from seven to fifteen million, while most cable series can succeed with just two or three million—diminishes the cultural relevance of single shows and necessitates the inclusion of an extensive range of series and the broader-level narrative analysis evident in subsequent chapters. [27]

Frameworks for Understanding Televised Masculinities

"Masculine" was long simply assumed to be an adjective describing how "men" are and as designating the opposite of "feminine." Gender studies and sociological theories developed since the start of the second-wave feminist and gay rights movements have led to much richer and more complicated understandings of masculinities and to the employment of a myriad of words such as "dominant," "hegemonic," "preferred," and endless others to modify "masculinity" to various ends. In many cases these modifiers denote different aspects of the relationship between men and power, which is perhaps best encapsulated in the term "patriarchy." Patriarchal ideologies are the functional opposite of feminist ideologies in that patriarchy seeks to allow special privileges and authority for men—and particularly straight, white, affluent or educated men— and to reinforce men's dominant gender status in society. Following bell hooks and several other feminist theorists, I view feminism as

> not simply a struggle to end male chauvinism or a movement to ensure
> that women will have equal rights with men; it is a commitment to eradi-
> cating the ideology of domination that permeates Western culture on
> various levels—sex, race, and class, to name a few—and a commitment to
> reorganizing U.S. society so that the self-development of people can take
> precedence over imperialism, economic expansion, and material desires.[28]

Importantly, then, this conception of feminism does not seek to replace men's dominance with dominance by women, but to dismantle all ideologies supporting inequality.

American television has offered many different types of men, but whether it be the western hero, the television newsman, or the domestic comedy's head of household, patriarchal constructions of masculinity have dominated. There is not a singular or consistent patriarchal masculinity, but rather, masculinities that reinforce men's dominant gender status in the culture include aspects such as behaviors and attitudes that assert men's "natural" place as leaders and their superiority over women and that commonly position certain men—specifically, those who are white, heterosexual, physically powerful, and educated or financially prosperous—as having greater power than others.[29] Patriarchal masculinities affirm both single bachelorhood or coupling with a woman, so long as men desire women, and often suggest that men have such voracious sexual needs as to require more than one sexual partner. Patriarchal men were typically presented as family breadwinners, though often also as capable problem solvers at home. Men who deviated from the patriarchal masculinity might function as antagonists or "bad" men in an episode, but television's male protagonists consistently have been infallible and well intentioned and their authority rarely questioned.

In order to discuss the varied masculinities of different characters across different shows, the analysis in this book presumes that a spectrum of masculinities exists on US television that might be plotted between poles of "patriarchal" and "feminist." Embodiment of purely patriarchal or feminist masculinities is undoubtedly rare and fairly unimaginable. Rather, characters embody a variety of attributes that can be tied to both patriarchal power structures and the feminist endeavors that seek to dismantle them. This book does not engage in historical analysis, and I leave it to another scholar to illustrate how the masculinities displayed by characters before second-wave feminism embodied or contested patriarchal aspects. Analysis here centers on evidence of how contemporary characters negotiate prevailing patriarchal masculinities with aspects of a more feminist masculinity. This process of contesting patriarchal masculinities yields masculinities "reconstructed" by feminism, so that a series might inhabit many "degrees" of reconstruction

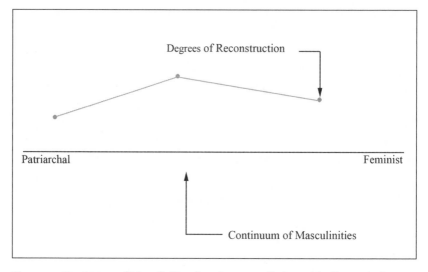

Figure 1.3. Continuum of Masculinities. Seeming contradictions and adjustments in contemporary masculinities can be mapped on a continuum between patriarchal and feminist masculinities for more meaningful analysis than dichotomies of "progressive" or "reactionary" allow.

that exist on this spectrum of masculinities. The point of analysis is not to presume a linear progression or to dwell on creating hierarchies, but to tease apart the process of these shifts and identify evidence of changing norms in the aspects of masculinities most affirmed—and those still uncontested—on television in the post–second wave context.

Such a framework for analysis—with its conceptualization of a spectrum of reconstructed masculinities and varied possible combinations of patriarchal and feminist aspects—provides a tool for expanding the analysis of masculinity on television. While this precise spectrum need not be replicated in the analysis of masculinities in other texts, its use illustrates a strategy for avoiding the stymied "on the one hand it is progressive, but on the other it contains those progressive impulses" type of analysis that allows for the ideological complexity of texts but often provides unsatisfying analytic conclusions. Its use in contextualized analysis that specifically places the characters in a cultural milieu, acknowledges simultaneous and recently resolved social dilemmas, and considers factors beyond gender, such as generation, ethnicity, class, and sexuality, adds depth to analyses and provides more grounded cases. Its use in the study here of a particular time and set of narrative forms enables deeper exploration of the way popular culture negotiates changing social norms and the way a construct such as masculinity changes over time, which is not possible by simply categorizing shows as enacting either a progressive or a reactionary masculinity.

Another term used particularly in this analysis is "hegemonic masculinity," which originates in sociological literature. R. W. Connell defines "hegemonic masculinity" as a "culturally idealized form of masculine character," and is important because those in accord with hegemonic masculinities are afforded greater privilege.[30] Connell's early work in this area endeavored to create ways for thinking and talking about the complicated nature of masculinity and power in society that were not commonly assumed. In modifying "masculinity" with "hegemonic," scholars sought to intervene in the tendency to speak of the existence of a singular masculinity. Such an approach commonly placed masculinity and femininity in opposition, which did little to explain the nuances and power involved in the oft-unacknowledged multiplicity of masculinities or femininities and instead relied upon assumptions of essentialized, presumably biologically determined sex roles. Labeling certain traits or tendencies as characteristic of hegemonic masculinity draws attention to the constructed nature of those deployments of masculinity that are particularly culturally rewarded, and conceiving of masculinity as plural and varied is crucial to contesting beliefs that certain behaviors are inherently and "naturally" male traits. The idea that there is a multiplicity of masculinities and that greater power is afforded to some masculinities than others is central to this book's arguments about how several of the series depict men as conflicted over different constructions of masculinity and the book's exploration of the consequences of their negotiation among them.

Importantly, the leading sociological theorists always viewed hegemonic masculinity as flexible in design; as Connell writes, "'Hegemonic masculinity' is not a fixed character type, always and everywhere the same. It is, rather, the masculinity that occupies the hegemonic position in a given pattern of gender relations, a position always contestable."[31] Connell provides a conceptualization of hegemonic masculinity that is both changeable and contestable. In acknowledging its lack of fixedness, Connell explains the mutability of variations in the hegemonic masculinity of different class or ethnic subcultures, which remain powerful in those groups despite deviating from what is perceived to be the hegemonic masculinity of the dominant culture.[32] Such mutability is also helpful for conceptualizing differences among hegemonic masculinities present in various cultural forms—as I argue that there is not a single hegemonic masculinity on twenty-first-century television, and therefore I construct analyses sensitive to discerning the hegemonic masculinity of each series' narrative universe. Understanding hegemonic masculinity as contestable ties it to neo-Marxist explanations of the operation of hegemony, discussed in greater detail below. Most basically, the idea of contestability acknowledges that power relations are not fixed, which enables an analysis of how aspects of the series indicate contestation and adjustment from patriarchal masculinities. I intentionally avoid using "dominant masculinity" because it suggests a singularity and steadfastness that is difficult to prove—dominant where, for whom, when?—and is inadequate for explaining the breadth of masculinities evident in contemporary television. Although arguably a less readily accessible and inherently "academic" term, "hegemonic" as an adjectival modifier better asserts the complexity of how power operates to make certain embodiments of masculinity seem natural. Analysis throughout the book thus considers shifting norms and the negotiations among aspects of patriarchal and feminist masculinities in the early twenty-first century and evidence of how they might be dominant, residual, or emergent, per Williams's conceptualization.[33]

Despite the flexibility presumed by sociological gender theory, the concept of hegemonic masculinity has been awkwardly used in media analyses. My deployment of hegemonic masculinity is strategic and somewhat at odds with how it often has been used in media scholarship, which typically begins by establishing essential traits of hegemonic masculinity and then endeavors to identify them in the media texts being studied. For example, in his 1994 analysis of media representations of the baseball player Nolan Ryan, Nick Trujillo used a five-part definition of hegemonic masculinity as "defined in terms of physical force and control," "defined through occupational achievement," "patriarchy," "symbolized by the daring, romantic, frontiersman," and "heterosexually defined," and then identifies evidence of aspects of this masculinity in the way the media represent Ryan.[34] As Robert Hanke adeptly critiques, the reduction of hegemonic masculinity into such a seemingly absolute and static entity risks conflating any such definition of masculinity with a normative definition of what it is to be a man while evacuating any notion of the complex operation of hegemony through which those in power must continuously seek the consent of those they subordinate.[35] Such a deployment of hegemonic masculinity does little to address the multiple and sometimes conflicting attributes associated with "being a man" that might be found throughout a culture and the manner in which cultural forms such as television provide a venue for the debate, modification, and reassertion of cultural ideals.

Even sidelining what may seem esoteric concerns about accounting for contestation as central to the operation of hegemony, it is infeasible to establish a consistent rubric of *a* static hegemonic masculinity that would be identifiable across a broad range of television texts. This medium that simultaneously offers us staid and stoic newsmen, wrestlers oozing testosterone, and the paternal assurances of fathers who know best makes simple typologies of hegemonic masculinity of little analytic value. Static notions of hegemonic masculinity have been used by others to examine television with somewhat greater nuance although, notably, such studies typically consider masculinity in only one or two series or as a discourse surrounding a particular news subject rather than considering the broader swaths of television programming examined here.[36] Studies that enumerate characteristics of hegemonic masculinity and then endeavor to find them lack a mechanism for identifying emergent masculinities or the way masculinities may be contested and negotiated within a particular cultural form. In a broader study of 1980s television, John Fiske identified that "[t]he 'macho' characteristics of goal centeredness, assertiveness, and the morality of the strongest" were most likely to be characteristics of the villain, not the hero, in television melodrama, suggesting the need for analysis that begins by examining texts, not by looking for specific qualities within a text.[37] Although it may be possible to derive a static definition of hegemonic masculinity from the sociocultural context and then find it in particular texts, such analysis fails to account for significant components of how ideology functions and the existence of other masculinities.

Instead, this analysis follows the approach of critical media and television studies and begins from the context of various television series and explores what types of male behaviors and perspectives are affirmed within a particular narrative universe or what behaviors are supported as proper, ideal, or heroic within the situation of the show. I use "hegemonic" to indicate deployment of masculinities that are presented as "natural" and that receive support *within that narrative* as acceptable or preferred; hegemonic masculinities are often idealized in narratives or connected with characters that are heroic or positioned for viewer identification. Each narrative universe has its own hegemonic masculinity as well as competing variations. Importantly, it is not the case that there is extreme variation among hegemonic masculinities in different shows—particularly among the cable dramas considered here. Yet this approach to analysis provides a means for interrogating tensions and negotiations in series that explicitly explore the difficulty these male characters experience in their self-presentation and relationships with other men. This terminological strategy aids in the book's focus on examining the relationship among various masculinities.

Such a conceptualization of hegemonic masculinities emphasizes their capacity to be fluid and shifting. In some cases the hegemonic masculinities in a series align with patriarchal masculinities; however, many aspects of patriarchal masculinities are no longer hegemonic. For example, the gender dynamics of the 1960s-set *Mad Men* frequently displays behaviors and aspects of masculinity common among straight, white, upper-class men that were hegemonic at the time but that now seem shockingly unacceptable: regular fraternizing among men and their secretaries; the necessity for women to be virginal in order to be desirable; or even just norms in practices such as childbirth, where women are made unconscious for the process and a father would rather spend the day at the office than sit in the waiting room, let alone be present for the birth.[38] It is also the case that the hegemonic masculinities in these shows do differ markedly from some others on television, such as those of "real men" reality shows such as *Ice Road Truckers* or *Deadliest Catch*, the self- and gratification-obsessed masculinities of *Jersey Shore*, or several of those series noted in this book's introduction.

In terms of my critical standpoint, I draw from an Althusserian and Gramscian concept of hegemony in which the operation of hegemony is a constant process of struggle through which more powerful groups attempt to convince those with less power to consent to their own subordination. Per Althusser, emphasis must be placed on the constancy of struggle and perpetual reassertion of dominant perspectives, and a medium such as popular television is an important site to examine because of the way its stories contribute to the ideological state apparatus—social institutions such as family, churches, education systems, and the media that teach and enforce "proper" ways of being, thinking, and believing within society.[39] The affirmation of aspects of patriarchal masculinities within media texts helps sustain patriarchy within society, and thus, a key strand of analysis throughout the book examines the negotiation of patriarchal masculinities evident in constructions of masculinity in television storytelling in the twenty-first century. The analysis remains attuned to the way emergent hegemonic masculinities may continue to be patriarchal, even if in different ways, as well as to indications of hegemonic masculinities that evince the incorporation of feminism.

For the most part, the analysis in the following chapters demonstrates evidence that feminist masculinities have been incorporated into the hegemonic masculinities of the television storytelling considered here, but asserts that tensions remain present and that various aspects of masculinities negotiate the challenges of decreased patriarchal privilege in different ways. Although "feminism" does not receive the blame for the struggles depicted, some patriarchal behaviors and perspectives persist—at times openly questioned, while uncommented upon in others. With an emphasis on dissecting the negotiation performed by television storytelling, the analysis attempts to address some of the inherent pessimism that can characterize the use of hegemony as a theoretical framework, as any "victory" of the subordinated inevitably can be argued to be a strategic allowance by the dominant. This ultimately points to a key limitation of textual analysis—that it tells us nothing of what texts and audiences do when they interact.

In terms of audiences, these shows—while featuring male protagonists—are not watched by audiences with a heavily male skew, and their cultural work is certainly important in terms of contributing to understandings not only of the gender roles men craft but also of those developed by women. There is an uncertain and complicated relationship between popular cultural texts and the ideas of societies that consume them and my sense of the potential influence of cultural texts is messy and nonlinear. To be clear, I do not assert that the confusion and struggle over how to be a man that characterizes many of the series considered here maps neatly onto the psyches of men of this time or even the men who watch these shows. I don't even have a certain argument on whether writers of these shows identified these conundrums in their own and peers' experiences of masculinity, so that television storytelling follows culture, or whether these ideas are "changing" the perceptions of men in a manner suggesting that television influences culture. There are empirical methods that can address such questions about audience effects, but my methods are not among them. Here I seek to prove various assertions about themes and representational trends present in an array of fictional television series. I suspect that for an audience to see cultural texts that preponderantly vilify aspects of patriarchal masculinities plays a role in the culture at large coming to adopt, or at least consider, those views as well, but this analysis cannot claim how or to what extent this happens for viewers. Identifying some of the uncommon constructions of gender and gender scripts that are present, such as the depiction of intimacy among heterosexual male friends in some of the series discussed in chapter 5, and explaining how thematically similar series deal differently with gay panic, for example, mark the contribution of careful textual analysis to broader scholarly projects. Although textual methods do not prove audience effects, critical analysis can posit that telling these stories contributes to real men imagining and experiencing different heterosexual relationships with other men and to women's thinking about men in different ways as well.

Contextualizing Twenty-First-Century Dramatic Portrayals of Men

A final crucial piece of context requires considering the broader storytelling environment of the series this book considers. Certainly, there are far more storytelling contexts that could be discussed than there is reasonable space for here. These shows cohere into one of many contemporary phenomena depicting men and masculinity. Absent here—but calling for others' analysis—are the masculinities of the winners and losers of reality competition shows, the real men depicted in docusoaps such as *Duck Dynasty*, *Wicked Tuna*, or *Hillbilly Handfishin'*, which provide glimpses into parts of America typically obscured from media view, and the juvenile humor and raunchy comedy of *Workaholics* and *Blue Mountain State*, targeting younger men. Moreover, the field desperately needs systematic historical analysis of men and masculinity on television in nearly any era of the medium, be it the 1950s patriarchs, 1960s suave action heroes, or grizzled detectives of the 1970s.

The most relevant part of the vast, largely unconsidered history of men and masculinity on television to the analysis here begins in the early 1980s as many of the storytelling spaces that remained predominantly male provinces began incorporating female characters. Such series often emphasized contested gender norms and blamed the discord on women or identified aspects of femininity as incompatible with the male professional sphere. The emphasis on changing gender scripts as the problem of women alone continued to perpetuate the invisibility of masculinity.

But while hostile toward women's entry into professionalized workspaces, some television series also began to present an open challenge to patriarchal masculinities through characters commonly termed "new men." Such characters exhibited a masculinity either changed by the women's movement or at least less antagonistic toward women's changing social roles than counterparts who were characterized as deeply committed to patriarchal masculinity. Although the precise attributes of new men were often unclear when referenced in popular writing, Nickianne Moody succinctly defines new men as embodying "a set of developing constructions of masculinity that (in the wake of shifts in the terrain of sexual politics and the rise of lifestyle marketing) eschewed traditional, 'armour-plated' machismo in favour of a more emotionally literate masculine ideal."[40] These so-called new men were typically white, upper-middle-class professionals and members of the tail end of the Baby Boom generation who had feminist women—or at least those with a post-second-wave consciousness—in their lives.

Such characters emerged most consistently in the 1980s, although many characters in 1970s series embodied cracks in the façade of common patriarchal masculinities. New men espoused antisexist ideas with varying explicitness, but departed significantly from the bombastic patriarchal masculinity of their predecessors; consider *All in the Family*'s (1968–1979) Archie Bunker (Carroll O'Connor) as a classic depiction of patriarchal masculinity, while his son-in-law Michael Stivic (Rob Reiner) contrastingly embodied many of the emerging characteristics of the new man. Although most discussion of the new man on television develops in examinations of *thirtysomething* (1987–1991), traces of this distinctive masculinity were apparent in earlier characters, such as Stivic, Jim Rockford (James Garner) of *The Rockford Files* (1974–1980), and Alan Alda's Hawkeye in *M*A*S*H* (1972–1983), which indicated an initial emergence of feminist-conscious masculinities that became more common in the 1980s. This new man masculinity was hardly uniform or dominant, as even when such a character did appear, his masculinity was typically one of many displayed in a series. The "new male masculinity" is also a key subject of contemporaneous film criticism.[41]

Though new men may have disregarded some aspects of patriarchal masculinities, they were by no means feminist either. Indicating the ambivalence with which feminist critics received these new men in the contentious moment of late 1980s backlash, Hanke's analysis of *thirtysomething* emphasizes how male characters alternatively described as "sensitive," as "nurturing," and as offering a "new view of manhood" existed in narratives that still glossed over "questions of power, real gender inequities, and capitalist work relations."[42] Hanke ultimately reconciles these contradictions to assert that the presentation and negotiation of masculinity in *thirtysomething* was an illustration of hegemonic masculinity shifting in order to maintain its status, and Sasha Torres, who approaches *thirtysomething*'s depictions of men and masculinity through the framework of feminist and film theory, reaches a similar assessment.[43] Like Hanke, she digs past the surface appearance of *thirtysomething*'s male protagonists' "new masculinity" to identify the various ways in which hegemonic gender relations still operate.

The new man indicated the emergence of a new archetype rather than a wholesale transition in the masculinities common on television. *New York Times* columnist Peter J. Boyer argued that the new man was already passé in 1986—notably, a year before *thirtysomething* (1987–1991) even debuted—citing as evidence what he identified as "hard-boiled" men such as those in *Miami Vice* (1984–1989), Ted Danson's Sam Malone character on *Cheers* (1982–1993), and Bruce Willis's David Addison on *Moonlighting* (1985–1989).[44] But the return of macho men that Boyer identifies precisely illustrates the contentious complexity of televised prime-time masculinity throughout the 1980s, as the characters he notes did not dominate their narrative universes in the manner of many previous male characters, nor were they the most prevalent or popular across television schedules. Scholars Jonathan David Tankel and Barbara Jane Banks refute Boyer's assertion and note that with the exception of the *Miami Vice* detectives, all of Boyer's new hard-boiled heroes are paired with a strong female character with whom they "exist in a constant state of tension."[45] Tankel and Banks argue, "An alternative interpretation of prime-time programs featuring sexist male leads is that these programs function as a forum where the conflict between old and new gender roles is enacted over and over, much as it is in society."[46]

Tankel and Banks thus identify how changes in women's depictions in the post-second-wave milieu begin to affect the range of viable masculinities. Their contextual point about the presence of strong *female* characters is important, but so too are the range of men also present alongside boorish, macho characters. In addition to the variation in masculinities evident across series in the late 1980s, there was often considerable variation in the masculinities present within a single series; consider *Hill Street Blues'* contrast among Frank Furillo (Daniel J. Travanti) and Howard Hunter (James Sikking) as a particularly strong illustration of this, but even consider the further variation offered by Andy Renko (Charles Haid), Mick Belker (Bruce Weitz), or J. D. LaRue (Kiel Martin).

In these waning days of broadcast network dominance and the gathering of mass audiences, an exceptional chasm in the masculinities asserted by central male characters could be found in prime-time television's most successful shows. As popular attention like Boyer's article suggests, as well as others in *TV Guide* and the *Washington Post,* television's "regular" men were now being implicated in debates about manhood and shifting masculinities, not just the usual suspects of westerns, action shows, and detective series.[47] A cycle of comedies about single dads further compounded the complexity of televised masculinities in the 1980s; series that turned new attention to men as primary caregivers included *Diff'rent Strokes* (1978–1986), *Gimme a Break* (1981–1087), *Silver Spoons* (1982–1986), *Double Trouble* (1984–1985), *My Two Dads* (1987–1990), *Full House* (1987–1995), and *Blossom* (1991–1995). Even the short-lived series *Love, Sidney* (1981–1983), which presented cloaked queerness, indicated the range of masculinities available as US television's network era drew to a close.

The mid-1980s through early 1990s can be characterized as a period in which the gender politics of television dramas offered many different masculinities. One way to understand this variation is as a competitive tactic aimed at offering multiple points of identification given the real contestation of these ideas occurring simultaneously.[48] But by the mid- to late 1980s, the new cultural dynamic of a post-network environment of niche hits was increasingly evident. Although *thirtysomething*, *Moonlighting*, and *Miami Vice* provided considerable fodder for journalists and academics who generally commented about the exceptionality of these shows' stylistic and narrative innovations, as well as their gender dynamics, these were not broad or long-term hits. *Thirtysomething* never cracked the top thirty most popular shows among television households, *Miami Vice* ranked at best ninth in 1985–1986 and tied for twenty-sixth in 1986–1987, and *Moonlighting* ranked twenty-fourth in 1985–1986, ninth in 1986–1987, and tied for twelfth in 1987–1988, though these were strong performers among the younger 18–49-year-old demographic.[49] In general, comedies such as *The Cosby Show*, *Family Ties*, *Cheers*, and *The Golden Girls* dominated among household ratings in this era, but dramas featuring more patriarchal masculinities, such as *Dallas*, *Matlock*, and *Highway to Heaven,* typically outranked series that offered new men and that openly negotiated masculinity.[50] By the mid-1980s, household ratings had grown less important to the networks, which were increasingly worried about maintaining the younger and affluent audience groups most likely to be early adopters of the cable services and VCRs that now added to nightly competition; and this audience was more likely to view shows such as *thirtysomething*. The mid- to late 1980s began to evince viewing patterns that remain relevant to understanding the dynamics of male portrayals that continued through the early 2000s as the hegemonic masculinity of male characters in niche hits began to deviate more and more from that of the male characters populating mainstream series. This bifurcation—which to a large degree is replicated and becomes even more exaggerated the broader the survey of genres—requires careful and contextualized assessment of television's many competing masculinities.

Where these 1980s series offered contrasting masculinities that allowed explicit negotiation of male identity and gender scripts, this contestation between patriarchal and new man masculinities became less explicit throughout the 1990s. Although some of these series that placed new men and their dilemmas in the foreground continued to air into the 1990s, the negotiation of gender politics became more muted in many shows of this decade. A range of ensemble dramas such as *Northern Exposure* (1990–1995), *L.A. Law* (1986–1994), and *Homicide: Life on the Street* (1993–1999) dominated critical discussions and integrated a range of masculinities, while diminishing the focus on the exceptionality of "new man" perspectives.[51] The high-profile 1993 debut of *NYPD Blue* (1993–2005) again returned more explicit attention to changing masculinities through the pairing of David Caruso's John Kelly and Dennis Franz's Andy Sipowicz. The fact that this long-running detective series ultimately became the story of the reformation of the patriarchal, racist, and sexist Sipowicz—perhaps because of Caruso's early decision to leave the show—allowed the cumulative narrative of *NYPD Blue* to comment on the transitions in masculinities that were not especially noticeable in the course of week-in, week-out procedural stories. In fact, a similar argument can be made of *Homicide: Life on the Street* in terms of the terrain it covered—in bits and pieces each week—in the making of Tim Bayliss (Kyle Secor) as a detective and in relation to the masculinities of the various detectives surrounding him. By the end of the 1990s—as the series considered here begin—this negotiation between patriarchal and new man masculinities achieved some resolution as many characteristics of the new man became part of the hegemonic masculinities found in most dramas and Boomer protagonists began to be replaced by leading men young enough to have been acculturated in a post-second-wave milieu.

Accomplishments of the women's movement that seemed tenuous in the late 1980s were not revoked throughout the 1990s, but became steadily entrenched, and new men continued to proliferate until the prototypic patriarchal or "unreconstructed" male became increasingly uncommon except as a subject of reform (Sipowicz) or as an object for critique or parody, as seen in the treatment of characters such as Richard Fish (Greg Germann) in *Ally McBeal* (1997–2002) and Denny Crane (William Shatner) in *Boston Legal* (2004–2008). The new man consequently became unexceptional, expected, and common—arguably hegemonic—throughout US dramas in the 1990s. Men worked side by side with women in various professional realms and were decreasingly depicted as questioning women's ability to be both mothers and workers, and the gender politics of the workplaces that dominated narrative settings also decreasingly remarked upon gender. Except for *Ally McBeal*, which returned to gender politics—particularly sexual harassment—as a central narrative subject, most workplace dramas by the late 1990s simply adopted the expectation of nonhostile workplaces that became standard as a product of cultural discussion and corporate policies in the wake of Anita Hill's testimony. Men in dramas were increasingly depicted as also challenged by the need to balance work and home in the manner that had long plagued their female counterparts, as evidenced by male characters in series such as *ER* and *Law & Order* who scaled back their professional commitments to fulfill family duties or lost their families due to overcommitment to careers.

Many aspects of second-wave activism became integrated into the hegemonic representation of women throughout the 1990s as well, and the changing representations and stories told about women had implications for their male counterparts. Women became commonly depicted as able workers with highly professionalized careers, and were almost always white, straight, and, most often, single. The emergence of a multitude of female characters that transcended previous stereotypes as wives, mothers, and sex objects necessitated the development of male characters that reflected such adjustments. Once women became regularly portrayed as equals and superiors onscreen, there was decreasing space for unreconstructed patriarchal masculinity to be heroic or preferred—at least in these narrative universes. These new women required male characters who offered a revised masculinity, a trend particularly pronounced as women infiltrated the action drama as protagonists—as in such series as *Buffy the Vampire Slayer*, *Charmed*, *Dark Angel*, and *Alias*. Such series deviated from the paternalistic masculinity of predecessors such as *Charlie's Angels* or *Wonder Woman* and often allocated depictions of patriarchal masculinity to villains.

The centrality of gay politics throughout the 1990s also enabled the proposition of a "post-closet" era of representation that likewise reconfigured the range of masculinities on offer. Gay male identity was absent or made to seem aberrant in popular culture until the 1990s, at which point television scholar Ron Becker documents a "startling increase" in gay and gay-themed US television programming.[52] Becker constructs a sophisticated analysis of the way television's industrial dynamics and cultural politics produce this representational change that in many ways initiates the interrogation of patriarchal masculinities continued in the series considered here.

Becker proposes the term "post-closet TV" to describe a representational context evident by the late 1990s in which openly gay men on television become banal and explores how television narratives began to construct *not* being out as the pathology that had once been attributed to gay identity in TV portrayals.[53] The transformation of television's norms regarding the representation of gay men—from absence to occasional pathologized or mocked characters to a context where gay identity is banal and being closeted is pathologized—in less than two decades marks a trajectory of amazing speed and indicates a clear contestation of heteronormativity unquestionably relevant to the analysis of televised masculinities that *Cable Guys* explores. Paradoxically, the series considered here introduce a conundrum of featuring masculinities enabled by and characteristic of a US culture considerably cognizant of gay identity—the post-closet milieu Becker suggests; however, they simultaneously remain firmly heteronormative in their presentation of male sexuality despite the inclusiveness of the broader television space. Gay characters—particularly men—are decreasingly exceptional as cast members, yet it does remain the case that no mainstream series has featured a central gay protagonist (outside of a channel particularly identified as targeting gay audiences),[54] and few dramas— *Oz, Queer as Folk, The L Word, Brothers & Sisters*, and *Glee*—have offered complicated and sustained treatment of gay identity or sexuality.[55] Despite the common presence of gay characters, the male-centered serials explored in the next two chapters feature a complicated disavowal of gay male identity and exclude gay characters to an extent uncharacteristic of the television series aired contemporaneously. The maintenance of heteronormativity as an aspect of patriarchal masculinities, despite other challenges, is a significant limitation of these texts and a crucial part of the analysis that follows.

Finally, I must briefly acknowledge the broader media context surrounding television in the early twenty-first century. Contemporaneous popular film similarly provided indicators of cultural reconsideration of gender scripts and hegemonic masculinities. Although more artistically esteemed productions such as *Fight Club* (David Fincher, 1999) and *Brokeback Mountain* (Ang Lee, 2005) inspired analysis, few have done much to make sense of the wellspring of juvenile masculinities at play in what Peter Alilunas describes as "dude flicks" that dominated popular film comedy in this decade. Alilunas focuses on comedies that "construct their humor from the inadequacies and failures of white male masculinity," such as *Old School* (2003, Todd Phillips) and *Dodgeball* (2004, Rawson Marshall Thurber)—most any film of the 2000s starring members of the "frat pack" of Owen Wilson, Will Ferrell, Adam Sandler, Vince Vaughn, and Ben Stiller.[56] Although Alilunas conflates them, a second type of dude flick—that written, directed, or produced by Judd Apatow—comes to dominate popular film comedy of the era. Apatow's films similarly feature a pack of actors, but a group about a decade younger than those above (Paul Rudd, Michael Cera, Evan Goldberg, Jason Segal, Jonah Hill, and Seth Rogan). Apatow's oeuvre of films—*The 40-Year-Old Virgin* (2005), *Knocked Up* (2007), *Superbad* (2007), and *Funny People* (2009), among others—have been discussed in popular criticism in terms of depicting a crisis in masculinity among the "man-boys," sometimes also termed "beta males," that populate his films, which perhaps have avoided attention of film scholars because their crass, stoner humor can be dismissed as the sophomoric joking of boys.[57]

Despite appearances, there are many layers to these films that are clearly wrestling, although at times clumsily, with emerging masculinities, male friendships, and heterosexuality among post-second-wave characters. Apatow and his films take further what David Greven terms "new forms of American Masculinity" in his analysis of the teen comedies at the turn to the twenty-first century that immediately preceded Apatow's success, such as *American Pie* (1999), *Dude, Where's My Car?* (2000), *Loser* (2000), *American Pie 2* (2001), and *Saving Silverman* (2001).[58] Greven valuably explores how the films reflect and struggle with the issues of changing gender roles and notions of manhood in what might be perceived as forgettable teen films. Yet the role of teen films in the acculturation to adulthood for a particular cohort underscores the social relevance of the shifting gender scripts he identifies. More recently, queer studies scholar Jack Halberstam has identified the masculinity common in these films as "a new form of parasitical masculinity," but offers only casual analysis focused on the prevalence of males exhibiting slacker masculinities who partner with ambitious, attractive women.[59]

* * *

As new paradigmatic gender roles became established in 1990s television, the medium's competitive environment entered a period of rapid and significant transition. Broadcast networks identified formulas featuring mixed-gender workplaces devoid of gender-based tensions that would appeal to broad audiences, but were then faced with competition from cable channels that began developing series from an entirely different playbook. The next chapter traces the way cable channels created series that deviated from the ensembles dominant in broadcast dramas and focused on male protagonists frequently described as antiheroes to create the subgenre I distinguish as the "male-centered serial." The most distinctly new phenomenon considered in this book, the male-centered serial introduces the latest construct to the evolving array of male types and a reworking of the new man. The men at the center of these shows embody reconstructed masculinities in ways different from the new man, yet continue to struggle with some aspects of patriarchal masculinities.

2

Trying to Man Up

Struggling with Contemporary Masculinities
in Cable's Male-Centered Serials

"Tortured souls are the new breed of antihero."

"Sensitive men take TV by storm."

"They steal, they cheat, they lie, and we wouldn't have it any other way—the timeless appeal of the anti-hero."

"TV's role: Produce male leads. Shows shift attention to more mature complex characters."[1]

This epigraph collects titles from a range of popular-press articles in the mid-2000s commenting about the changing faces and characterizations of men on television. Though these characters ranged from so-called antiheroes to so-called sensitive men, profound character depth increasingly became a hallmark of a subset of television storytelling in the 2000s. As Lynn Smith, writing for the *Los Angeles Times*, described it, "Original shows, on cable as well as network TV, are shifting attention to more mature and complex characters. The small screen is now crowded with charming, smart, confident, humorous grown-up men." *New York Times* critic Alessandra Stanley considered the phenomenon and opined, "From *The Sopranos* to *House*, men marked the last 10 years of television less as hellions or healers than as analysands—fragile bullies who recognized they were damaged and sought help. The 21ˢᵗ century was ushered in by a He Decade: 10 years of men gazing at their navels."[2] Using words such as "self-doubting," "eccentric," and "unorthodox," Stanley catalogs the way dramas of the decade such as those considered here, as well as *Monk* and *Law & Order: Criminal Intent*, "focused narrowly on the male mind" to offer what I describe as exceptional character interiority.[3]

Considerable character depth emerges as an attribute of many series of this era.[4] Important back story about protagonists added growing complexity to characters even in series that featured the stories of multiple protagonists, such as *The Wire* or *Deadwood,* or were driven by the narrative strategies of episodic procedurals, as in *Monk, Burn Notice,* and *Leverage.*[5] Horace Newcomb identifies such rich characterization as early as *Magnum, P.I.* (1980–1988), but this strategy grows more commonplace on broadcast television in the late 1990s.[6] Illustrations include the profound, but sporadically invoked, effect of Claire Kincaid's (Jill Hennessy) death by drunk driver on district attorney Jack McCoy (Sam Waterston) on *Law & Order* or the occasional acknowledgment of John Carter's (Noah Wyle) privileged upbringing and the childhood death of his brother on *ER.* These nuggets of character depth were often emphasized only in particular episodes and offered additional texture to the character for those viewers who had seen the episode or episodes revealing the back story. Indeed, many casual viewers were probably unaware of this layer of characterization and the narratives still made sense without this knowledge; these audiences just missed out on the supplementary significance. Even the procedurals that sated the pleasure of the broadest audiences, such as *Law & Order, CSI,* and those built from their episodic, plot-driven template, increasingly populated their series with more complicated characters at this time—consider *CSI's* Gil Grissom (William Peterson) or *House, M.D.'s* Dr. Gregory House (Hugh Laurie).[7]

But a difference in the characters, nearly to the one, could be correlated with whether a broadcast network or cable channel originated the series. As *San Francisco Chronicle* critic Tim Goodman observes, "starkly simple black-and-white characterizations are most often portrayed on broadcast television, where appealing to a wide audience is necessary for survival. In cable, a niche environment that seized on more sophisticated adult renderings of fictional characters, chance-taking is a must." Seeking to stake its claim as a channel that thought so far outside of the box that it branded itself with the slogan "There Is No Box" in late 2007, FX launched *The Shield* in 2002, a series frequently compared to *The Sopranos* for its focus on a sympathetic but bad protagonist and its willingness to push the boundaries of television propriety. This time with a character ostensibly on the right side of the law in a fictional interpretation of Los Angeles' scandalized Rampart division, *The Shield's* protagonist, Vic Mackey (Michael Chiklis), initially just bends the rules to control gang- and drug-ridden streets. The series' seven seasons chart the increasingly criminal acts he must pursue to maintain the house of cards required to cover up the initial indiscretions of his "strike team" unit. FX followed *The Shield* with *Nip/Tuck* (2003–2010), *Rescue Me* (2004–2011), and *Sons of Anarchy* (2008–), building a particular brand of programming targeting mature viewers desiring more complicated plotting and characterization with an array of shows inconspicuously investigating men's existence in contemporary America.

Other cable channels quickly joined the examination of modern masculinities. Showtime entered the game in 2006 and seemed to up the ante to a breaking point with *Dexter* (2006–2013), a series about a serial killer whose work defines grizzly. At *Dexter's* launch, many opined that the form had reached too great an excess with its serial killer protagonist, but as the series completed its third season in 2008, *Boston Globe* columnist Matthew Gilbert noted that "[y]ou can't help but recoil from Dexter Morgan . . . but you can't help but love him too," indicating the skillful characterization and plotting that made it possible for audiences to understand Dexter's (Michael C. Hall) killing of evildoers who escaped the justice system.[8] In these and series such as *Huff* (Showtime, 2004–2006), *Brotherhood* (Showtime, 2006–2008), *Californication* (Showtime, 2007–), *Breaking Bad* (AMC, 2008–2013), *In Treatment* (HBO, 2008–2010), *Hung* (HBO, 2009–2011), and *Men of a Certain Age* (TNT, 2009–2011), several cable series relentlessly probed distressed male minds and souls and took audiences to their most dark and damaged places. Shawn Ryan, creator and executive producer of *The Shield*, reflected on the changes in television's leading characters, noting that television storytelling had long been based on the comfort provided by characters that would not let audiences down. He explains that for decades, television "showed its heroes making a choice between right and wrong and the audience knew that the choice would be right."[9] Acknowledging the way cable television in particular moved away from this standard, Goodman describes the distinction of cable in this way:

"Networks stay away from anti-heroes precisely because . . . they know that most Americans, like nervous 4–year-olds watching scary parts of a Disney film, want to know it's all going to turn out OK in the end. On a network, it always does." On cable, "there's no such safety net."[10]

To contextualize these assertions of Ryan and Goodman, it is more apt to acknowledge that *some* television storytelling in the twenty-first century showed characters making wrong decisions, but that these characters existed nearly exclusively on shows originating from cable channels. Broadcast networks experimented with characters, offering greater character depth and some unconventionality—for example, Dr. Gregory House's antisociality or the back story of Patrick Jane of *The Mentalist* as a con man feigning psychic ability—but still in 2013, morally ambiguous protagonists remained the exclusive terrain of cable's niche audiences. The other key narrative differentiation between broadcast and cable was in the balance between episodic and serial storytelling each offered. Cable channels were far more willing to allow the seriality that proved crucial to constructing a gradual process of character self-discovery that enabled the exploration of characters struggling with broad constructs such as contemporary masculinity and their place in relation to it.

Distinguishing the Male-Centered Serial

Male characters have been central to television storytelling since the medium's origins, which may lead some to suggest that there is considerable redundancy in the term "male-centered serial." The "centeredness" in these shows is more extensive than simply including male characters, so that these series become essentially about the protagonist. This focus enables a particular type of narrative that allows for the telling of stories about the *entirety of men's lives*—both the personal and professional spheres. Male-centered serials divide narrative time between stories of the protagonists' work and home lives and provide considerable exploration of their motivations, dilemmas, and underlying neuroses. In some cases (*Dexter, Hung,* later seasons of *Sons of Anarchy*), interior monologues presented through voice-overs make the viewer privy to the character's understandings and assessments of events, although audiences also see his fallibility and misperceptions. His worldview is just one part of the broader narrative universe the viewer accesses, not an omniscient perspective. Likewise, *Rescue Me, The Sopranos,* and *Dexter* use dream sequences or hallucinations to texture the characterization of their protagonists beyond that possible in the realist space of the narrative. Most series, however, simply provide this interiority by exposing the viewer to the entire world of the protagonist so that viewers see the code shifts and variation in information meted out to loved ones versus coworkers or, in the case of *The Sopranos, Rescue Me,* and *In Treatment,* to a psychiatrist. The viewer consequently knows more about the character at any point than any other character with which he interacts, and in many cases, has a better understanding of the character than he is presented to have of himself.

Male-centered serials emphasize characterization; their narratives explain and meditate on the men and their actions so that viewers can understand or assess their misdeeds and contradictions. At a most basic level, male-centered serials can be described as shows about a particular character or characters (*The Shield* is the story of Vic Mackey). Even though other descriptors might also offer accurate categorization (*The Shield* is a cop show), the tension driving the cumulative narrative— or the series in its entirety—is a case study of a particular man, which reinforces the sense of the series being "the story" of its protagonist. Like any other show, then, male-centered serials simultaneously blend established narrative strategies and formulas and add uncommon characterization and seriality that allow both aspects of similarity and differentiation from other textual forms. As a cop show, *The Shield* merges textual attributes such as the solving of crimes, the negotiation of departmental politics, and depictions of primarily male workplaces that connect it with shows such as *Miami Vice, Homicide: Life on the Street,* and even *Dragnet.* But its extensive depiction of Vic's home life, the centrality of his family as a motivation for his actions, and its examination of his struggles to synch the illegal and amoral things he does with why he claims to do them make the series about him more than "the job." The totality of the series is a story about Vic Mackey with various policing narratives that complicate, but only provide part of, his story.

Importantly, I'm not proposing these categorizations as rigid binaries—male-centered serials or not—but rather position them on a spectrum; and my desire isn't to police strict boundaries or to suggest that the characters and explorations of masculinities in these series are more important than those of other series. Mostly, the category emerges from a need to acknowledge and name the distinctive narrative possibilities of series that aren't primarily workplace procedurals or ensemble dramas and to identify that a different type of storytelling about men's lives emerges in these shows at this time. Accordingly, the demarcation of the male-centered serial and its preliminary focus results from the need to acknowledge that some of the exceptionality of the stories these series explore—such as their engagement with men's identity struggles—is enabled by this narrative distinction. Although the male-centered serial by no means provides the only or most significant development in relation to television's narrative constructions of men in the early twenty-first century, a variety of character attributes and narrative themes are preponderant in the male-centered serial in such a way as to allow for the identification of a discrete narrative form. The male-centered serial allows for a balance of identity-shaping components of life to bear upon the characterization of its protagonist. This breadth of identity construction, which enables characters to do more than stand in for general "dads" or "detectives" but offers the stories of specific individuals, in concert with the seriality and long-term character development possible through television storytelling, creates a distinctive space for televised constructions of men and masculinity.

Notably, when broadcast networks have attempted series more like the male-centered serials, they primarily diverged from the cable formula by decreasing the serial narrative and emphasizing episodic "work" narratives—as in the case-of-the-week settled on *Shark* (CBS, 2006–2008) or *Eli Stone* (ABC, 2008–2009), the philanthropic mission-of-the-week on *The Philanthropist* (NBC, 2009), or the crime-of-the-week on *Life* (NBC, 2007–2009).[11] None of the broadcast efforts proved commercially successful, though it is impossible to pinpoint whether the cause of failure relates to plotting, character type, or the happenstance of forces such as scheduling and marketing.

The telling of detailed stories about multifaceted aspects of men's lives in male-centered serials enables these shows to interrogate submerged sentiments about gender scripts that lurk beneath the surface of largely reconstructed masculinities. The characters at the center of these dramas present conflicted figures upon which the difficult process of negotiating contrary gender norms is mapped and explore uncertainty about contemporary manhood in a manner that does not presume that reinstating women's subordination is the solution, as had been suggested by previous narratives or as may be suggested by discourses in other television forms. These series make explicit the contestation involved in the struggle over hegemonic masculinities required by post-second-wave gender politics by depicting the consequences that result for men.

Instead of providing the easy image of reconfigured gender relations often offered by broadcast dramas, the male-centered serials narrativize the process of working though discontentment with and uncertainty about contemporary gender scripts in a constructive, but not unproblematic manner.[12] The series feature protagonists unsure of how to be men and of what is expected of them in a society substantially different from the worlds of their fathers. The men make missteps, but stories construct their situations as complicated and avoid the once-common trope of blaming women and feminism for unmooring men from the gender scripts and cultural privileges of the past. Much of the serial narrative of these shows is simply the story of how these men "turn out," of whether they figure out how to be who they are meant to be. The seriality prevents the stasis more common of television series. In a few of the male-centered serials, the characters are in a constant process of change, but most of the men exist in a state of being endlessly bewildered by how to handle situations in their lives in a way never fully or clearly resolved at the conclusion of each episode.

In their meditation on contemporary masculinity, the series depict being a father—and trying to be a good father—as a central component of how to be a man, while very few cases depict men who succeed at being good husbands. Parental, if not paternal, duties—particularly the notion of providing for one's family—consistently emerge as the men's primary motivator, one that they pursue by any means necessary, and often lead to the illegal endeavors explored in the next chapter. These series consistently avoid stories of the career-driven man common in broadcast dramas, and instead frequently explore stories about non-college-educated characters in nonprofessional trades. This leads the series to tell a particularly class-marked set of stories about men's struggles with work and family roles. Also, generation emerges as an explicit feature of male identity through the awkward relationships most of the men are depicted to have with their own fathers. The relevance of second-wave feminism's role in redefining hegemonic masculinities becomes clear here as unmistakable tensions emerge as a result of the way the characters and their fathers embody their masculinities. Significantly, these series examine the lives of straight white men in narrative worlds extraordinarily devoid of gay men or women, and limited ethnic difference enters these series only through secondary and tertiary characters. This narrowness is notable both because it is a culturally specific look at men's struggles and because it is somewhat peculiar relative to the more extensive—albeit limited—diversity more commonly on offer on US television.

In total, the series primarily deviate from patriarchal masculinities through the affirmation of companionate marriages of equals, despite the men's struggles to achieve this, and in affirming parental involvement and placing a priority on care giving. The expansion in expectations of men's participation in home life introduces challenges for several who must negotiate growing familial demands with workplaces and traditional responsibilities of provision. Other aspects of patriarchal masculinities, particularly heteronormativity, simultaneously persist to construct worlds for men in some ways much different than, and in others very much the same as, those of their fathers.

Why Male-Centered Serials? Why Now?

Identifying clear causes or likely correlations for the consistencies among the male-centered serials beyond the interconnecting sociocultural factors outlined in the last chapter is difficult. The patriarchal masculinity long dominant in US society unquestionably continued to permeate some regions of the television world, but this masculinity arguably lost its dominant status in the prime-time drama sometime during the last decade of the twentieth century. This can be explained by both narrative and audience considerations: dramas are particularly reliant on characterization for complexity so that examination and introspection of character can occur here in ways less available to other genres; women commonly dominate drama audiences, making it more likely that shows are populated with men who do not threaten or denigrate them; and the characterizations of women in dramas expanded considerably in the 1990s and this greater range of roles and empowerment required adjustments in the characterizations of men.

The characters in the series explored here embody a shift from a preponderant story that attributed the "male crisis" of the late twentieth century to feminism and women's gains as they came to fruition in the 1980s and much of the 1990s.[13] I avoid the terminology of "crisis" following the well-made case by Kimmel and other masculinity scholars that it is meaningless to speak of male crisis having contemporary urgency because this condition can be traced from the late 1700s through the present. This sense of "crisis" is really the hegemonic contestation of acceptable masculinities that began well before the modern media era and has been part of gender identity in all times.[14] Instead, I consider how the stories told by male-centered serials in the early 2000s opened important spaces for assessing men and masculinities in an era after the substantial, yet incomplete, gains of second-wave feminism and the entrenchment of those gains after their contestation through what some have characterized as a period of backlash.[15] The uncommon interiority of the male-centered serials allows the characters in these series to give voice to anxieties about transitioning gender scripts in a manner that interrogates the challenges of men in twenty-first-century America.

Explaining why male-centered serials emerge on US television at this time draws on the broader contextual examination offered in chapter 1, as well as some more particular narrative trends. First, it is important to remember the relative youth of original cable narrative series. Shows lasting more than a season could be counted on one's fingers by the end of the nineties, yet a subgenre of male-centered serials had emerged just a decade later. By 2010 some clear distinction between the series typically produced by broadcast and cable was evident, and even among cable series alone there were at least two different types of series with male leads: male-centered serials and procedurals with a male protagonist such as *Monk*, *Burn Notice*, *Royal Pains*, and *Leverage*. The procedurals, several of which indeed centered on male characters, featured narratives predominantly driven by episodic "case-of-the-week" plots that made these shows much more similar to episodic procedurals on broadcast networks. Series such as *Monk*, *Burn Notice*, *Royal Pains*, and *White Collar* are primarily about a single male protagonist, with narratives focused on the plot exposition of the case-of-the-week instead of the character development and inner-life probing common to the male-centered serials.[16]

The antecedents and causes of the male-centered serial can be traced to a variety of industrial imperatives and generic developments. As of 2013, the male-centered serial was a narrative phenomenon particular to cable. The economic structure of cable channels—which are funded both through subscription fees and advertising—enabled these channels to create or license series with unconventional protagonists likely to be considered "edgy." Where the strategy of the *broad*caster is to erect a big tent that welcomes heterogeneous audiences with content unlikely to easily offend, niche entities such as cable channels succeed by developing programming that strongly interpellates narrower sections of viewers with content that connects deeply with their beliefs or interests. Cable had considerable success with series that on some level were character studies—typically of quirky, somewhat flawed, or unconventional leading characters.

Setting aside the industrial distinction of cable momentarily, the emphasis on characterization borrowed a page from the playbook that had led many female-centered dramas to fill broadcast schedules in the latter part of the 1990s. Indeed, none of these shows featured protagonists that pushed moral codes or legal standards, as emerges de rigueur with male characters, but they did break from a trajectory of "role model" depictions of women and instead interrogated the challenges of contemporary life by depicting fraught and flawed heroines who struggle but abide. Throughout the late 1990s and early 2000s, broadcast networks experienced surprising success with shows, such as *Ally McBeal* (1997–2002), *Judging Amy* (1999–2005), *Providence* (1999–2002), *Gilmore Girls* (2000–2007), and *Alias* (2001–2006), that focused their narratives on female characters and defied the long-held industry lore that shows had to be about men in order to be successful.[17] Series creators built shows upon careful algorithms blending family drama, procedural workplace settings, and multidimensional flawed and evolving characters to produce a subgenre whose repeated success surprised many. Broadcast networks did attempt to rework this formula with male characters at the helm in the early 2000s in shows such as *Ed* (NBC, 2000–2004), *Citizen Baines* (CBS, 2001), and *The Education of Max*

Bickford (CBS, 2001), but achieved only limited success for no clear reason.[18] These series anticipated the male-centered serials, although they featured unmarried protagonists and did not offer the introspection or flawed characters that emerged a few years later in cable series.

Other precursors to the male-centered serial include an array of original cable series that offered masculinities that varied from the "new man" character and indicated preliminary efforts toward depicting characters that were uncertain about how to negotiate the patriarchal masculinities hegemonic in the past with some of the feminist masculinities also increasingly available to men. ESPN's 2003 series *Playmakers* featured an ensemble of characters dealing with conflicts between the identities expected of them as professional athletes—and football players at that—and their true identities, or the men they sought to be. And even before *The Sopranos*, HBO delved deeply into masculine crisis in the prison series *Oz* (1997–2003) and in the context of a broader family drama in *Six Feet Under* (2001–2005). HBO never identified itself as offering gender-specific narratives, but many of its shows disproportionately centered on male characters and offered intricate examinations of their uncertain negotiation of modern male identity (*Oz, The Sopranos, Six Feet Under, The Wire, Entourage, Hung*).[19] Showtime also began its efforts in original series production with the American version of the British-originated *Queer as Folk* (2000–2005) in this period.

Back on broadcast television, a character such as *NYPD Blue*'s Andy Sipowicz offered an important progenitor of the characters considered here. Significantly, Sipowicz belongs to the older guard of a previous generation, which in some ways distinguishes the worldview of his character from those I consider. *NYPD Blue* is also about Sipowicz's gradual redemption, where the misdeeds of the male-centered serials' protagonists are often beyond atonement. The male-centered serials foremost depict men working through the negotiation of contemporary masculinities—so that the gradual narrative development is as important as, if not more important than, any sense of resolution provided by the end of the series and the men's status at that moment. The shows are not guides or lessons that might instruct men on how to deal with the dilemmas of uncertain gender scripts, but tell cautionary tales that at least offer the suggestion that one is not alone in this confusion.

The other antecedent narrative phenomenon—the one that particularly gives rise to the male characters and show form found on cable networks—was *The Sopranos*. *The Sopranos* provided the template through which I suspect nearly all the shows discussed in this chapter are imagined—if not by their creators, then by the network executives who developed them. *The Sopranos* offered two lessons that changed television creativity: the protagonist does not have to be a good man; and cable channels can offer compelling original series and their storytelling is advantaged by smaller audiences.

The discourse referring to the protagonists of these series as "antiheroes" that becomes common in discussion of the shows examined in this and the next chapter emerges first in descriptions of Tony Soprano (James Gandolfini). According to literary theory, "antihero" is actually a misnomer, or at least imprecise. Literary theory characterizes the antihero as lacking nobility and magnanimity, or as one who lacks the attributes of the traditional protagonist or hero, such as courage, honesty, or grace.[20] Describing these men as "flawed protagonists" seems a more apt characterization, though a less remarkable turn of phrase, as the men at the center of these series certainly do not lack courage and nearly all believe their cause is noble. These protagonists clearly are not the traditional heroes that might inspire audience emulation or identification. In many cases, they are obviously "bad" men by dominant social and legal, if not moral, norms. Yet most of the series also probe the circumstances and conditions that have led them to transgress the bounds of propriety, and the series depict them struggling with their responses to circumstances not entirely of their making.

To a significant extent, the series raise questions about which immoral actions can be justified and under what conditions. The protagonists are mostly driven by motivations related to families—a need either to provide for or to reconstitute them. The narratives are not heavy handed in their defense of wrong actions but do construct events and situations that are morally ambiguous. The motivation of family need—and this is a noble cause in the narratives—leads to stories that engage viewers in a way that calls on them to interrogate presumptions of good and bad, the characters' actions, moral relativism, and mostly how the men navigate their personal and professional choices. *The Shield*'s Ryan explains that in comparison with putting characters in a position where they inevitably make the right choice, "it is far more interesting to put your main character in a position where he or she has to choose between two wrongs,"[21] which describes the scenarios that the protagonists of the male-centered serials commonly occupy. Or, as television scholar Newcomb explains, "It's the agony of their choices. When you see Vic Mackey with his autistic children, you think, here's a guy who's done terrible things, and he's trying to protect the people around him. There's a deep moral ambiguity."[22] Although television series may have featured morally contentious characters in the past, the severity of the transgressions on offer in these series consistently surpasses in comparison.

Turning to the second lesson offered by HBO, until its success with *The Sopranos* and *Sex and the City*, general expectations of original scripted series from cable channels were quite low. Some channels found modest success with niche audiences, success adequate to warrant the production of multiple seasons, but no series had become a cultural phenomenon of the chattering class of *New York Times* readers whose previous most likely comment in regard to television had been to proclaim that they did not own one.[23] The prestige cable hit of the moment now provokes endless discussion in popular-culture outlets targeting college-educated, upper-class demographics, be it *The Sopranos, Mad Men*, or *Girls*. Much more can be said about how *The Sopranos* and *Sex and the City* might be identified as emblematic of a seismic shift in television production than is relevant here—and if it hadn't been these shows, then it would have been others. Nevertheless, these shows were essential forebears to those I consider because they began shifting viewers' expectations of cable series, established that original cable narrative series could offer rich and popular stories, and proved that producers could effectively monetize them through various old and new distribution platforms.[24]

We Don't Need an Antihero: Protagonists of Male-Centered Cable Serials

Writing about the lead characters of *Dexter*, *The Wire*, *Deadwood*, *The Shield*, and *The Sopranos*, Diane Holloway notes, "These terrible, tortured souls are the new breed of antiheroes, and they are startling in their portrayals of pure evil and compromised souls."[25] Indeed, a common thread among popular discussion of these shows in the mid-2000s—particularly in the wake of *Dexter*'s compelling characterization of a serial killer and scenes of marital rape by *Rescue Me*'s Tommy Gavin (Denis Leary)—was a query of "how dark can we go" as successive series continued to push boundaries of making characters relatable and their potential for redemption increasingly infeasible.[26] The extents of these cases are significant because they were widely acknowledged and discussed as aberrant and going too far; but we also lose something if we reduce these series to these events or components instead of engaging the robust storytelling that surrounds the characters' antisocial and illegal deeds. Rather than emphasize the extremes, it is important to construct a sense of the general norms and notable commonalities among the protagonists of these series.

Of the at least fourteen shows that meet the rough categorization of the male-centered serial—*The Sopranos, The Shield, Nip/Tuck, Rescue Me, Huff, Dexter, Brotherhood, Californication, Sons of Anarchy, Breaking Bad, In Treatment, Hung, Men of a Certain Age,* and *Justified*—I focus on nine as particularly archetypal in establishing common tropes or as achieving a certain level of success and cultural discussion: *The Sopranos, The Shield, Nip/Tuck, Rescue Me, Dexter, Sons of Anarchy, Breaking Bad, Hung,* and *Men of a Certain Age.*[27] The next two sections identify what might be viewed as common taxonomic features of the series' characters and narratives: occupation and family life. In addition to the narrative characteristics that distinguish the male-centered serial, they consistently feature various themes, which further supports the consideration of male-centered serials as a distinctive form and one that is centrally engaged in examining the dilemmas and struggles of negotiating contemporary masculinities.

Men at Work

Engaging in "work" appears preponderantly across the series, an unsurprising aspect of depiction relative to the past and present history of male television characters. Notable of the general trend in the depiction of work in these series, however, is the fairly even split between jobs that do and do not require college educations and the socioeconomic status afforded to these characters as a result.[28] Although the percentage of the US population that completes college is below 30 percent,[29] the upper- and upper-middle-class world predominantly on offer in fictional television commonly depicts characters in highly professionalized careers that require, at minimum, a college education. College is obviously not required for the extralegal activities of *The Sopranos'* Mafia dealings or the black market entrepreneurship of the *Sons of Anarchy's* motorcycle club. It is also unnecessary—though not uncommon—for public service careers with their own academies, such as firefighting (*Rescue Me*) and police work (*The Shield*). The trio of central characters in *Men of a Certain Age*—Joe (Ray Romano), Owen (Andre Braugher), and Terry (Scott Bakula)—are acknowledged to have attended college, although they pursue careers that do not necessarily require advanced education. Joe is a small-scale entrepreneur as the owner of a party store, Owen sells cars, and Terry is a sporadically employed actor who pays his bills through temp work and then joins Owen selling cars as well. College educations are to be assumed for high school teachers (*Breaking Bad*, *Hung*), forensic scientists (*Dexter*), and plastic surgeons (*Nip/Tuck*).

This distribution of occupation and educational attainment is notable relative to a variety of narrative norms and in terms of the opportunities allowed and not allowed to the characters accordingly. First, these work roles lead to the presentation of characters who occupy a far truer depiction of middle-class life than typically found on television, where the ubiquity of doctors, lawyers, and to some extent detectives creates a norm of highly professionalized work that affords upper-class privilege and makes any suggestion that families struggle with how to pay the bills a rarity. Further, the presentation of public school teachers in *Breaking Bad* and *Hung* somewhat extends the view of middle-class life typical of the non–college educated, given the comparatively low pay of teaching relative to many professions requiring college education, especially in terms of depicting men in these occupations and the need in these cases to earn a "family wage" as sole breadwinners.[30] Importantly, these occupations are never played for laughs in the manner of comedies that often mock or critique blue-collar work. These series treat the men and their occupations respectfully, although they also acknowledge the frustrations and lack of fulfillment resultant from the men's limited agency.

As discussed further in the next section, occupation plays a key role in the "problems" that protagonists struggle with in their lives and that produce the narrative complication for the characters and the series. Many male-centered serials depict the crisis of inadequate means faced by the middle-class white male in the twenty-first century: cops can't provide a comfortable life and autism experts for families without skimming (*The Shield*), the risk of public service careers after 9/11 adjusts the risk-versus-reward calculation of these jobs for the non–college educated (*Rescue Me*); teachers can't afford housing and to provide for their family (*Hung*) or have inadequate health care (*Breaking Bad*), which necessitates participating in illegal trades to earn supplementary income; or those raised in a motorcycle-club subculture lack marketable skills to earn a living outside of it (*Sons of Anarchy*).

It is also worth considering the occupational status of these characters relative to those common among the women in concurrent "female-centered dramas." Women in such series remained overwhelmingly in highly professionalized careers such as law (*Damages, Drop Dead Diva, The Good Wife*), medicine (*Hawthorne, Nurse Jackie*), or high-level law enforcement (*Saving Grace, The Closer, Rizoli and Isles, In Plain Sight, Body of Proof*).[31] This comparison illustrates the disjuncture among depictions of common occupations of men and women and further underscores the exceptionality of the male-centered serial's attention to characters lacking college educations or in professions with middle-class ceilings.

In addition to acknowledging the differences these series provide from broadcast narratives that tend to feature men in highly professionalized careers, the other relevant juxtaposition is with the trend of unscripted series in the mid-2000s built around men working as deep sea fishermen (*Deadliest Catch*), oil riggers (*Black Gold*), arctic long-haul truckers (*Ice Road Truckers*), and tree fellers (*Ax Men*). Such "real men" docusoaps present men working in jobs requiring extensive physical labor, bearing considerable bodily risk, and offering rewards that are directly dependent on performance.[32] These series expanded unscripted series' reliance on targeting men through traditional constructions of men's work in *American Chopper, Monster Garage*, or *Dirty Jobs* or in survival series such as *Man v. Wild* and *Survivorman*.

Although twenty-first-century television offered various work lives for men, there was considerable stratification by form or genre. The occupations of protagonists in many of the male-centered serials occupied a middle ground in between the white-collar professional careers common to male characters in scripted broadcast and ensemble series and these reality series depicting jobs based on hard labor that offered the dramatic tension of survival. The 2000s indeed provided a range of stories about men and work, but only viewers sampling a variety of shows and channels would know it.

The negotiation of contemporary gender scripts offered by the male-centered serials consequently did not isolate the uncertainties and dilemmas faced by their characters to men of a privileged class status, as could be said of the "new men" of *thirtysomething* in the 1980s or in terms of coterminous discourses about nonpatriarchal "metrosexuality" in the 2000s that was commonly the province of men in professional fields. Not only were the male-centered serials about men grappling with how to be a man in post-second-wave society, but several deliberately presented this as a struggle of a class of men uncommonly represented in US scripted television.

Men at Home

Men have had opportunities to eschew domestic life and still maintain masculinities that were culturally acceptable. Partnering has been less a focus of the narratives for single or divorced male characters than it has been for women; unmarried men in dramas simply have primarily been depicted as workers without the suggestion that they might need to be more than that. The presence of and attention to domestic affairs is one of the primary distinctions of the male-centered serial, which features considerable thematic consistency in depicting the men's home lives. However, where it was unsurprising to find the characters uniformly engaged in work, it is more remarkable that the protagonists of the male-centered serials are uniformly fathers. The characters' marital status is more difficult to classify; it is the case that unstable marital relationships are by far the norm, and in most cases, the cumulative narratives of the series chart the uncoupling, negotiations, and in some cases recoupling of the men and their spouses.

Perhaps more than anything else, desire to fulfill the responsibility of fatherhood propels the characters in these series. The men specifically value fatherhood, not simply a reconstitution of family, which would presume an equivalent importance of marital reconstitution. Paternal duty is consistently affirmed in the series, and it is not simply accorded symbolic value or afforded lip service, but instead, the shows depict the men going to great lengths to be involved with and to secure their children's needs. Though filled with good intentions, these men are flawed fathers who are shown trying, but mostly coming up short. Unlike the befuddled father of comedies, who could also be described in this way, the dramatic context makes these flaws and failures often heartbreaking and tragic. The audience sees the men really trying, but some alchemy of chance, personality, and circumstance prevents things from working out as they intend.

It is not the case in these series that the men are unaware of the importance of family and need to be taught this over the course of the narrative (as in a film narrative such as *The Family Man*, 2000); rather, most know this from the start, but are in some way impaired from or unable to succeed in fulfilling this role, often for reasons beyond their control. Many of the men no longer share the same domestic space as their children, but for the most part, this does not result from any failure as fathers but from their failings as husbands, which is a notable distinction in terms of the stories the series explore and their constructions of hegemonic masculinity. These series depict the men as willing and eager dads whose failures in other arenas require them to struggle to regain parental privileges.

Further evidence of the narrative importance of fatherhood as an aspect of male identity in these shows—and not just a matter of coincidence or hegemony—is made clear by juxtaposing them with the episodically organized series centering on male characters (*Monk, Burn Notice, Royal Pains, Leverage*) that uniformly feature childless, single men. This difference in paternal status that correlates with narrative type is significant and underscores my argument about the distinction of the male-centered serial as a narrative form that conspicuously enables the examination of aspects of men's lives such as the intersection of work and family in a manner different from other narrative forms. Further, the male-centered serials often include the actors who play the roles of their children as part of the regular cast, another indi-cation of the intentionality and significance of constructing these men as fathers. Although the child actors do not appear in every episode, this structural casting distinction leads to children who are not merely referenced but actually seen, and suggests the importance of these roles relative to those of series that have guest actors appear as protagonists' children in rare episodes.

The male-centered serials construct paternity as a crucial component of men's identity. Much of the feminist criticism of television and its female characters has long lamented the overemphasis on maternity as the central and defining experience in female characters' lives. The shows considered here arguably make paternity no more important or no greater a source of dramatic conflict than has been the case of maternity in narratives about women, but paternity has not been cen-tral to the identity of men, especially in dramas. Men have been fathers in comedies, but these stories have neither offered significant reflec-tion on the role of the father, nor have they depicted men struggling in meaningful ways with its consequences. The few dramatic portray-als of fathers typically have been located in family dramas, and here, too, series rarely linked being a father with the problematic of the series or episodes; instead, fathers were steadfast, well grounded, and reliable. (The WB's *Everwood* [2002–2006]—a family drama airing cotermi-nously with these male-centered serials—is a notable exception.) This thematic of the father who cares deeply but struggles in his attempts to figure out how to be the father that he wants to be, needs to be, and is expected to be consequently diverges significantly from established television narratives about men and provides a notable shift from sto-rytelling that has consistently asserted fatherhood as uncomplicated or natural. The responsibility of co-parenting this suggests is indicative of an aspect of masculinity that has moved from the more rigid patriar-chal gender norms that required women to bear the primary burden of parental duties to a more feminist reconstruction of male roles.

In contrast to this emphasis on men engaged with paternal duties, marital bonds are depicted as fragile and permeable, and these rela-tionships provide much of the personal dramatic tension of the series. Importantly, many wives are depicted as active agents in the marital conflict characteristic of the series, and some are as lost and self-destructive as their (ex-)husbands. Generalizing a cause of the failed marriages is far more difficult than noting that disrupted matrimony is preponderantly the case; some series attend little to explaining the familial fractures, and among those that do offer greater detail, common themes are lacking. It is also difficult to classify the complicated status of these relationships, as in most cases it varies considerably throughout the series. Many shows feature couples that are intact at a series' beginning but that separate or divorce by its end (*The Shield, Breaking Bad, Nip/Tuck, In Treatment*; Dexter's wife is murdered), with some that reconcile (*The Sopranos, Rescue Me*).[33] In others, the couple is separated before the beginning of the narrative, although the ex-wife continues to be part of the character's life (*Rescue Me, Hung, Californication*, Joe in *Men of a Certain Age*). The marital status of many of the characters varies by season and remains static from start to finish in only one case (Owen in *Men of a Certain Age*). This preponderance of instability is telling on its own—is it not possible to offer deep character studies of steadily monogamous men?—but this too may be a function of generic type and the need for sources of melodramatic tension.[34]

The reasons why the marital relationships fail vary, but narratives typically depict failings on the part of the male protagonist as the root cause. In several cases, the marital failure directly relates to the wife's disapproval of her husband's illegal actions, while in other cases, it is due to the protagonist's distancing and emotional unavailability—which is often a result of keeping his illegal dalliances from his spouse. In *The Shield*, Corrine (Cathy Cahlin Ryan) isn't completely privy to the extent of Vic's wrongdoing. Her suspicions grow season by season, and ultimately it is physical threat to their family that results from retribution against Vic that motivates her decision to separate from and divorce Vic, and then to move the kids away permanently through witness relocation. *Breaking Bad*'s Walt loses his family after his wife learns he's been cooking methamphetamine to pay health bills related to his cancer treatment and in an effort to leave his family solvent if his cancer proves terminal. He and Skyler (Anna Gunn) reconcile enough to have a working relationship—she helps him launder his profits. As she becomes aware of the extent of his criminality, it is clear that she cannot rationalize his illegal means in the same way he can, and this becomes an insurmountable gulf in their relationship. In other cases, the narrative sides with the male protagonist. *Hung* examines the dead end faced by a one-time high school sports star after he hits the middle-class ceiling of being his family's sole earner as a high school teacher and his wife leaves him. But even here, as the break-up is afforded more depth over subsequent seasons, viewers learn that his inattentiveness to his wife and lack of understanding of how to be an engaged partner contributed to her dissatisfaction.[35]

Some of the characters do achieve full reconstitution of their families. Although the final scene of *The Sopranos* was full of uncertainty, the selection of this banal family moment for the final scene made clear that at least this part of Tony's life was in place. *Rescue Me* concludes with a tenuous reconstitution as Janet gives birth to a child very much positioned to be Tommy's opportunity for paternal redemption. Tommy has filed his retirement papers, but in a final scene Janet (Andrea Ross) permits him to return to work. Given the tumult of the relationship's preceding six years it seems unlikely that the domestic harmony will last, but if Tommy has indeed grown throughout the series, a new era in the relationship may indeed be possible.

Beyond the shifting status of the relationships, the disposition of the women in these series must be acknowledged. None of these women is depicted as passive, and all seek marital relationships that are partnerships even if domestic duties primarily fall to them. The women openly express dissatisfaction when their husbands fail them and take action when situations become unacceptable. *The Shield*'s Corinne gradually goes back to full-time work as a nurse during the series in order to rely less upon Vic. Janet (*Rescue Me*) and Skyler (*Breaking Bad*) are occasionally depicted doing office work, although both also primarily stay home to care for young children. Only Tara (Maggie Siff) in *Sons of Anarchy*, who begins the series as an ex-girlfriend, then becomes girlfriend, fiancée, and wife, explicitly pursues a career; and with the exception of Tara, all of the women are the primary caretakers of their children. Although it is unsurprising that these men would couple with women of a similar socioeconomic status, such a preponderance of female characters without highly professionalized careers is unusual for contemporary television series. This dynamic serves to place a greater burden on the male characters as sole providers, and presumably contributes to the desperation that leads them to engage in illegal activities.

Regardless of the varied degrees of relationship discord that these series depict, they all feature characters engaged in what might be termed "companionate marriages" that are depicted as partnerships. Neither husband nor wife appears able to make unilateral decisions for the family, as would be characteristic of the norm of the patriarchal pater-familiar structure, but nearly all the characters struggle with balancing individual desires, needs, or duties with their role in the partnership. With the exception of Owen, the sole contentedly married character, all of the characters are to some degree challenged by how to negotiate the dynamics of their companionate marriages, and in most cases, things begin to go wrong when the men keep secrets or feel they must find solutions for problems without including their wives. Importantly, Owen's marriage is not depicted as being without challenge. He and his wife struggle over how to manage her return to work and his dissatisfaction with his career, but they are depicted discussing the challenges with the aim of a mutually satisfactory outcome—as though common contentment is the greatest goal. Of the various relationships, Owen's provides the clearest blueprint of what a marriage of equals— the more feminist construct of marriage—would look like. Across the series, the narrative universes the characters inhabit support such marriages, yet the male character's inability to relinquish greater responsibility for family provision leads to his failure to engage fully in this equality. As discussed later, this exclusion of the wife emerges from the male protagonist's sense that a man's duty is to provide for his family, regardless of the fact that he is not positioned as the traditional head of it. As the next chapter explores, the burdens he takes on in provision consistently end poorly for him and his family.

Daddy Issues

The context of the protagonists' relationships with their own fathers— a matter attended to in fair detail in several of the series—also proves useful to understanding the characters' motivations, dilemmas, and actions as fathers. In all the instances in which the men's fathers are referenced or included, the series feature contentious relationships, and the change in hegemonic gender scripts between the generations figures as a source of the acrimony. The relationships that the men have with their fathers are quite different from those that they seek to have with their own children, and many pursue a parenting strategy that deliberately contradicts their own experience. Across the series, the protagonists' fathers embody previous patriarchal norms that afforded fathers little responsibility in child raising and expected minimal involvement. This contrasts with protagonists who consistently struggle to participate in the lives of their children in ways their fathers never considered.

In *Rescue Me*, Tommy and his father are explicitly depicted as embodying two different generations—of firefighters, husbands, fathers, and men. The awkwardness of their communication is made humorous in one episode when the deeper meaning of a conversation about sports is subtitled on screen to make clear the implicit, more personal communication, but Tommy's awareness that his father cannot be the model for his efforts to restore his family is also presented as part of Tommy's conflicted feelings when his father dies. The series charts Tommy's efforts to be involved in—even micromanage—aspects of the lives of his own children, though like his father, he too struggles to express his love in ways they desire.

In *Men of a Certain Age*, Owen's primary storyline examines his relationship with his father, who is also his employer. Owen's father, Owen Thoreau Sr., has belittled Owen as son, employee, and man, and the series chronicles Owen reaching his breaking point once he reflects on his own life at middle age and anticipates his father's plans to pass him over upon retirement. Although they reconcile, the relationship returns to crisis when Owen realizes that the dealership is deeply in debt and perceives his father as saddling him with a doomed legacy. After Owen gains some traction and begins turning the dealership around—albeit by being a very different manager than his father—his father takes steps to sell the dealership without consulting Owen, having not considered the practical or sentimental implications for him.[36]

Fathers are significant to protagonists' identity negotiations even when absent. As a section of the next chapter chronicles, dead fathers can be particularly challenging figures for young men struggling with their masculinity and approach to fatherhood. The specter of deceased fathers particularly haunts protagonists born into outlaw worlds such as Tony Soprano, Dexter Morgan, and Jax Teller (*Sons of Anarchy*).

The absence of the fathers often leads the protagonists to project their anxieties about how they are not achieving the same measure of manhood as their fathers would expect, anxieties that lead to dreams and panic attacks for Soprano and are played out in imagined conversations with Dexter's dead father in *Dexter*. Though not absent due to death, Christian (Julian McMahon, *Nip/Tuck*) attributes much of his selfishness and inability to care for others to his own childhood of abuse and being raised in foster homes. His surgical partner Sean (Dylan Walsh) also struggles with a sense that he let his father down, as he recalls disagreement between his father and mother over surgical repair for his harelip as the reason for his parents' separation and the paternal absence in his life. This life experience contributes to Sean's career choice and continues to affect him when he is faced with his own son's surgical needs.[37] Notably, many male characters in other series at this time also suffer conflicted relationships with their fathers or experience generational tension over optimal fathering techniques. This is a common aspect of characterization among several of the male protagonists in *Lost* and a central narrative tension between father Zeek (Craig T. Nelson) and son Adam (Peter Krause) in *Parenthood* and Jay Pritchett (Ed O'Neill) and son-in-law Phil Dunphy (Ty Burrell) in *Modern Family*.

In all the cases explored in the male-centered serials, the series depict a textually explicit struggle by the protagonists over the fact that the way they choose to be fathers and men differs considerably from the relationships modeled for them. Their fathers, and the attributes of masculinity hegemonic among their fathers' generation, are consistently opposed to the masculinities required of the protagonists. Perhaps more than anyone or anything else, the fathers attract the men's resentment over their inability to find a way to be the men they need to be. The consistency of this portrayal is surprising, especially in the absence of a defining cultural crisis or more common acknowledgment of this tension within broader cultural discourse. The protagonists understand that many of the patriarchal aspects of masculinities common to their fathers' generation have been made unacceptable; unable to embody an alternative and frustrated by the older generation's unwillingness to acknowledge the bankruptcy of its legacy, they remain perplexed by who they are to be.

Who These Men Are Not

A few additional features of the series and their protagonists warrant acknowledgment. Although probably already assumed, it is worth explicitly noting that none of the characters is gay. In fact, the series are so surprisingly devoid of even secondary characters exhibiting gay sexuality that these shows might warrant classification as something even more resolute than heteronormative—maybe heterocentric—to acknowledge how uncommon it is to have such a complete evacuation of gay identity in television texts of this era, especially among those targeting upscale audiences.[38] It could be that the characteristics of the male-centered serial I address create this heterocentricity, but I think a stronger explanation derives from the potential threat of homosexuality to straight masculinities depicted as being in contestation. Similarly family-based series organized around female protagonists, such as *Nurse Jackie* and *United States of Tara*, include gay male characters—in some cases with storylines about their sexuality.[39] But in the male-centered serials, gay identity is "too much" for this already overwrought negotiation of patriarchal masculinity to acknowledge, and thus this process of working through contemporary tensions in masculinities mandates a narrative universe devoid of the possibility of gay identity. Notably, then, despite the many ways in which male-centered serials offer a sophisticated context for exploring male identity, there is seemingly no room for homosexuality to enter into these men's negotiation of self—a clear limitation of the more feminist ideological work evident in these series. The male-centered serials may avoid aspects of patriarchal masculinities, but heternormativity remains uncontested here.

The uniformity of whiteness among the protagonists and their families must also be acknowledged in the context of reading the absences and presences of these shows. Significantly, one situation in which media scholars have identified male stereotypes occurs when men are also members of other nondominant groups. Stories about the particular experience of masculinity for these men are often marginalized in the male-centered serials or exist as significant structuring absences. Many of my claims regarding the negotiation of masculinity are thus particular to straight white men who have most easily accessed hegemonic masculinity and enjoyed patriarchal privilege. Despite the uncommon socioeconomic diversity of these series, it must be acknowledged that they are blindingly white.

The racial difference of the sole nonwhite leading character, Owen in *Men of a Certain Age*, is unacknowledged in the narrative, a conspicuous absence given the back story that the three men have been friends since their 1960s childhood. In many cases, the whiteness of these characters is ethnically marked—as in Tony Soprano's (James Gandolfini) Italian identity or Tommy Gavin's Irishness. Several series do include multicultural secondary casts: Latino Captain Aceveda (Benito Martinez) and African American patrol cop Julian (Michael Jace) are developed and afforded their own storylines in *The Shield*;[40] *Rescue Me*'s firehouse includes a Puerto Rican and African American among its brotherhood and often speaks of race—albeit in the series' uncertain and politically incorrect tone; *Breaking Bad*'s New Mexico border drug trade involves a variety of Mexican and Mexican American characters;[41] and within his Miami setting, Dexter works in a multicultural homicide squad. As these examples suggest, the nonwhite characters are arguably even more tertiary than secondary characters; series that offer their protagonists a community of friends make closest confidants white—as is the case of Vic's strike team,[42] Walt's partner Jesse (Aaron Paul), and Tommy's closest friends in the firehouse.[43]

Finally, a note about where these characters make their homes, as sense of place or geographically specific issues develop in many of the series that reflect on which men are engaged in these negotiations of masculinity. All but one of the series are set in major metropolitan areas and highlight this setting—although many place their action in cities not ordinarily featured as television locales. The series nevertheless simultaneously and contradictorily ignore the characteristics of urban life in a way that opens identification with these characters to men outside of such environs so it doesn't seem that these are problems and situations that only men in urban spaces would encounter. An uncommon number of the series are set in Los Angeles: *The Shield, Californication, Nip/Tuck,* and *Men of a Certain Age.* Even with the base of the entertainment industry being in LA, this is an unusual percentage of series to be located in the city, and all craft narratives specific to LA. *The Shield* never references the entertainment industry, but the city's Rampart division scandal and the racial diversity of its urban neighborhoods function centrally in the series' policing storylines. *Californication, Men of a Certain Age*, and *Nip/Tuck* flirt with the edges of the entertainment industry in a manner that leads these shows to feature stories that could only happen in LA.

Only *Rescue Me*, set in New York City, locates its story in the Northeast—an uncommon fact given the tendency of series to be set in the major cities along the northern Atlantic seaboard. New York functions centrally as the location of the 9/11 attacks; thus this series could not be told anywhere else. With the exception of *Hung*, set in ex-urban Detroit, these series are also explicitly situated outside of the Midwest. Notably, *Hung's* opening sequence features considerable use of urban Detroit to reinforce the themes of industrial decay and shifting fortunes—for the region, and particularly for its non-college-educated white men—although most series' action is located in less urban settings such as Ray's demolished home on a lake, coffee shops, and the high school. Of the others, *Dexter* and the first seasons of *Nip/Tuck* take place in Miami and *Breaking Bad*, in Albuquerque. For the most part, although visually distinctive, these settings are interchangeable with any other metropolitan area.[44]

In most cases, family homes are neither explicitly signified as urban nor clearly marked as suburban, as in *The Sopranos*. The exception, *Sons of Anarchy*, is set in a rural California town named Charming—an ironic moniker given its occurrences of drug and weapon trade, molestation, and white supremacy. Here, location in a small town functions importantly in the narrative, as the more patriarchal masculinity hegemonic within the motorcycle club derives its power from being outside of urban and industrialized areas in which education is more likely to secure the greatest accumulation of capital.

Notably, though, these stories do not, for the most part, take place in small-to-midsized towns, but are tales of men in cities.[45] Yet paradoxically, with the exception of *Rescue Me*, the specificity of urban life is hidden: characters all drive on uncrowded surface streets, exterior shots of homes offer run-of-the-mill architecture, homes are in neighborhoods that could be many places, and the lives of these men are presented as those of men anywhere. The series thus simultaneously are very specifically located yet attempt a placelessness that works to make the series' contemplation of contemporary masculinities more broadly relevant.

"What Does a Man Do, Walt?"

Laying bare the motivation of its protagonist, *Breaking Bad* poses the question used here as a subheading to its protagonist by Gus Fring (Giancarlo Esposito), who is trying to convince Walt (Bryan Cranston) to continue making meth. Walt has earned the money he needed to support his family if his cancer proved terminal, and it even appears that his cancer is in remission. In a key moment in which Walt's character arc turns and he begins to transition from hapless victim reduced to earn for his family by any means possible to a willing and complicit agent in the drug trade, Gus answers the question for him: "A man provides; and he does it even when he is not appreciated, or respected, or even loved. He simply bears up and he does it, because he's a man."[46]

Similarly, in describing *Rescue Me*, co-creator, producer, writer, and lead actor Denis Leary articulated the central premise of his show as follows: "The show is ultimately about male ego, male pride, being a man, that's the heart of the show: 'What is it to be a man?'"[47] Beyond the narrative organization that unites the shows considered here, such moments of explicitness make very clear what all of the shows wear plainly, yet unremarkably, on their surface; these shows are meditations on what it is to be a straight white man, on what they do or feel they must do in the particular time of the beginning of the twenty-first century in the United States.

Much more so than previous trends in male characterization such as the new man, these characters and their struggles do not indicate a knee-jerk retort to a previous norm. So-called new men of the 1980s contradicted many aspects of patriarchal masculinities and perhaps were men before their time; they were what you might conjure up if you were tasked with imagining men changed by the feminist movement. In contrast, the men of the male-centered serials are characters that embody the complexity of experiencing the gradual changes related to opening the public sphere to women, as has occurred over the past twenty to thirty years. And just as the possibilities for women have changed, so to have men witnessed adjustments in the attributes of masculinities affirmed within the culture.

The men in male-centered serials seem legitimately bewildered at times by how to act or respond to the events of their lives. They look to their fathers and disregard that masculinity without nostalgia, but eliminating that set of gender scripts does little to call alternatives into existence. In each of the series considered here, it seems as though series' writers began with an idea for a troubled protagonist, but had little expectation of where that character would end up. The result is that the series often unfold like a meditation on the challenges men face in negotiating their identity in a post-second-wave world instead of providing a blueprint for contemporary masculinity typical of a role model. Throughout these stories the viewer is no more certain of who these men should be than the characters are, and although the audience may be able to identify when the character goes wrong, viewers are also made to understand the confusion and uncertainty that leads to wrong action.

The characters at the center of the male-centered serials are compelling protagonists. Their series artfully offer them depth and nuanced characterization that allows audiences to root for them even though they clearly do bad things and also very well may be bad men. Yet, most remain seemingly redeemable and desirable in a manner that creates a complicated relationship among viewer, story, and character. In many cases, it is the intricate intersection of the causes of these flaws and failures that makes the series and characters so compelling. As Goodman notes, "On a great drama, the writers are constantly challenging you as a viewer."[48] Thus the protagonists of the male-centered serials create a viewing pleasure that is not about identification with the character, but instead perhaps about the stimulation of considering one's own moral compass or of parsing the mixed emotions the shows introduce as viewers face a dilemma of wanting the criminal protagonists to elude apprehension so that the narrative can continue, while nevertheless knowing that apprehension is the deserved fate.

The methods employed here cannot definitively answer questions about the audience, but narrative analysis makes clear that the male-centered serials preponderantly present deep character studies and conflicted men previously rare on US television. Although the particular narrative attributes of the male-centered serial explain some of the openings for attention to men's struggles in reconciling post-second-wave gender scripts for work, family, and the measure of what it is to be a man, the consistency of the themes presented in this chapter are too predominant for happenstance and instead are suggestive of broader cultural anxiety. Interesting, and still unexplainable in my mind, is the impetus that stimulates stories about men's struggles. Some sort of catalyzing event remains elusive, so that these preponderant themes and stories of struggle seem instead to be an organic bubbling to the surface of largely unconsidered and unspoken challenges for men. Chapter 3 now delves more deeply into several of these series to identify the commonalities and divergences among the illegal dalliances of these series' protagonists and what this common defiance of structures of law and order suggests about the opportunities available to men.

3

Any Men and Outlaws

The Unbearable Burden of Straight White Man

We meet Walter White on the day he turns fifty. A white man in Albuquerque, New Mexico, he is the sole earner for his family, which includes a teen son and a wife expecting their second child. Walt teaches high school chemistry and moonlights at a car wash for extra money. After collapsing at the car wash and learning he has inoperable lung cancer, he begins cooking crystal methamphetamine, ostensibly to pay for the medical bills uncovered by his insurance and to build a nest egg for his family's survival after his impending death, but also to live a life less mundane in the time remaining.

Ray Drecker coaches baseball and basketball for the high school team he once starred upon. He married his high school sweetheart but the stardom has faded and the sweetheart has left him for the class nerd, who is now an affluent dermatologist. He falls farther from his planned life when the lake home he lives in—his childhood home—burns down and lapsed insurance payments leave him without means to rebuild. Ray refuses the offer of his McMansion-dwelling neighbor, who wants to buy the property and raze the out-of-place bungalow, and instead sets up a tent on his property and endeavors upon a second career as a male prostitute to earn the income he needs to rebuild the home, and hopefully his family.

Vic Mackey shares his suburban home with his three children and loving wife. Police work in the inner city is tough, and he begins to cut corners and bend rules. At first he and his detective team use some cash and drugs pocketed from busts to incentivize informants to help them do their jobs and make the streets safer. But when they need to cover up minor duplicitous dealings, their actions and the stakes rapidly escalate until there is little difference between the detectives and those they arrest.

These men, whose tales animate *Breaking Bad*, *Hung*, and *The Shield*, respectively, are protagonists in various stages of being undone. They are not necessarily bad men, or at least none starts out that way, but a series of choices—including engaging in illegal behavior—lead at least Walt and Vic far outside the moral bounds of society. In addition to these stories of three relatively "any man" characters, who break the law in an effort to provide for, restore, or maintain their families, are series about those who have less of a choice. Tony Soprano (*The Sopranos*) and Jax Teller (Charlie Hunnam, *Sons of Anarchy*) were born into lives enmeshed in illegal trades. Their patrilineal legacy destined them to be leaders of men who exist in worlds outside the law and society, and despite their longing for lives in "normal" worlds, it seems doubtful either could ever have such a life. Destiny was similarly cruel to Dexter Morgan of the eponymous *Dexter*, who witnessed the brutal murder of his mother as a three-year-old and then spent days trapped with her bloody corpse in a cargo container. His adoptive police-officer father chooses to channel his resulting sociopathic and homicidal impulses, refining Dexter into a serial killer compelled to murder the guilty who escape justice. As an adult, Dexter evades detection, but also finds himself lonely, separate, and feeling not fully human.

These show premises highlight the consistent criminal behavior characteristic of the protagonists of male-centered serials. Hank Moody (David Duchovny), who unintentionally yet inevitably commits consensual statutory rape in *Californication*, and Joe Tranelli (*Men of a Certain Age*), who battles a gambling addiction, complete the list of men whose transgressions, while still illegal, seem practically benign among the pack of men who have taken another's life.[1] This composite of series' descriptions indicates how—in addition to telling stories about the entire lives of richly drawn characters—several of the male-centered serials focus on protagonists who attempt to solve what might be termed the principal problematic of their lives through illegal means.

The fact that so many of these men—uniformly white, straight, and either physically or intellectually formidable—must transgress the bounds of law and order suggests that all is not well in the lives of men. This turn to illegality may be assumed to be a reaction against fading patriarchal power, but the intricately constructed characters and their stories reveal a far more complicated engagement with changing gender roles and social norms than might be presumed.[2] All the series depict the men facing crises that challenge their core priority—which is typically the maintenance or reconstitution of family—but vary in how the protagonists balance their own desires with what is best for their families and in the reasons why the men choose these routes. The series consistently tell stories of men who are floundering in their efforts to be the men they want to be and have the things they most want. Their difficulty in "being men" indicates a masculine identity crisis that derives, at least in part, from difficulty merging newly valorized aspects of masculinity, such as paternal involvement and nonpatriarchal marital relations, with residual patriarchal masculinities that require great responsibility of men for familial provision. The men believe in equitable partner relationships yet are unable to free themselves of a sense that they alone must bear the burdens that lead them to seek illegal solutions.

Another notable component of these men's struggles is what the stories blame and do not blame for their protagonists' dilemmas. Women, wives, and feminism are never constructed as in any way responsible for the situations with which the men contend. Rather, allocation of blame can be indentified in the complicated relationships with and anger the men express toward their fathers. This blaming of the father, which is commonly implicit, though sometimes explicit, maps easily onto a blaming of patriarchy and the patriarchal masculinity the fathers are depicted to possess.

This chapter explores how and why these men—who rank among the most privileged in American culture—find themselves needing to break the law to support or restore their families and what these stories tell us about the dilemmas and challenges of contemporary masculinities. The chapter conceives of all of these men as outlaws, but distinguishes between those characters who begin as "any men" in stories that tell tales of men who go bad and those born into the outlaw life.

Television's Outlaw Heroes

Outlaw protagonists that are truly bad men have been rare on television.[3] Leading men have been socially awkward, womanizers, and otherwise unlikely heroes, but depicting a protagonist engaged in extralegal activities has defied the standards and practices of television—if not in actual prohibition, then as mandated by industry lore regarding what audiences will tolerate. *The Fugitive*'s Richard Kimball may come closest to offering a criminal protagonist, but even here viewers know he was wrongly accused. Television storytelling has historically eschewed nonheroic protagonists or characters that challenge simple dichotomies of good or bad, so that even those who are supposedly bad are known to be good. Some protagonists in male-centered serials aren't actually criminals—as is the case of *Rescue Me*'s Tommy Gavin, who never clearly violates laws of the state beyond drunken disorderliness but can be endlessly cruel and impudent to friends and family. Most of the rest are felons. Some, such as Dexter, only do bad things to bad people (except when mistaken or on the verge of being discovered), while Vic Mackey, Walter White, and Tony Soprano may once have been able to rationalize their misdeeds in terms of situational ethics, but ultimately commit acts of depravity beyond justification. In comparison with these murderers, Ray Drecker's work as a prostitute seems benign, especially in the stories depicted, which construct his encounters as offering emotional growth for him and valued service to his clients, who otherwise lack opportunities for intimacy. Yet the offenses of the nine protagonists are significant: eight commit prosecutable offenses, two are irredeemably selfish in their personal lives, and five murder repeatedly.[4]

Despite offenses ranging from being egocentric rakes to being first-degree felons, these characters exist in narratives that may not go so far as to seek audience empathy, but construct circumstances so that audiences understand how the characters reach this point of action. Unlike the common television character perceived as likely to inspire viewer identification, these characters are relatable versions of a good self that has gone bad, who come to make wrong—very wrong—choices. Many of the narratives encourage viewers to hope the characters elude law enforcement and, at the least, not to perceive them as villains. Some of the shows feature protagonists that change over time—a narrative tool available to television's ongoing storytelling, but rarely used. Neither Walter White nor Vic Mackey begins as the monster he becomes, illustrating another strategy these series use to explore nonheroic protagonists in defiance of conventional norms.

Although few protagonists in television history have so unrepen-
tantly resorted to the illegal acts common to those of the male-centered
serial, male characters have long faced and responded to problems;
and at a narrative level, these outlaw stories are just a more extreme
variation of such storytelling. Much of the programming of prime-
time television's early years emphasized stories that were confined to
an episode so that the gradual process of making a difficult choice was
abbreviated, the consequences of the action were narratively insignificant, and the implications of the action were typically limited to the
man's professional life. The problem motivating the plot was a case that
needed to be solved, a legal trial requiring adjudication, or a patient
needing treatment. For example, in the episode of *Hill Street Blues*
titled "Trial by Fury," police captain Frank Furillo is under public pressure for successful prosecution in a case in which a nun has been raped
and murdered. Faced with a lack of evidence, he tries to solicit a con-
fession by only charging two suspects whom he is confident are guilty
of the rape and murder with possession of stolen property (obtained
from the church), hoping that the suspects' fear of vigilante justice if
they are released will lead them to confess. One confesses and agrees
to testify against the other for a second-degree murder plea. Although
this is portrayed as a difficult situation and decision for Furillo, and
one that leaves his girlfriend, public defender Joyce Davenport (Veron-
ica Hamel), angry enough to suggest he sleep elsewhere that night, all
is returned to normal in the next episode and this action lacks linger-
ing implications. As Jeffrey Sconce describes, throughout much of US
television history the storytelling of the medium has been dominated
by "a world of static exposition, repetitive second-act 'complications,'
and artificial closure."[5] A range of serial features grew increasingly
common by the end of the twentieth century, whether that of featuring
multi-episode plot arcs or offering serial "personal" storylines inter-
mixed within series focused on an "occupational" episodic story. Part
of what earns the male-centered serials their distinction is the narrative priority afforded to ongoing storytelling about issues and relationships in the life of a man. So while the male characters of series past
would have reasonably struggled with similar problems, television's
dominant narrative strategies diminished these inter- and intraper-
sonal crises through episodic resolution.

Although the "new men" that populated series such as *thirtysome-thing*, *Hill Street Blues*, and *St. Elsewhere* and progeny such as *NYPD Blue* and *ER* were increasingly depicted as wrestling with persistent personal problems, all of these characters negotiated these challenges within the realm of legal society. *NYPD Blue*'s Andy Sipowicz is probably the closest precursor to the outlaws of the male-centered serials, but the flaws that differentiate Sipowicz from a hero in his time, primarily his deep-seated racism and alcoholism, are largely personal. He is only—and only initially—presented as morally irredeemable; he is never a criminal, and it is clear from the outset that his tale is one of redemption, especially as he faces an inconceivable range of melodramatic torture over his twelve seasons on *NYPD Blue*: the death of his son, wife, and two partners; single parenthood; cancer. Still, his character offers a preliminary version of the type of storytelling that receives much greater focus in the male-centered serials, stories that in their preponderance question whether the men depicted in these shows can exist within the confines of law-abiding society.

What's to Blame? Disentangling Gender and Class

Illustrating that the protagonists in the male-centered serials preponderantly seek solutions outside the boundaries of social norms requires only simple descriptive analysis, but interrogating what enables the prevalence of this story and what this trend suggests about men's social status proves more complicated. Though the men categorically engage in illegal behavior, the reasons why are varied and developed with inconsistent nuance across the series. Most clear, however, is the structuring absence of what is not blamed: women.

Television's "new men" of the mid- to late 1980s—the most recent male character type to contrast patriarchal masculinities prior to the male-centered serials—also suffered problems and uncertainties that hadn't previously been emphasized in depicting the male experience. But these men's problems could be predominantly traced to difficulties negotiating women's changing gender roles as enabled by second-wave activism. Because new men were almost always those of upper-middle-class privilege, they most profoundly experienced the consequences of women's increased access to the public sphere in professional careers or encountered romantic interests with similar aspirations. The problems these men faced were, with varying degrees of subtlety, attributed to a world being changed by women's demands. In some cases, these changes were affirmed as a necessary social transition, and the shows explored the benefits this might have for men as well as women. Others presented women's changing roles as a loss of male privilege and an unreasonable imposition by women.

The male-centered serials, however, recast the source of men's troubles—often obscuring an easily identifiable cause—but unequivocally refuse to blame women. The men's relationships with the women in their lives are often troubled, but this is most commonly acknowledged as a result of the men's failure to live up to what the narrative presents as reasonable expectations of them. Women are spared blame, but gender roles are nonetheless implicated as a cause of men's problems: it is men's social roles and the characters' struggle with the expectations of men, fathers, and husbands that lead to their predicaments.

The critical analyst who queries "how did he get here" finds a hazy blend of causes most precisely expressed as the challenge of negotiating male gender scripts in post-second-wave, postindustrial, neoliberal societies. Transcending the academic jargon, the problems these men face emerge from a realignment of gender norms that has connected with unintended or unrelated adjustments such as the decline in the family wage and considerable growth in basic fixed costs for US families. Although unnamed, economic changes such as the erosion of the middle class and reduced access to safe housing and competitive schools—especially for the non–college educated—bears considerable responsibility for the crises the men in these series experience.[6] These series do not emphasize a simple, individualized cause of the men's struggles, such as alcoholism, joblessness, or infidelity; rather, the problems are structural and institutional. Admittedly, the series do not emphasize these structural causes; hints of the sources of the men's uncertainties are often only cursorily referenced in pilot exposition and rarely developed. But the viewer who stops to reflect on the question of "how did he get here" finds that the blame is not placed on individual failing.

Though financial crises primarily inspire the illegal actions of the three "any man" protagonists that begin their series as law-abiding citizens, gender is just as centrally implicated in this economic crisis because the gender script the men adhere to in their personal pride and sense of self leads them to make crises involving the support of the family theirs alone to bear.[7] These are not men harped upon by nagging wives or pushed by others to take on great burdens; instead, they are driven by internalized expectations of their role as men *to provide*— as the scene from *Breaking Bad* discussed in the conclusion of the last chapter highlights. Any effort to pinpoint a cause of their predicament must acknowledge the cumulative, intertwined influences of economic crisis and residual gender scripts: economic crises cause the initial problematic, but adherence to a patriarchal gender script that demands that a "man" behave in certain ways exceptionally limits the range of solutions available.

The complicated intersection of gender and economics as a cause is furthered to the degree that many of the series present men struggling with a parallel to the work/family dilemmas identified as "women's problems" in the context of second-wave feminism. Historian Stephanie Coontz has written recently about a "masculine mystique" to addresses how narrow and increasingly contradictory expectations of men straightjacket them into proscribed gender roles, much as was the case of the feminine mystique.[8] The mystique Betty Friedan wrote of can be described as women's dissatisfaction with hegemonic gender roles that suggested women should be fulfilled by performing the duties of femininity: "cooking, cleaning, washing, bearing children."[9] What Coontz terms a "masculine mystique" likewise acknowledges hegemonic gender roles; she explains, "Men are now experiencing a set of limits—externally enforced as well as self-imposed—strikingly similar to the ones Betty Friedan set out to combat in 1963, when she identified a 'feminine mystique' that constrained women's self-image and options."[10] Longitudinal research from the Families and Work Institute has identified a significant rise in reports among men in dual-earner couples who report work/family conflict from 35 percent in 1977 to 60 percent in 2008, while for women, this conflict has only risen from 41 to 47 percent.

Other aspects of their survey led the institute's researchers to conclude that a "new male mystique" had come to replace the "traditional male mystique."[11] As they use the term, the "traditional male mystique" asserts "pressure to be the primary financial providers for their families" or mandates that "men should seek fulfillment at work and strive to be successful as financial providers for their families."[12] They use the terminology of a "new male mystique" to describe the feeling among men that they must simultaneously live up to the traditional male mystique while also being a much more involved partner and father. The significant growth in the experience of work/family conflict results because unchanged workplaces have "created pressure for men to, essentially, do it all in order to have it all."[13] In their analysis, the institute's researchers explain,

> The new male mystique suggests that men today are facing two opposing forces—greater value placed on involvement with their families versus social structures, systems and norms that do not make it easy for them to spend less time working and more time with their families. . . . For some men—those with work-centric or strong traditional values—the world has changed too much, while for others—especially those with family responsibilities—the world has not yet changed enough.[14]

At their core, the terms "male mystique" or "masculine mystique" are really just another, perhaps more accessible way of saying "hegemonic masculinities"—in this case referencing the way masculinity is constructed in the broader culture, rather than in particular narrative universes. In their surveys, the Families and Work Institute uncovers the situation of real men that is reflected in the struggles depicted by the protagonists of the male-centered serials. Though the issues the characters face are more extreme manifestations of work/family crisis, the protagonists endeavor, in a manner consistent with the institute's analysis, to embody persistent patriarchal masculinities that enforce their role as provider while at the same time adhering to reconstructed masculinities that demand they prioritize being involved partners and fathers.

A work/family conflict develops for men for whom work is still tied so closely with masculine identity that they cannot choose not to work, and the tension that evolves from what the man must do and who he must be as a worker leads to his alienation from his family. Even thirty years after feminist intervention and the realignment of public and private gender scripts it introduced, no mainstream cultural discourse poses an option for men of *not* being a worker.[15] The men in these series are depicted as caught in a web of gender roles and capitalist inequality that derive in part from the failure of men's gender scripts to acknowledge how greater domestic involvement affects occupational duties. Shifting norms of paternal gender scripts enable and encourage men to be more active participants in children's lives at the same time that there has been no loosening of professional demands, and considerable uncertainty regarding how this reflects on one's masculinity persists.[16] Some of the confusion over and inability to be "good men" that plays out in these series results from male characters bumping up against changing expectations that don't acknowledge the double bind contemporary men face in reconciling duties as fathers, husbands, and workers. For example, the marital separation of Janet and Tommy before the start of *Rescue Me* is blamed on Tommy's detachment from his family—a detachment that results from the absence created by working the three jobs that are needed to provide for the family and allow Janet to not work outside the home. This preexisting detachment exacerbates Tommy's sense of guilt, grief, and isolation after 9/11, which fuels his alcohol abuse, which then causes further estrangement.

To be certain, men do not face the discriminatory laws and subordination to structures of power experienced by women of the 1950s and 1960s, nor is my argument that men face greater burdens than women or that their struggles should be viewed as paramount to those of women. Coontz identifies evidence of real men struggling with social regulations of identity, and here I identify narratives exploring this struggle. Importantly, the narrative universes of these series are sufficiently informed by feminism as to presume the uninhabitablity of victimhood for these men. Although many appear to be and express feeling desperate, they do not complain, but, in Gus's words, they "bear up," in a manner suggesting that the fault is not with with the new masculinities but with uncertainty over how to manage the increasing, and sometimes contradictory, scope of culturally desirable masculinities. Thus it is necessary to consider the stories' acknowledgment of the negative consequences shifting gender norms have for men without presuming that this acknowledgment suggests a backlash against feminism.

The series construct the core problem the men face as related to limited financial means, though gender roles are inextricable from issues of men's work, "duty" of provision, and earning power. Importantly, the series pose economic crisis as an explicitly manifest problem and present it with greater verisimilitude than the often-artificial treatment of economic struggle, which is most commonly a structuring absence within US television. In choosing illegal means, the men do not set out in search of great riches but rather pursue modest goals: Walt initially endeavors just to pay for cancer treatments and establish a nest egg to compensate for the loss of his income; Ray seeks enough money to rebuild his stark cabin home. Unlike in *The Sopranos*, these series do not depict the men and their families seeking or living lives of extraordinary means.[17] These series offer some of the most "realistic" depictions of the mise-en-scène of the truly median family income of approximately forty thousand dollars for 2010 US society. Where the common absence of attention to economic conditions in US television leads to a depiction of spacious, newly constructed homes and Pottery Barn–style furnishings as the typical trappings of the "middle class"— when this is more likely achieved only by the top 10 percent of wage earners—the homes of the characters in these series are comparatively claustrophobic, sometimes kitschy, and not overwhelmed by conspicuous consumption or the common aspirational style and décor.

Even though a better economic situation appears the solution to the characters' central problem, the illegally gained money does not provide a solution but instead introduces new crises. It quickly becomes apparent that the men don't need money so much as a path to acquisition that lacks the consequences of their illegal trades. The male protagonists are depicted as caught in dilemmas resulting from existing in a moment of incomplete transition into feminist masculinities. They embrace changed gender scripts through more equitable marriages and greater participation in the lives of their children, but are not yet able to disregard the sense that a man must provide. In retaining aspects of patriarchal masculinity that assume the duty of familial provision, many of the men miss out on the availability of able help from marital companions. It is possible to imagine very different outcomes in many of the series if the protagonists had openly shared problems with their wives and sought to solve their problems together.[18]

The following sections explore the challenges that lead the men of male-centered serials to resort to extralegal activities and the consequences depicted for them and their families. The first section gathers the cases of "any man" characters, while the second section explores the men born into illegal worlds. The analysis reveals the nuances among similar stories—for example, how Walt's motivation in *Breaking Bad* blends patriarchal duty with midlife crisis while *Hung* emphasizes shifts in the US economy and cultural values. The any man tales foreground characters struggling with ego, pride, and responsibility in narratives that differentiate heroes and villains according to how men take responsibility for themselves and their obligations. The outlaw stories explored subsequently tell more particular stories about younger men attempting to reconcile legacies left by deceased fathers with their own sense of how to be a man in contemporary society.

Bad Teachers: Men Gone Bad in *Hung* and *Breaking Bad*

There are considerable structural similarities among the shows that feature "any man" characters despite appreciable variation in where they end up. These men begin their stories living relatively ordinary lives but come to pursue life paths far from ordinary. In their entirety, the series explore the protagonists' responses to notable challenges—typically introduced in the pilot episode—and then trace their reactions and the way they deal with the outcomes of their choices. *Breaking Bad*, *Hung*, and *The Shield* provide the most apt illustrations of any man narratives, though the former two shows receive the greatest focus here. *The Shield* was one of the first male-centered serials and is ostensibly about Vic Mackey, but its plotting utilizes its ensemble cast with fairly extensive episodic B and C storylines that require it to afford less narrative attention to Vic's character in comparison with those of other male-centered serials. Despite this, clear parallels between the stories of Walter White and Vic Mackey warrant acknowledgment of *The Shield* and illustrate how this narrative phenomenon may exist more broadly.

Of the any man series, *Hung* provides exceptional explicitness in voicing its protagonist's struggle to find his place in the world. *Hung*— as well as *Dexter*, which is explored in the next section—provides voice-over narration by its lead character that makes clear the inner dimensions of the character's struggles; similarly, in its fifth season, *Sons of Anarchy* begins using Jax's journal entries, meant for his young sons, to allow viewers a sense of his perspective. These series consequently don't simply tell stories about events that happen to these men, but explore how these events lead the men to grapple with their sense of self and place in the world. The voice-overs make explicit what is often implicit or uncovered only through close analysis in other series; yet the voice-overs are not of omniscient narrators, but rather express the protagonist's perspective. The viewer consequently often sees things that are obscured to the character and is afforded the ability to see the limits of the character's interpretation of the events surrounding him while also understanding the internal motivations and perspectives of the character.

More than in other series, the crises of Ray Drecker (Thomas Jane) are connected implicitly and explicitly with macroeconomic changes in American society. Ray's narration opens the series over visuals of Detroit's symbols of fading glory—Tiger Stadium being demolished, shuttered auto manufacturing plants, magnificent works of architecture now crumbling:

> Everything is falling apart, and it all starts right here in Detroit, the headwaters of a river of failure. Thank god my parents aren't around to watch the country they loved go to shit. They were proud Americans. They had normal jobs and made a normal living. They fit in. They weren't kicked up the ass every day of their lives by property taxes, homeowner's associations, and greedy, beauty queen, ex-wives. What would I tell them if they saw me now? That I'm not to blame? That it's not my fault? They didn't raise me that way. They taught me to take responsibility and get the job done, no excuses. You do your best with whatever gifts god gave you.[19]

And so we find Drecker, not seething with anger, but lost, struggling, and humbled.

In many ways *Hung* tells the story of a conventional American character—the golden boy and hometown all-star—but picks up on his story twenty years after the the story usually ends. Ray earned a college baseball scholarship, married his high school sweetheart, and was recruited into the major league, which is typically where this story concludes. But for Ray, an injury ends his career as a player and leads him to return home to middle-class, suburban Detroit to become a high school teacher, the "second most-winningest" coach in school history, and a father. By the time we meet him, the high school sweetheart has left him, his team has been on a losing streak, and tight finances lead to a lapsed home insurance bill and homelessness after a house fire. Ray acknowledges that he feels that "I wasted my youth and now I look around and everybody seems to have something but me. I don't have anything. I got a burned out house, a job that pays shit; I can't afford to pay my taxes on time; I can't even afford to buy my son a ticket to a rock and roll show."[20]

Such feelings of desperation lead Ray to attend a hotel ballroom seminar on "Unleashing Your Inner Entrepreneur," during which he is encouraged to identify and market a hidden talent. The only "talent" Ray can identify is the praise he's received from women for being, as the series' title notes, "hung." As the series opens, audiences consequently find Ray on the way to his first attempt to moonlight as a prostitute. He explains himself, not by making excuses but by noting,

> Desperate times call for desperate measures. Do you know what a public school teacher makes these days—okay, so maybe we make a little more in Michigan than the national average—but what is the national average: more than a waiter, less than a plumber, about half of what it takes to live a normal life. So what do you do when your career pays crap? You do a side gig; used to be stocks, now ebay, tutoring.[21]

Ray's decision to opt against such conventional salary enhancements and instead pursue prostitution is part of the series' strategy of exploring Ray's crisis as something larger than a personal situation, but related to changing gender norms and economic fortunes. Ray's homelessness is just the latest in a series of lost privileges that begins with his career-ending injury, return home, and wife Jessica (Anne Heche) leaving him. As his voice-over explains, "What happened to my life? I used to be a big deal. I used to be going somewhere. Now all I ever seem to do is try not to drown. When did life become something that you buy?"[22] In Ray's mind, then, a combination of early personal success, the economic reality of postindustrial America, and a society obsessed with consumption have eroded what he speaks of as "normal" in his parents' lives and left him without a script of what to do. The conspicuous Detroit setting makes clear that *Hung* is a story of the fading of American exceptionalism and the male privilege that was part of it.

Gender crisis is at the heart of *Hung* and yet is somehow regularly obscured by economic crises in plotlines and characters' understanding of situations. The role reversal of a man entering women's "oldest profession" and the management of his career by two women offer complicated, yet underdeveloped, avenues for exploring gender politics: *Hung*'s stories instead emphasize the peculiar personalities of the women and their rivalry. Where the decision to write a story about a male prostitute appears clearly to be a strategic plot device—would the show have seemed exceptional enough to warrant creation if Ray simply chose to earn extra income tutoring or offering private sports lessons?—it consistently fails to examine the gendered nature of this endeavor. Ray's escort work is routinely less about sex and much more about the challenges of intimacy that lead women to request his services. These women, and his efforts to satisfy them, teach Ray lessons relevant to his quest to not be the man of the circumstances we first find him in, while also offering at least brief glimpses of the dissatisfactions women experience in this post-second-wave, postindustrial, consumerist society. But these stories engage little, if at all, with the gendered nature and politics of sex work.

The series ultimately tells the story of one man who may be challenged by the broader social changes that have reorganized American culture in the last quarter-century, but who can only attempt to change much smaller pieces; he is not crusading to restore the family wage for factory workers, but trying to rebuild a house so that his children, and perhaps his ex-wife, will again live with him. Notably, his difficulties with Jessica are not related to her career aspirations. The precise circumstances of her decision to leave him are not made clear, but Jessica does not seek a particularly post-second-wave femininity for herself. She appears happy to be the "kept woman" of patriarchal masculinities past and leaves Ray for a man who can provide greater financial support, but apparently little else; when he experiences financial crisis, she reevaluates the relationship and leaves him too.

In comparison with the other protagonists and series considered here, Ray's crimes of sex for pay seem negligible, and the series' emphasis on the comedic rather than melodramatic aspects of his exploits further lightens the moral and legal concerns of his actions. Ray is never in danger of arrest—although exposure of his second career to Jessica, his children, or the school district is posed as a clearly embarrassing and emasculating consequence.[23] The other series delve much more deeply into broader moralistic questions of good and bad; Ray never seems a bad man and the series never suggests that his actions hurt others. *Hung* also emphasizes broader sociocultural changes as a root cause of the protagonist's economic and familial troubles to a degree less evident in other series, in many ways offering a face to the tide of un- and underemployed Americans who were part of the "mancession" that the series anticipated. Ray's story is consistent with the others, though, as a tale in which a male character struggles with his place in the world in a particularly gendered way and of a man unable to provide for or restore his family without resorting to unconventional and illegal means.

On the surface, Ray and the version of Walter White audiences meet at the beginning of *Breaking Bad* appear quite similar. Both are dissatisfied schoolteachers: overwhelmed and underpaid. Yet, though similarly reliant on archetypal male-centered serial protagonists, *Hung* and *Breaking Bad* are profoundly different shows. *Hung* is light, Ray's travails are comedic, and his voice-over exposes his motivations by explaining his worldview and actions, while *Breaking Bad* takes viewers on the dark journey of turning Walter White from a mild-mannered chemistry teacher into a heartless, egotistic drug kingpin with nearly imperceptible clues as to why Walt takes this path.[24] *Breaking Bad* displayed considerable audacity as a television series by defying expectations that it would eventually devolve into a conventional redemption tale. As the stories and Walt's actions grew ever darker in each subsequent season, series creator and lead writer Vince Gilligan insisted that Walt's journey would not end happily ever after, and Gilligan repeatedly described the central conceit of the show as answering the question, What might it look like to turn Mr. Chips into Scarface?[25]

More than any of the other series, *Breaking Bad* charts the undoing of a man as he—to use a southern colloquialism—"breaks bad" and becomes a different man from the one who begins the series. Gilligan seemingly dares the audience to continue to hold sympathy for Walt, who is introduced as a decent, well intentioned, by-the-rules-though-milquetoast family man who isn't dealt the hand in life that American mythology and American television typically affirm. Being good and doing the right thing haven't paid off for Walt. He lost a true love (Gretchen) and budding career after inexplicably leaving her and his research to a graduate school partner (Elliot), who has used their science training, and possibly Walt's research, to earn billions. Walt nevertheless finds himself a satisfactory life—perhaps one he would have contentedly coasted through—yet is about to lose even this at an early age.[26]

Unlike in *Hung*, where voice-over narration provides clear motivations and introspection, in *Breaking Bad*, viewers must interpret subtle gestures and vague comments to gain insight into Walt's mind—and even these clues are often inconsistent.[27] Only the viewer—not other characters—might interpret Walt's decision to cook and sell methamphetamine as a strategy for family provision in the series' early episodes in which he keeps his terminal cancer diagnosis a secret. To his wife, Skyler, and cooking partner, Jesse, his erratic behavior seems more consistent with a midlife crisis. Days before his collapse and diagnosis—in fact at his surprise fiftieth birthday party—Walt watches news footage of his brother-in-law Hank, a Drug Enforcement Administration (DEA) agent making an enormous meth and cash siege. Clearly impressed by the quantity of cash, he asks how much money the DEA seized, to which Hank replies, "About $700 grand." At that moment, Walt brushes aside Hank's offer to let him ride along with him, but days later, after Walt and the audience learn that he is dying, Walt pursues Hank's offer and learns of the involvement of his former student, Jesse, during the drug bust he observes.

Although there is a recognizable logic to the idea that Walt endeavors upon a life-changing path of meth making as an effort to pay medical bills and support his family in case of his death, this motivation is often in subtle tension with the proposition that Walt simply wishes a richer life experience in his last days. Walt is clearly beaten by the mundaneness of his life: by students who care nothing of the science he is passionate about or humiliate him as he cleans their cars at the car wash; by managers at school or the car wash who subordinate him; and even by the family life that he indeed loves but finds stifling. Just as a full understanding of Ray Drecker's pursuit of illegal cash must acknowledge that his anxiety about being a washed-out high school hero affects his effort to restore his family, so too must Walt's endeavor as a meth maker, then dealer, then kingpin, acknowledge that he starts on this path in rebellion against a life that has been safe, ordinary, and full of regret about leaving his research, losing Gretchen, and missing the windfall of the company he founded with Elliot because he sold his shares so early.

Without the insight of voice-over narration, it is more difficult to assess Walt's primary versus secondary motivations and what he intentionally pursues as opposed to what happens unintentionally. The series makes clear that the White family is financially strained even before Walt's diagnosis. His life mirrors Ray Drecker's assessment that a public school teacher earns "half of what is needed for a normal life": in addition to Walt's after-school job at the car wash, the series depicts Skyler haggling with a creditor on the phone, reprimanding Walt for using the "wrong" credit card, and shopping at a discount store for new jeans for Walt Jr. The set decoration of the family home—a small, claustrophobic ranch with narrow hallways—further underscores their economic limitations.

After his diagnosis, Walt struggles to contain increasingly seething anger over the disappointment of missed opportunity that leads to his life as a science teacher rather than scientist. The camera lingers for just a moment in the pilot on a plaque on the wall in the White home that recognizes Walt as a contributor to research on a project earning a Nobel Prize. Walt's back story as a scientist is circuitously and incompletely explained. Colleagues from graduate school regard him as a master of crystallography, but he inexplicably left that world of big ideas that has yielded great riches for Gretchen and Elliot.[28] The series never explains Walt's decision to become an educator—and a high school teacher at that—despite advanced degrees in chemistry. Walt met Skyler, who worked as a cashier at a restaurant he frequented, in graduate school, but flashbacks reveal far greater intimacy—intellectual and personal—with Gretchen than he ever displays for Skyler. The audience thus never knows why Walt missed the opportunity that continuing with his research and the company he shared with Elliot would have allowed.

Walt's dissatisfaction bubbles just below the surface, occasionally exploding in outbursts such as when he quits his job at the car wash after being asked to leave his post as cashier to dry cars once too often, or when he blows up at Skyler, who reasonably interrogates him about why a former student (Jesse) has begun calling him. Walt's explosions make sense to viewers who are aware of the stress of the cancer diagnosis and his forays into the meth trade, but these details are unknown, at this point, to those in his life. A rare moment of self-expression occurs after he tells his family about the cancer and his intention to forgo treatment. They stage an intervention as an effort to persuade him to undergo treatment, and when finally given an opportunity to explain himself, Walt tells them,

> What I want, what I want, what I need, is a choice. Sometimes I feel like I never actually make any of my own, choices, I mean. My entire life it just seems I never had, you know, a real say about any of it. This last one, cancer, all I have left is how I choose to approach this. . . . What good is it to survive if I'm too sick to work, enjoy a meal, to make love. For what time I have left, I want to live in my own house, I want to sleep in my own bed. . . . You, cleaning up after me, me with a, some dead man, some artificially alive, just marking time, no, no, and that's how you would remember me. That's the worst part. . . . I choose not to do it.[29]

Walt reverses his choice and assents to treatment the next morning, apparently in acknowledgment of his family's feeling that choosing against treatment suggests his life with them is not worth fighting for. In the fourth season, Walt recounts his father's early death from Parkinson's disease to Walt Jr., and it becomes clear that his fears of how he'll be remembered originate from these memories. Regardless, the cancer quickly becomes insignificant to the story. It importantly provides a preliminary catalyst for his vocational transition, but his cancer goes into remission at the end of the second season, leaving the rest of the series to follow the consequences of the life his diagnosis leads him to take.[30] Or Gilligan provides another way to understand the significance of cancer in the series by noting that "he [Walt] is the cancer of the show."[31]

As the subsequent seasons play out, it becomes increasingly apparent that providing for his family was largely a rationalization for a decision Walt made for far more egotistical reasons. In accord with his expressed desire to "make his own choices," Walt's diagnosis jostles him into recognizing his dissatisfaction with the banality of his life, so that while Walt claims providing for his family as the cause, this seems a facile reading and the truth Walt would like to believe.[32] In the pilot episode, when Jesse seeks an explanation for Walt's desire to cook meth—Jesse actually phrases it as "breaking bad"—Walt responds, "I am awake." In season four, after Skyler has learned of his involvement in the meth trade and becomes complicit in covering it up, Walt chafes at having to hide his great genius and success from the rest of his family, and it is this hubris that eventually leads to Hank's detection of Walt. He repeatedly makes evading detection more difficult by refusing to quietly cook his valuably pure drug and letting the credit—though also the blame— go to others. The serial plot of season four traces the struggle between Walt and Gus—who has built an elaborate façade to conceal his meth enterprise and employs Walt and Jesse as cooks. After the tense, season-long contest that apparently will only end with the death of Walt or Gus, Walt understands Gus's demise as evidence that he "won," an expression not only of this battle with Gus, but of his entire post-cancer-diagnosis endeavor, through which he has proven himself and his life's purpose. And in the series' final scene between he and Skyler, in which she rejects further declarations of what Walt did for the family, even Walt at last admits that "I did for me, I liked it, I was good at it, and I was really, I was alive."

Assessing the masculinities in *Breaking Bad* is difficult. Walt's prediagnosis sleepwalking through life certainly isn't venerated, but neither is the egotist that he becomes as he quickly overcompensates for his previous deferential existence. As Walt becomes increasingly self-centered during season four, Jesse's character becomes progressively more central as the hero of the narrative. Jesse begins the series as an immature, irresponsible druggie who has been cast off by affluent parents focused on raising his younger, intellectually gifted brother.[33] Unlike Walt—who can easily rationalize his involvement in murder as necessary to maintain the safety of his family—Jesse is unable to accept the lives taken in the course of his misadventures with Walt and is tortured by guilt over his complicity and actions. The series depicts both men looking for meaning in their lives, but where Walt searches for prestige and a sense of accomplishment in making the best meth and building an empire to rival the one he passed up, Jesse searches for meaning through human connection. Likewise, brother-in-law Hank provides a rich site for considering contrasting masculinities. He begins the series embodying a blustering patriarchal masculinity, which he maintains in front of the other DEA agents. Viewers see Hank suffer panic attacks as he moves into a more dangerous field role and then see how he struggles to preserve his sense of his manliness after being shot and confined to a wheelchair, all of which provide subtle meditations on the challenges of occupying an acceptable masculinity.

The story of Vic Mackey in *The Shield* somewhat parallels Walter White's story. Viewers begin the series with little sense of Mackey's back story, and meet a version of Mackey who is an arrogant, corrupt, yet compelling character who murders a fellow team member after learning he was building a federal case against him. The series airs a flashback episode in its second season that provides the origin story of the unconventional unit that houses Mackey's strike team and the detectives and officers working there. Here, audiences see Vic as a detective lobbying then-Commander Gilroy for the opportunity to lead the new unit. Vic is a different man, softer, confident but not arrogant, and intimate and engaged in conversation with his wife—rather than speaking at her, as is the norm otherwise in the series. The episode tells the story of the first case of Mackey's "strike team" and shows the considerable pressure on Vic to deliver quick results. The team ultimately elects to bend the rules by planting evidence on a drug dealer they know to be guilty of murdering a prostitute and then coercing one of his underlings to provide probable cause so they can send a team of officers in to find it. In discussing the illegal technique, Vic—seemingly with sincerity—suggests that the team will do it "just this once" and then "go back to doing it the right way" once the pressure is off. As the episode ends, Vic and team member Shane marvel at how easy the setup was, preparing the premise of the series and the origins of the unit's corruption. The strike team extends beyond illegal tactics to convict known criminals and begins engaging actively in the drug trade by eliminating a competitor for a drug dealer who helps Mackey by giving him tips and kickbacks. The strategy of the strike team fails to completely eradicate the drug trade, but they justify their actions as promoting community safety because the controlled drug monopoly reduces violence resulting from competing trade.

This first small bad act begets many subsequent ones as acts of increasing illegality are required to cover up earlier wrongdoing. Once Mackey goes so far as to kill a fellow officer, the illegal actions of the strike team escalate beyond rogue police techniques such as stealing from drug dealers to provide money to incent informants, to outright thievery for personal gain. Their gravest acts are done to prevent exposure. Despite the fact that the series ends with the protagonist having lost his job and family and having utterly destroyed his friends, the downfall of Vic Mackey is very different from that of Walter White. Walt deliberately chooses his path and understands his choices to have a series of outcomes; Vic doesn't realize the enormity of his choices in the moment, so much of the series traces his efforts to restore the stasis of family and work life that is imperiled by the threats he introduces.

The any man tales affirm the masculinity of men who take responsibility for themselves and their obligations. Walt—at the beginning of his journey, at least, and arguably in the very end—and Ray are faced with a challenge, and both do something about it rather than wallow in the situation or expect someone else to provide a remedy. It is notable that both Ray and Walt had legal routes available to them, but dismissed them, arguably, out of pride. Such choices raise questions regarding the relationship between pride and masculinity and whether these shows tell tales that affirm prideful men or suggest pride as their downfall, as the series diverge with respect to the consequences of the men's actions. Elliot first offered Walt a job and then to pay for his cancer treatment and Walt declines both overtures, which creates a complicated matrix of lies as he initially hides his drug income by telling Skyler that Elliot is paying for the treatment. Walt is too prideful to accept money from Elliot, but not so prideful as to be bothered by Skyler thinking that he accepts the money, suggesting that it is not just pride, but aspects of ego and selfishness that are confirmed by Walt's subsequent inability to stop cooking meth after achieving his initial financial goal and being diagnosed as in remission.[34] Walt's refusal of Elliot's offers contributes significantly to my argument that family provision is not the core or sole motivation behind his entry into the meth trade.[35] *Breaking Bad* depicts excessive pride as Walt's downfall and his need to prove himself as a shallow and egotistical act. Although milquetoast Walter White is regarded as a meager man, his growing daring as drug dealer does not enhance his masculinity. The series more consistently courts sympathy for Jesse—who errs, but suffers with regret and guilt—as the "better man," or for Hank, who suffers a nearly fatal and emasculating injury because of Walt's actions against the cartel.

Ray could have sold his property to his neighbor and restarted his life but *chooses* to decline this offer. Ray's pridefulness does not have the severe ramifications that Walt's does—largely because the countersolution he pursues is less extreme. Ray does initially ask Jessica for financial help, which the audience sees as difficult for him and a sacrifice of pride. And his choice seems less prideful given that the lake house has sentimental value to Ray, and his neighbor in many ways represents the rampant consumerism he perceives as at the core of all the things going wrong with America. Ray seems more determined than prideful, and his actions put him at risk of minor legal complications and engender no threat to his family.

Vic Mackey's pride—evident in his belief that he can solve the escalating need to cover up prior bad acts—is also punished within the narrative. Vic's choices lead him to lose his family and friends—in some cases in truly devastating fashion. The series ends with an image of Mackey having lost his relationships and his vocation and with no suggestion that he's worthy of sympathy. These series thus cannot and do not end in redemption, where all live happily ever after in the end; and, in some cases, the men pay fully and tragically for their misdeeds, so that the series can retrospectively be read as the undoing of the men.[36]

Returning to the questions of why men of such privilege risk their families and freedom and what their willingness to take these risks indicates, it is clear that the characters embark on their journeys as a result of desperation. Ray is desperate to have his kids, if not his wife, back, and his nostalgia somewhat necessitates repairing his home rather than starting over. Walt is desperate to live his remaining days in a manner that has been lacking and to leave his family provided for. The instigations of their actions—Ray's fire and Walt's cancer—do not lead to easy blame—but provide the conditions for examining how these men respond to crisis. Indeed, the fire and cancer are only catalysts; the conditions of each man were established earlier through vocational decisions and spousal choices that contributed to making them the desperate men they become.

Born to Be Bad Men: Absent Patriarchs and Their Legacies in *Dexter* and *Sons of Anarchy*

In juxtaposition with these series, which chart the transition of ordinary "any men" who venture deliberately into illegal trades, are series featuring protagonists born into outlaw worlds that have codes and norms different from those of conventional society. Like the any men who make choices that estrange them from the world they live in, the outlaws seek to leave the world they were born into, feel confined by the identities available to them, and similarly seek to alter their destiny. Consequently, both parallels and clear demarcations can be identified between the situations of any men resorting to illegal means and outlaws who are forced into choices that position them outside the realm of society.

The outlaw shows feature protagonists who profoundly transcend the moral bounds of television series that have long offered protagonists that were simultaneously heroes. Series such as *Sons of Anarchy*, *Dexter*, and *The Sopranos* seemingly provide realist narratives with action set in the conventional modern-day world governed by commonly known technologies and rules of physics, yet their characters exist in an alternate subculture within this conventional universe that seems more similar to science fiction series than other realist narratives set in law-abiding worlds. In large part, it is this device of the subcultural space that enables storytelling about bad men as heroes, because in their world, they are not bad men.

Yet, it would be patently incorrect to assert that these subcultural worlds are lawless. Indeed, their guiding rules and codes of justice differ from those of American society, but clear codes prescribing behavior exist nonetheless. For example, though protagonist Jax Teller has killed several men and is clearly a murderer by the standard of American society, within the moral universe of the club, killing those who have first committed offenses against him, the club, or his family conforms to the code of this universe and doesn't lead Jax to the moral anguish expected of an any man who would perpetrate the same acts. *Dexter* is set in less of a formal subculture, but likewise requires viewers to accept the terms of its story and the conceit that Dexter is a sociopath who must kill in the same way others must eat or sleep. As long as he follows

Harry's Code—the rules developed by his adoptive father to help him evade capture—the meaning of these deaths differs from the murders committed by any man characters who are responsible to the laws of US society.

The characters born into these worlds of alternative laws are not subject to the same moral quandaries that trouble the any men, but they too are chafed by the expectations and boundaries their worlds place upon them. Dexter struggles with the sense that he is missing out on something by not being human and finds that his charade of performing being a human leads him ever deeper into human rituals and conventions such as marriage and fatherhood. Jax and Tony Soprano—to varying degrees—imagine a better life in the "normal" world. Being a member of law-abiding society would eliminate the ever-present threat of incarceration and appears to offer Jax access to being the type of father he seeks to be, while Tony seems more to just long for a life that is not the one of familial and Mafioso demands he finds crushing, though part of the show's endeavor is exploring the parallels between mob management and that of any manager. Curiously, then, in many ways, the outlaws' desires and subsequent actions are like those of the any men in that they deviate from the norms of the world into which they are born. But where the any men's actions lead them to defy US law, the outlaws seek to trade the conditions of their deviant world for those of dominant US society.

Although *Sons of Anarchy* and *Dexter* fit together neatly as illustrations of men struggling with aspects of masculinity in an outlaw context, they ultimately explore quite different stories. Jax's journey features some of the most explicit interpersonal crises of any of the series, and the threats to family and Jax's efforts to thwart them offer thematic consistencies with the struggles of the any men. At a level of surface description, *Dexter* bears great similarity with the other series featuring protagonists engaged in illegal deeds; however, *Dexter* proves to be somewhat separate from the other shows considered here because its protagonist struggles more with his *humanity* than his masculinity. Despite this, both *Sons of Anarchy* and *Dexter* highlight storylines about an absent patriarch whose ghostly legacy features importantly in his son's effort to negotiate competing aspects of masculinity.

Sons of Anarchy

Sons of Anarchy is a family melodrama with Shakespearean overtones set in the Sons of Anarchy Motorcycle Club, Redwood Original chapter, often identified by the acronym SAMCRO in the narrative. The central protagonist, Jackson (Jax) Teller, is in his early thirties at the series' start. Jax is the son of one of the club's founders, John (JT) Teller, who died when Jax was a boy. JT's best friend, Clay Morrow (Ron Perlman), took over as president of the club, married Jax's mother, Gemma (Katey Sagal), and raised him. In the fourth season, Jax learns that Clay is responsible for his father's death, although the audience—who learns this well before Jax—also knows that Clay and Gemma were having an affair and that Gemma is also complicit in JT's death. The club is based in a rural, central California town called Charming and engages in a range of illegal enterprises. Selling illegal guns provided by the Real Irish Republican Army (RIRA) is their primary trade, although they also engage in some sectors of pornography, prostitution, and protection. In season four they traffic, but do not sell, drugs for a Mexican cartel. The series blends episodic and serial storylines, although most storytelling is ongoing. Most seasons are organized by an external threat to the club, such as legal prosecution by the Bureau of Alcohol, Tobacco, and Firearms or the US Attorney's Office, a turf challenge by an Aryan gang seeking to bring drug trade to Charming, and complications in relationships with the RIRA or various other motorcycle clubs and gangs. Considerable internal struggle also plays out among the members of the club and among Jax, Clay, Gemma, and Jax's eventual wife, Tara. The series' depiction of the club and the lives of its members neither particularly romanticizes nor critiques its world. The series utilizes melodrama and the narrative tools of the soap opera much more than the other series considered in this book. Despite the action sequences of gunfights and motorcycle chases, its most suspenseful tensions result from the management of secrets and information.

Where *The Sopranos* introduces Tony during midlife crisis and follows his life at a point when substantial change isn't really possible, *Sons of Anarchy* introduces the youngest of the protagonists considered here and traces Jax's journey through the process of deciding what kind of man he will become. As *Sons'* creator and executive producer Kurt

Sutter describes him, "He's more a Christopher or Shane than he is a Tony or Vic," referencing the junior characters of *The Sopranos* and *The Shield*, respectively, the two series *Sons* is most commonly compared with, and the latter of which employed Sutter as a writer.[37] Relative to the dominant themes across the male-centered serials explored in the last chapter, it is notable that becoming a father inspires the introspection that leads Jax to reassess the world of the motorcycle club and his place within it. As his prematurely born son struggles to stay alive, Jax becomes better acquainted with his father when he finds and reads the manifesto John wrote some twenty years earlier, just before his death. Both JT—at the time of writing—and Jax—at the time he reads—are disenchanted with how the club had "lost its way."[38] Jax first tries the easier path of trying to reform the club from within in seasons one and two. But after having his son kidnapped in retribution for club-related RIRA dealings and then fathering a second son before serving a fourteen-month prison sentence—during which he suffers a nearly fatal stabbing wound—he resolves at the beginning of season four that he cannot be the father or husband he seeks to be while a member of the club. The fourth season traces his attempt to extricate himself from the club so that he can take his fiancée and sons out of the dangerous world he's always known. At the end of the season, plot contrivances force him to stay and lead to his ascension to club president, where he once again tries to reform from within while not being corrupted into the type of leader who has led the club to need reformation.[39]

Determining the hegemonic masculinity within *Sons* is made complicated by Jax's straddling of the world of the club and his desire to leave it or, more precisely, by his desire to be part of a different kind of club. Indeed, the masculinity affirmed by the motorcycle club (MC) is profoundly patriarchal, but the MC is not idealized; the errors of its ways, such as its reliance on physical violence and association with criminal enterprise, are what Jax identifies as incompatible with being the father and husband he seeks to be. The world of the MC is one in which men do still "take care" of women, so provision for family is clearly something Jax must do. The means by which a man provides for his family and remains loyal to the club aren't particularly important and may reasonably require violation of the rules of "regular" society. A man may be hot-tempered or stoic, physically violent or psychologically manipulative without priority—so long as he takes care of his family and remains loyal.

Yet, while Jax as protagonist is positioned by the narrative to embody the hegemonic ideal, he is a figure in transition—much like Walter White, although on a very different journey. It is often unclear how much distance Jax seeks from the norms of the club. He recognizes that the violence and illegal acts create an unsafe environment for his family. His romantic relationship with Tara—his young love who left Charming, trained as a neonatal surgeon, and returns after Jax has married and divorced his first son's drug-addicted mother—appears far more companionate than patriarchal. Indeed, Jax's struggles with the contradictions of transitioning masculinities are often clearest in regard to Tara. Given the remuneration of her successful professional career, Tara could support them if Jax left the club. In posing his plan to leave, Jax explains, "I don't have any skills Tara. I'm an okay mechanic with a GED. The only thing I ever did well was outlaw. I just need to make some bank; set myself up with something." Though she replies, "I can go anywhere, I make good money," Jax shakes his head, dismissing this idea with "pshaw, I'm not going to live off my wife. I can't." Knowing this to be the case, Tara doesn't push him.[40] Yet his need to be the provider keeps him in the club in pursuit of a big payday in season four—at considerable physical and legal risk—and leads to the situation in which it becomes untenable for him to leave and hence to further personal tragedy.[41]

Jax best embodies the struggle of cobbling together a culturally acceptable masculinity from all those available. In a sense, he must choose between two different paternal legacies: Clay's clearly patriarchal version that has led the club from its origins in fraternity to one involved in increasingly criminal acts in an effort to secure better livelihoods for its members; and that of JT, whose absence makes him uncertain and unknown, but at the least, a contrast to Clay. Jax seeks for the MC to provide a source of fraternity without an attendant threat of incarceration that would disable his role as father and husband. He desperately wants to be able to provide for his family, support his club, and fulfill JT's hopes for him, but struggles with the irreconcilability of these desires.

Jax is consequently faced with a sense of duty to a range of conflicting entities. His choice at the beginning of the fourth season to leave the MC in order to preserve the family he has sired, a choice against the family that raised him, is only trumped when it is evident that his departure from the club will result in the club's destruction and either his incarceration or a life on the run from the law. The central crises, and richest melodrama, result when he must choose between duty to family and loyalty to friends, extended family, and the club, which notably was also a common theme of series such as *Buffy the Vampire Slayer*, *Xena: Warrior Princess*, and *Charmed*, which often forced complicated choices of prioritization on their heroines, who likewise occupied alternative realms.[42] Elsewhere I argue that the balancing of competing interests in these series functions as an allegory for the demands on women to "have it all" in which they are constantly required to choose between needs of family and work, a relevant parallel to my argument here about the connections between these men's struggles and those named as problems for women.[43]

Dexter

Like Jax, Dexter Morgan desires to escape the world he inhabits—a world that separates him from the mainstream. But unlike Jax, Dexter isn't really part of a subculture; he is isolated in a world belonging only to him—particularly after his father's death. The series first introduces Dexter as not fully human. Indeed, his adoptive father, Harry (James Remar), understands him in this way: as a sociopath, as someone so damaged as to be unfixable. Harry consequently develops what Dexter comes to call "Harry's Code," to teach the sociopathic Dexter how to kill and evade capture and what type of person to kill. Harry's Code enables Dexter to kill those able to circumvent the justice system due to technicalities, and thus, within the situational ethics of the series, offers viewers a narrative justification for understanding a sociopathic serial killer as a narrative hero, or at the least, enables viewers to remain invested enough in his story to follow it to its conclusion. As in *Hung*, *Dexter* features a first-person narration that allows the viewer a sense of Dexter's view of the world, which is probably the only way to remind audiences that a character who looks so normal is to be understood as not fully human. Series creator James Manos describes Dexter as the "most sane" and "most honest" character within a narrative universe

otherwise depicted as largely dysfunctional, but that too is a component of the central concept of the series: that an inhuman character can
effectively play at being human.[44]

Over the course of the series Dexter improves his performance of
being human, although his voice-overs often remind the audience of his
own uncertainty regarding the distinction between the performance of
being human and authentic human response. He begins acts of human
performance that gradually make him seem like he may be bridging his
isolation, as when he enters into a romantic relationship with a woman
so emotionally damaged that her distrust of intimacy obscures Dexter's
peculiarities, allowing him a cloak of conventionality. Despite his longing to be human, the mythology of the series suggests that he can never
attain this end if he is indeed a sociopath.[45] Where *Sons of Anarchy* can
pose life outside the MC as a possibility for Jax, the cumulative narrative of *Dexter* is much less ends based. In order to remain true to its
mythology, the question propelling narrative action is more a matter of
"how will things turn out for Dexter?" than "will he become human?"
We can only wonder whether he'll be caught, because the series maintains that his fate as sociopath is sealed and there is no redemption story
available until its final season, when it introduces the psychiatrist who
treated Dexter as a child and helped develop Harry's Code. This final
season plot allows the series to rewrite its origin story. Interactions with
sister Deb after she learns Dexter's truth and the return of love interest
Hannah reveal Dexter to have emotions, which the psychiatrist asserts
he should be incapable of as a sociopath, and in the end, suggest he
can overcome his nature. The series cultivates viewers' interest through
the search for season-specific antagonists and the insertion of Dexter's
inhuman character into mundane situations, such as marriage, fatherhood, and religion, that require proficiency in human socialization.

Consequently, though *Dexter* bears many surface similarities with
the male-centered serials—as a story about the entire life of a man who
is driven to try to create and then restore a family—the show is ultimately quite different from the others because Dexter's struggle is less
that of a man struggling with masculinities than that of someone so
damaged that he struggles to be fully human. If analysis of other male-
centered serials has emphasized what the series' narrative similarities suggest about the experience of being a man in contemporary US

society, *Dexter* offers less meaningful insight because of the tenuousness of understanding Dexter as a man. Yet still, in its own way, *Dexter* enters into conversation with notions of masculinity, primarily in the way the series makes the performative nature of masculinity more evident than most. The guises Dexter dons to hide his difference make clear a hierarchy of things "men" must do to pass as men within society: engage in coupling, be able to banter when among the guys, express concern for others, prioritize care for his son and sister. But it is much less clear whether this is a matter of performing humanity or performing masculinity. Notably, Dexter's desire to start a new life with Hannah seems to domesticate him out of his need to kill.

Negotiating Patrilineal Destiny with Lost Fathers

The father/son relationship figures centrally in nearly all the male-centered serials, but unlike in the relationships fraught with contradictory understandings of men's roles and masculinity depicted in the series discussed in the last chapter, the absence of the father becomes central to the journey of men such as Jax and Dexter. Where series such as *Rescue Me* and *Men of a Certain Age* depict conflict resulting from the protagonists' refusal to perpetuate the patriarchal masculinity of their fathers, the absent and somewhat unknown fathers of Jax and Dexter bestow a distinct patrilineal legacy and become at once a site of nostalgia and rebellion. Jax never really knew his father, and tries to piece a sense of him together throughout the series through the often contradictory and partial information he gleans from his father's manuscript and the competing accounts offered by his mother, Clay, other early club members, his father's Irish mistress, and the letters JT sent to her. Dexter's adoptive father also dies before the beginning of the series, but he is physically manifest in many episodes in Dexter's imagination, somewhat as a voice of conscience. Dexter too struggles to understand who his father was and to reconcile his memories as he learns about extramarital affairs—including with his biological mother, who worked as an informant—and that the cause of his death was not a heart attack, as was officially reported, but a suicide for which Dexter consequently feels responsible. The legacy of dead fathers similarly affects Tony

Soprano and Nate (Peter Krause) and David Fisher (Michael C. Hall) of *Six Feet Under* (2001–2005). Although Tony's father materializes only in dreams and flashbacks, he clearly exists as the measure of a man Tony evaluates himself against.[46] *Six Feet Under* verges on, but doesn't quite function as, a male-centered serial, but is worth acknowledging on this point. In this series, the family patriarch dies in the pilot, motivating the return home of eldest son Nate, who fled from his family and the family mortuary business. Much as with Harry Morgan, the ghost of Nathaniel Fisher (Richard Jenkins) haunts his sons as they learn their father's secrets and the series traces their efforts to reconcile who they are with the men they believe their father wanted them to be.

Jax's and Dexter's uncertainty about the values and beliefs of their fathers figures crucially in their difficulties establishing their own identities, accepting their masculinities, and determining how to be fathers. Jax's patrilineal legacy is to wield the gavel and lead SAMCRO, but Jax doesn't know how to be the man who leads the club. The mixed information he receives about JT leaves him uncertain as to how JT would have wanted him to lead—and if that is even the kind of leader Jax wants to be. Jax is sympathetic to JT in the first season because he finds the worldview in JT's manuscript appealing; however, seasons two through four depict Jax as increasingly lost as information about JT's infidelity and failure to right the club lead Jax to see him as weak and a failure. At the same time he sees how Clay's leadership nearly destroys the club and, like Tony Soprano, struggles with how to replicate the traditions and norms of his father's ventures in times that have changed.

Likewise, Dexter struggles with a sense of responsibility for Harry's suicide, fearing that it was seeing Dexter murder—in a fulfillment of Harry's lessons—that leads Harry to take his life, while for much of the series he simultaneously harbors great anger against Harry, wishing that he had rehabilitated Dexter so that he wouldn't find himself as such an outsider now. Absent and unknowable fathers consequently figure critically in creating a narrative in which young men work out how to be men. It is in the final scenes of the penultimate episode that Dexter confirms he no longer has the need to kill and Harry acknowledges that Dexter doesn't need him anymore, and his apparition disappears, presumably forever. The fathers of Jax and Dexter destine them to worlds of outsiders, so the sons struggle with whether they want to be part of that destiny and what refusing that world means in terms of forsaking their fathers.

Conclusion

Despite the common attributes of the protagonists of the male-centered serials outlined in the last chapter and the preponderant theme of these men seeking illegal solutions to their problems, this analysis reveals considerable variation in the stories the series ultimately tell. In some cases, men's struggles are foregrounded through voice-over and are indispensable to the storytelling, as is the case in *Hung*, while others are less centrally about the struggle over how to be a man, though they nevertheless provide further evidence of the complicated condition of contemporary men, as can be argued of *Breaking Bad*. Consistent with my argument for the distinction of the male-centered serial, all these series tell a story of the challenges experienced in the everyday lives of men who struggle with the responsibilities of family provision that burdened their fathers while simultaneously seeking to be a different kind of father, and often husband, than was common among the models of masculinity that preceded them. Many are not sure *who* to be, let alone *how* to be him.

The male-centered serials of this time tell stories about men unmoored from the certain legacy of patriarchal masculinities, and while depicted as befuddled and searching as a result, they consistently struggle for a way forward rather than a tether back. Many aspects of their struggles with the range of masculinities available to them resonate with challenges depicted for women in recent decades over how to choose among newly available femininities and gender scripts. Popular culture has rarely acknowledged such transitions in gender scripts without intertwining a reactionary solution, but these series resist a return to more distinctly patriarchal norms.

These series do important work in bringing the struggles of negotiating among patriarchal and feminist masculinities to the surface and suggest a need for greater engagement with the consequences of men's changing gender scripts and for sociological studies into experiences of men that parallel the second shift and other aspects of work/family double binds. Few popular-culture texts have meaningfully posed a choice of not working for men, nor have many featured relationships reflecting the shifts in wage earning that Hanna Rosin has identified as increasingly disadvantaging men with limited education.[47] The slow transitions in gender norms in the working world combine with generational shifts in attitudes toward parental and marital roles. Popular culture can play an especially salient role in depicting what nonpatriarchal relationships and masculinities might look like for those seeking alternatives to the models evident in their own upbringing, and is valuably combined with more expansive investigation of the implications of second-wave feminism for men and women and the culturally supported masculinities and femininities available to them.

4

Where Men Can Be Men

The Homosocial Enclave and Jocular Policing of Masculinity

The differences between male and female communication styles are a frequent topic for comedians. Women's perceived need to talk about everything, in detail, ad nauseam, is often mocked in such routines—typically by the male comedians who dominate the field—while men in these "conversations" hear only the "wha-wha-wha-wha" of adult-speak in *Peanuts* cartoons. But men talk too, and popular films and television have increasingly brought such talk into the open. Many comedic films of the early twenty-first century that Peter Alilunas calls "dude flicks" starring the "frat pack" and Judd Apatow's "man-boys," as well as the television series considered here, represent conversations among men as a constant, easy banter of humorous mocking and one-up-manship through which men nevertheless foster relationships and express sincere sentiment.[1] These films and several cable series centered on male characters in the early twenty-first century constructed spaces and relationships that depicted men interacting in all-male spaces and exposed the environ of "locker room" talk.

The conversations held among trusting groups of men offer a different perspective on men's struggles to negotiate among patriarchal and feminist masculinities than emerge through the male-centered serial. Series such as *Entourage* (HBO, 2004–2012), *The League* (FX, 2009–), *Rescue Me* (FX, 2004–2011), and *Men of a Certain Age* (TNT, 2009–2011) opened to public view conversations and relational posturing of men who deeply trust each other. Where the male-centered serials depict protagonists' interior efforts to make sense of contemporary male gender scripts, the all-male space of what I term the "homosocial enclave" reveals men collectively trying to work out contemporary expectations of masculinity and provides a setting in which close friends police each other's embodiments of masculinity. The multiplicity of male characters that inhabit any of these series creates a tableau that features a variety of masculinities—a component less evident in the male-centered serials—and allows examination of the attributes of the hegemonic masculinity supported and rejected in each series.

This chapter explores four series with dissimilar narrative organization and priorities that nevertheless all devote plot time to exploring the relationships among a group of men who share an intimate group relationship—either friends since school days or the close brotherhood of men who rely upon each other for their safety, in this case firefighters. The homosocial enclaves created in these series allow for performance of a masculinity that is much different from the way these men are depicted when they enter mixed-gender or "civilian" spaces and also reveal a particular type of men's talk that is uncensored by norms of social propriety. David Greven asserts that homosocial spaces "truly are private, special, enclosed," and thus allow the men to be "deliberately sequestered in a zone of intimacy in which they are safe to be themselves."[2] Such a zone distinguishes these series from the range of public contexts common in the male-centered serials in which protagonists interact with colleagues, heterosexual partners, and children, and is also distinct from the intimacy of the best-friend relationship explored in the next chapter.

The context of the homosocial enclave provides a different lens on men's anxiety about changing gender roles from those considered in other chapters. Where heteronormativity goes unquestioned in the male-centered serials and thus functions as a particularly persistent attribute of patriarchal masculinity, the homosocial enclave more openly negotiates heteronormativity as the men work to demarcate homosocial versus homosexual boundaries. The homosocial enclave provides the confidence of established male bonds, but its intimacy simultaneously introduces what Eve Kosofsky Sedgwick terms "homosexual panic."[3] Sedgwick argues that this panic derives from men's need for homosociality in order to properly perform male gender scripts but also to manage the often uncertain boundary between homosociality and prohibited homosexuality. Though gay identity and gay masculinities are more readily acknowledged, the series' politics regarding gay identity are varied and complicated. One series depicts characters genuinely confused by hegemonic heterosexual gender scripts that increasingly incorporate aspects of gay masculinity, others obsess over gay sex acts while seeming indifferent toward gay identity, and another makes no reference to gay identity or sexuality.

These series continue a trajectory of homosocial relationships found in various media, although uncommon on television. Unlike the Gothic novels Sedgwick considers, the shows examined here explore this negotiation in the context of what Ron Becker describes as a time of "straight panic" in which heterosexuals encounter a world in which the boundary between gay and straight identity is more and more insecure and society is more accepting of homosexuality. Straight panic can be used to conceptualize an adjustment in the formation of heteronormative ideology that enables media to include and often seemingly accept gay characters. In posing straight panic, Becker is not arguing the dismantlement of heteronormativity but acknowledging a shift in its terrain. The considerable contestation of gay rights in the 1990s through the early 2000s comingled with other adjustments to patriarchal masculinities that allow for emergent masculinities such as those Becker terms "queer-straight masculinity"[4] and "gay-friendly straight men."[5] These masculinities, which are among those evident in the series considered in this chapter, indicate more feminist versions of masculinity but also lead to uncertainty among the characters about how to embody these newly sanctioned forms of masculinity and whether and for whom they are truly acceptable.

The homosocial enclave is important for this book's broad investigation of the reconstruction of patriarchal masculinities because the negotiation of gay anxiety within the enclave attends to gay identity in a manner absent from the male-centered serials. Although the previous chapters make the case for significant feminist reconstruction of the masculinities evident in protagonists' dealings with their wives and in their attitudes toward the changed cultural milieu feminism has wrought, the heterocentricity of the male-centered serial enforced an absence of gay identity that inevitably affirms far more patriarchal masculinities in this respect. In this and the next chapter, the heteronormativity of patriarchal masculinities is acknowledged, and in some cases contested. Though these series importantly speak of gay identity, most persist in affirming heterosexuality. Through narratives that encompass a range of men with varying performances of masculinity, these series affirm the masculinities of some over others in order to more clearly demarcate a hegemonic masculinity within each narrative universe than is evident in series featuring a single protagonist. The following analysis consequently examines how the series affirm certain attributes of masculinity and what attributes are affirmed, or made hegemonic, identifying the way these relate to the spectrum of patriarchal and feminist masculinities.

Another significant contrast to the previous two chapters' focus on single male protagonists and storytelling of a more melodramatic nature derives from the reliance on comedic banter within the homosocial enclave and among friends, even when embedded in a broader narrative still classifiable as a drama. Importantly, the distinction of this chapter is not generic; it is *not* about shows that are comedies, nor is it about comedic techniques or strategies. Rather, it focuses on a group of heterosexual men with abiding friendships who engage in self-disclosure through banter-based conversation in a homosocial enclave. This enclave is a significant narrative component of each series, although each series creates the opportunity for this space differently. It is the case that almost all conversation in this space aims to make others laugh through what might be distinguished as jocular—or, dare I say, jockular—talk, despite the often serious topics and concerns addressed, and the analysis in this chapter examines how the men effectively and ineffectively use humor to jockey for status within the group.

Although the talk within the homosocial space may superficially appear as men "just joking," meaningful policing of masculinity occurs in this banter, and these conversations explicitly give voice to the men's concerns and uncertainties about who they are, who they are meant to be, and how they should "be men" in contemporary society. The selection of shows coincidentally provides a range of men at varied life stages, offering a more multifaceted look at men than the more generationally consistent protagonists of the male-centered serials. Although the series individually attend little to age as a crucial factor in masculinity construction, analyzing these series together indicates age to be considerably responsible for the central anxieties men face and the way we see them responding. *Entourage* and *Men of a Certain Age* provide endpoints on a continuum, from men who can't imagine a world that does not bend to their every desire to men who have been beaten down by the realities of life. Placed within this continuum, *The League*, occupied with what Heather Havrilesky aptly describes as "manchildren," depicts characters "in the early days of their surrender to adult responsibilities."[6] In slight variation, *Rescue Me* populates its ladder crew with men of two different generations. Although the series often tries to assert 9/11 as the defining distinction between older and younger members of the crew, plotlines chronicling characters suffering a heart attack and cancer reveal aging and disease as the biggest ongoing threats to the firefighters' virility, though the younger characters too face health concerns that originate from their work at Ground Zero.

Understanding Men's Talk, Comedy, and the Homosocial Enclave

Few linguists have studied the talk of men with other men, but the findings of existing studies reveal considerable similarity in the talk among men depicted in the television worlds discussed here and those of study subjects. In her book-length study, *Men Talk: Stories in the Making of Masculinities*, Jennifer Coates draws from thirty-two recorded conversations among all-male groups that are carefully transcribed in accord with the detailed norms of linguistic research.[7] Coates, who previously studied norms of women's conversations, identifies a variety of commonalities among the characteristics of men's talk with other men, particularly as it differs from conversational behaviors among women or in mixed-sex settings. She argues that the general cultural perception that men don't talk as much as women probably emerges from a difference in what men talk about. Citing research by Labov, Coates explains that men only find stories worth retelling if they violate the expected rule of behavior or feature experiences or events that are uncommon.[8] Analysis of men's conversations revealed that men's stories are about stereotypically male topics such as cars, technology, drinking, and travel, and the range of topics common in male conversation serves to regulate and reproduce the range of topics in accord with norms of masculinity.[9]

Men's talk rarely includes self-disclosure; however, men tell stories with male protagonists and often construct all-male storyworlds. A key part of storytelling in relation to masculinity is presentation of self; "collaboration"—conversation patterns that build the story through exchange—is much less common among men's conversations than in female talk. Men's stories attend closely to detail, which linguists explain as an important strategy that enables avoidance of talk of a more personal nature. Linguists theorize that the use of taboo words such as expletives and socially unacceptable or regulated words is key in performing and reinforcing hegemonic masculinity as both a means of verisimilitude—the ritual of talking the way "men" talk—and as a sign of toughness.[10]

Given the chapter's focus specifically on jocular talk and the prevalence of bantering in homosocial enclaves, it is worth noting that Coates finds that sharing laughter is highly valued and that "having a laugh is central to being acceptable as masculine."[11] Her studies have found men's conversations to have a "slightly manic feel" because conversations often switch between serious and nonserious frames.[12] Importantly, in terms of trying to understand how standards of masculinity might be enforced in a narrative played for comedic effect, Coates explains that "'having a laugh' often conceals other, more sensitive themes," and that "[m]en do deal with sensitive issues in their talk, but in tangential ways."[13]

I offer this insight from linguistic theory because much of the talk that occurs in the series considered here is precisely this kind of storytelling and bantering characteristic of men's talk. These series should be understood to deliberately create space within their broader narratives for this interaction among men—whether the diner breakfast ritual of *Men of a Certain Age*, the firehouse scenes of *Rescue Me*, conversations while hanging out in Vince's mansion or over meals in *Entourage*, or interactions in bars or while watching football in *The League*. The talk in these spaces serves the narrative function of deepening characterization and allowing self-disclosure, and it is precisely through this self-disclosure that the men give voice to, reveal, and negotiate their uncertainties about contemporary masculinities. To be clear, I understand the storyworlds considered here as scripted, fictional spaces and see little use in analysis that compares the real men's talk found in the linguists' studies with what is depicted in these shows. Given the considerable consistency among the real and scripted patterns of male talk, it is worth acknowledging the significance and roles of these talk behaviors that have been theorized by linguists, particularly the finding that the use of taboo talk provides a verbal display of toughness that is clearly implicated in the negotiation of the performance of masculinity. This insight helps explain some of the contradictions that emerge in the juxtaposition of the men's presentation of self in the homosocial enclave in contrast with the greater vulnerability evident in what audiences observe when the male characters are outside of these environments.

Television Comedy and the Politics of Jocular Talk

Given television studies' central interest in television's implication in the perpetuation of cultural power, scholars who have studied comedy have most frequently explored questions of how the comedy might work to reinforce or defy the dominant ideological order. Examining this possibility animates feminist media studies of the postwar domestic comedies as well as the "relevance" comedies of the 1970s that have provided rich fodder for feminist and critical race analysis.[14] Critical analysis has argued that comedy creates a space for the incorporation of nondominant ideologies and disenfranchised identities because of its ability to contain difference through its narrative imperative to "laugh at"—this is what, in the terms of the literature on humor, is classified as "superiority theory."[15] Despite the frequent use of comedy to contain difference, many have argued that even creating a space to acknowledge identities outside the mainstream serves an important first step, and that much humor remains open to readings that resist containment.[16]

The literature on television comedy in the twenty-first century is probably most useful for illustrating what these series aren't, or what they are not doing, as existing scholarship has not focused on what might be argued to be the transgressive middle ground that these series occupy. Unlike the satirical comedy considered by much coterminous television comedy scholarship, these series do not seem engaged in the same deliberately political enterprise, which is why I classify them as "transgressive," a distinction made by Michael Tueth, who proposes that "transgressive humor regresses to the infantile. Rather than portraying the objects of its humor in hopes that witty ridicule and public shame might provoke change, transgressive humor does not expect or even desire a change, for then the fun would end."[17] Tueth and Jonathan Gray, Jeffrey Jones, and Ethan Thompson argue that satirical comedy aims at some sort of reform—and that is clearly not the case of these series.[18] Yet at the same time, these series do deliberately defy the conventional safe approaches of most broadcast television comedy by violating norms of proper public speech and voicing perspectives uncensored by concern about consequences. These series may not be as openly engaged in political action or reform as satire, but this "exposure" of rude, offensive, or politically incorrect language does bring into public view otherwise hidden concerns or anxieties. Although this may not constitute political action, it does create an opportunity for the cultural work of negotiating anxieties that would be impossible if they remained publicly unspoken.

It is also worth acknowledging that none of the series considered here is the kind of conventional, proscenium-shot situation comedy that provides the context for most established theory about television comedy. The series considered here are either predominantly dramas or "drama-dies" that allow substantial character development or are comedies shot in single-camera, film style without a laugh track, or other comedic attributes such as the setup-joke-laugh timing common to proscenium-style, multicamera situation comedies. These formal components matter because of the role they play in positioning the audience and cueing it to respond and interpret in particular ways. As David Barker has illustrated through detailed study comparing the single-camera *M*A*S*H* with proscenium-style, multicamera *All in the Family*, the theatrical style and lack of reverse angles of proscenium shooting encouraged particular ideological readings; for example, it helped encode *All in the Family*'s Archie Bunker as a buffoonish character.[19] Likewise, Mills argues that the cues that tell you it is comedy provide a crucial feature of the form, and the laugh track is the most obvious feature of the sitcom. Without a laugh track, the content is often far more ambiguous in terms of what is meant to be funny and what is presented as the cause for amusement. Viewers of the shows considered here lack many of cues that have been standard in television comedy, which adds ambiguity to their ideological vantage point.

The Homosocial Enclave

David Greven explains that the term "homosocial" "succinctly describes the sphere and realms of same-sex relations—the relationships and spaces in which both male power and intimacy are concentrated."[20] For the series considered here, the homosocial enclave is defined by the exclusion of women to create an environment in which "boys can be boys." On one hand, the men are made safe either by the length of the relationships shared or by heightened responsibility created by the dangers they encounter, which lead them to depend upon each other for survival. The series often indicate, albeit implicitly, the security of these spaces through the distinctive performances of self and masculinity that characters embody inside and outside of the homosocial enclave.

In the aftermath of second-wave feminism, depictions of homosocial enclaves have been a rarity for contemporary television. Television producers were clearly aware of the well-founded critique of women's underrepresentation and of the importance of the female consumer to a commercial medium, as all-male enclaves became rare throughout 1980s and 1990s television despite the continued centrality of male characters or dyads. Admittedly, most series included at least a few female characters throughout television history; however, it was often the case, especially in workplace-set series, that these roles were minor or tangential to a degree that there might be considerable screen time afforded to scenes with only male characters. It goes without question in the contemporary industry that ensembles of regular characters should exhibit diversity—whether gender, racial, or, increasingly, sexual diversity, although this often leads to "token" representatives of underrepresented groups. Even token characters, though, typically disrupt what were previously all-male, white, and heterosexual spaces in significant and meaningful ways by rendering related sexism, racism, and homophobia more noticeable and thus less likely.

These series' efforts to create narrative opportunities for men to share a private world should be considered exceptional. As a distinctive narrative setting, the homosocial enclave relies on its totality; the male speech and relationships depicted within it are enabled by the exclusion of those not part of a trusted brotherhood. As subsequent analysis illustrates, access to the homosocial space is strictly policed, and jockeying for status within it is a constant activity even once access to the group has been secured. The casual bonds of most workplace settings are insufficient; the enclave requires the additional bonding that comes through dependence upon each other for survival and regular sequestered living—as is common among firefighters and soldiers.

Few series have created richer homosocial enclaves or devoted greater narrative time to them than the series considered here that construct a homosocial enclave and attend to men's speech and relationship maintenance within it. Thus it is not only the physical space of places such as the firehouse, diner, or context of shared meal or drink that is important but also these series' interest in exploring men's worlds through talk, often with little emphasis on forward plot development. Scenes depicting the homosocial enclave rarely advance plot action; rather, they provide moments for the type of intricate character development explained in chapter 2 and characteristic of the television storytelling emerging during the transition to the twenty-first century. None of these series is primarily about the "doing" of something, such as solving a crime, saving a patient, or securing justice; the logline for any of these shows could be "This series is about the relationships among a group of men." Plot is particularly minimal in *The League*, in which each episode strings together loosely connected scenes of interactions among the characters rather than following a traditional narrative arc. Likewise, *Men of a Certain Age* and *Entourage* typically provide little narrative closure within each episode and are constructed much more similarly to prime-time serials in terms of pacing and narrative resolution. On the whole, *Rescue Me* is most organized around a task—in this case firefighting—but responding to fire calls became less and less a focus of the series throughout its run, and the majority of episodes involve only the men's interactions in the firehouse and scenes from their private lives.

These series are not without precedent. HBO's short-lived *Mind of the Married Man* (2001–2002) attempted to take *Sex and the City*'s frank sex talk into the realm of married men, but failed to offer character depth beyond the men's interest in sex, and tales of infidelity bear significantly greater consequence—and thus diminished entertainment value—for those married than do the exploits of singles. The model for *Entourage* and *Men of a Certain Age*, in particular, probably can be

found in the BBC2 series *Manchild*, produced in 2002–2003 and aired
in the United States on BBCAmerica and some PBS stations in the early
part of the decade. This series replicated many aspects of HBO's *Sex and
the City*, but with a quartet of British men in their fifties, who negotiated life, love, accomplishment, and manhood at middle age. The series
was narrated by Terry, who was divorced yet enjoying the affluence of
a successful professional career. Terry set the tone for the series in an
opening voice-over in which he reflects that "[i]n a man's life, his teens
are a hormone-fueled quest for sex; 20s—finding a wife and a career;
30s—making serious money; 40s—unpicking the unholy mess marriage, families and work have made of your life . . . but time it right,
and your 50s can once again be a fulltime, fullon, hedonistic quest for
pleasure."[21] The demographically diverse quartet included Patrick, a
black, never-married antiquities dealer; James, a divorced, retired den-
tist, who suffers problems with impotence; and the still-married Gary,
who is suddenly wealthy due to an inheritance. The series produced just
fifteen episodes, though, and was better received in the United States
than in Britain. As some reviewers noted, the characters lacked any
sense of irony that would position the audience to laugh at the prepos-
terousness of these men so focused on a second youth. Nor did *Manchild* explore the uncertainties and ambivalences common among the
series addressed here, which may at times allow characters to inhabit
patriarchal masculinities but just as quickly reveal this as performance.

Other series featuring or built upon a homosocial enclave include
the episodic adventure series *The A-Team*, the prison drama *Oz*, and
war-based miniseries such as *Band of Brothers*, *Generation Kill*, and
The Pacific (as war-based series such as *M*A*S*H*, *China Beach*, and
Over There included women). Of these shows, the war-based miniseries probably have the most in common in terms of the depiction of
the jocular banter among a brotherhood of men; however, the exceptional circumstance of war produced very specific concerns for these
men that differ significantly from the contemplations available to their
civilian counterparts. The short-lived ESPN football drama *Playmakers*
(2003) also introduced these themes; however, it rarely made use of the
homosocial enclave and instead focused on the characters individually
by chronicling their off-field relationships. The BBC and Showtime versions of the series *Queer as Folk* also bear similarity in format in their

exploration of both homosocial and homosexual relationships among a group of male friends.

Few consistent features or attributes can be identified in the homo-social enclaves of all of these shows, given the various narrative strategies of the series and the range of life stages of their characters. Each series offers lessons about the negotiation of contemporary masculinities, and in some cases the divergences among the shows provide meaningful sites for analysis. Analyzing the series' joking and joke-based talk by examining what characters laugh at and how they laugh at it exposes the attributes of hegemonic masculinity operating in each show, the process of characters' contestation of norms of masculinity, and some of the fault lines most evident. Although variably emphasized, a maneuvering among the men for rank and prestige occurs within the homosocial enclave—the portrayal of which reaffirms certain aspects of masculinity and contributes to the affirmation of some masculinities over others.

All for One, One for All

Entourage was purportedly inspired by the life of movie star Mark Wahlberg, and follows the heartthrob and emerging movie star Vince (Adrian Grenier) and his "entourage," which includes his older brother, Johnny (Kevin Dillon), a rapidly fading, aging minor actor, and friends Eric (Kevin Connolly) and Turtle (Jerry Ferrera), all of whom are depicted as having grown up together in a working-class Queens neighborhood. The series follows the characters through their carefree and mostly cash-rich twenties in one of the world's most image-obsessed subcultures as Vince negotiates the perils of maintaining celebrity and being perceived as a legitimate actor as well as a pretty face. As the series moves away from its early celebration of star culture, each character works through personal narratives that necessitate that he find his own way and an eventual adult path for his life. Many of the series' central tensions result from the way the characters grow as individuals who revise their identity from their role in a group relationship established in boyhood. Eric is the first to define himself as something more than part of Vince's entourage, initially working as Vince's manager and then, needing greater self-determination, establishing a professional career as a manager of talent other than Vince. The others reach this milestone as the series concludes.[22]

The story of the youthful quartet begins with Vince's film premiere, and the tale of the highs and lows of Hollywood stardom affirms many attributes of patriarchal masculinity, although not without substantial critique of other aspects. This process of affirmation and critique is accomplished in the series by its prioritization of Vince's and Eric's masculinities and disavowal of the embodiments of masculinity performed by Johnny and Turtle. Unlike the case of *Sex and the City*—whose fans were regularly encouraged to report which of the characters they were most like—such an inquiry would never be posed of *Entourage* because it clearly establishes Vince and Eric as embodying masculinities unequivocally preferable to those enacted by Johnny and Turtle. Joking among the men is never done at the expense of Vince; and Eric is gently teased for behaviors such as his faithfulness to girlfriends, desire for monogamy, and ambition to have a career of his own. These values earn mockery in the common banter because they threaten the homosocial enclave, yet are affirmed in moments of sincerity. The criticism of Eric is much less frequent or barbed than the regular skewering of Johnny for his relentless hustling for roles, exaggeration of his past stardom, and aging, or of Turtle for his vulgar efforts to game any system, his embrace of merely being a part of Vince's entourage, or his lesser physique, looks, and attractiveness to women.

Despite the consistent affirmation of the masculinities of Eric and Vince, there is often jockeying for position within the group and for affirmation from Vince. Vince is afforded an unassailable and assumed position of dominance among the group of friends, presumably because of his role as provider. Eric, Turtle, and Johnny jockey among each other to see who can earn Vince's praise and be seen as the member of the entourage best serving Vince. Eric's petitions for leadership typically rely on knowledge appeals such as that he "understands the business," and he encourages Vince to make decisions based on strategy or values. Turtle defers more to Vince's desires—regardless of their rationality or strategic value—and more consistently supports his friend regardless of his own prerogatives. Johnny alternately relies either on a textually unsupported assumption that he has the stronger bond with Vince because he is his brother or that his experience as an actor makes him more knowledgeable about Vince's best interest.

Yet even though he embodies an idealized masculinity, Vince is an unpredictable leader. He rarely seems interested in occupying a dominant status among his friends, and might be swayed by any of their appeals depending on his broader psychological context at the moment. The result is that the series often appears fairly ambivalent in affirming the status of Eric, Turtle, or Johnny above one another *in the group*—and instead supports a sense that all seek to support Vince and maintain the homosocial relationship through different strategies.[23] Eric consistently provides the most direct challenge to Vince, whether by refusing to join the group on a shoot unless Vince officially makes him his manager or by walking away when Vince fires him at a time he's feeling vulnerable. As a result, Eric does at times lose status in the group in the short term, although his actions are consistently affirmed in the long run.

The use of joking to establish rank in *Entourage* ultimately suggests little about the value of different masculinities because characters' efforts or relative success are divorced from their identities by the inconsistency of Vince's actions and the series' affirmation that all the characters value the maintenance of the group. Instead, *Entourage* more clearly prioritizes masculinities through the characters' successes, failures, and general happiness outside of the group. By this measure, Eric's embodiment of masculinity is often affirmed through the series' construction of him as a character with goals and values that he adheres to and as able to mature beyond the status of a hanger-on into a man with a rewarding relationship with a woman and with his own career. The series affirms Turtle's and Johnny's loyalty to Vince, but their disinterest in leaving "the nest" is related to their nonidealized masculinity.

Grown Men and Their Jocular Jousting

Like *Entourage*, *The League* depicts the interworkings of relationships among a group of men with decades-long friendships, in this case, a group of friends since high school who participate in a fantasy football league. We meet *The League*'s men in their midthirties: Kevin (Stephen Rannazzisi), a lawyer, is married with a young daughter, and his wife, Jenny (Katie Aselton), also participates in the league; Pete (Mark Duplass) divorces at the opening of the series and is professionally employed but clearly just marking time; Kevin's slacker brother Taco

(Jonathan Lajoie) appears in each episode but is less integral to the group; Andre (Paul Scheer) is unmarried and a successful plastic surgeon, and Ruxin (Nick Kroll), also a lawyer—but more committed to maintaining professional appearances—has a trophy wife and infant son. For the most part, each episode of *The League* excerpts the men from their broader lives and depicts what might be a week's worth of their casual interactions, most of which revolve around discussion of their fantasy football league. There is commonly little plot to the show and instead it offers a collection of scenes depicting the men bantering, mocking, and trying to provoke each other to comic effect. *The League* is the most purely comedic of the series, offers minimal character development, and lacks the more serious registers of the other series.

Despite the show's irreverence and somewhat willful refusal of serious matters, the comic bantering still reveals sources of gender anxiety and the policing of acceptable masculinities. To a large degree the story of each season follows the competition to win the fantasy football league, and while prowess in fantasy football connects with patriarchal masculinities, even success in this realm cannot help men otherwise outside the hegemonic masculinity overcome their status. Winning the annual league competition provides an explicit measure of manhood, but even beyond this, *The League*, like *Entourage*, identifies its hegemonic masculinity primarily through disavowal of characteristics and behaviors that are presented as not part of its hegemonic masculinity.

Pete and Kevin embody the most idealized masculinities and their friendship is acknowledged as the deepest dyadic relationship within the group. Pete and Kevin, however, are fairly dissimilar, suggesting broad variety in embodiments of hegemonic masculinity so long as men are confident and secure in their identity. Kevin is depicted as having an equitable marital relationship and as being an involved father. In one case in which Andre tries to disparage Kevin because he can't join the others because he has to care for his daughter, Kevin makes clear that he doesn't regard the childcare commitment as a chore. The men do tease Kevin for their suspicion that his wife Jenny plays a considerable role in selecting his team lineups—which viewers know is indeed the case—but this offense isn't presented as the significant critique of Kevin's manliness that one might expect. In considerable contrast to Kevin, Pete is divorced, rarely depicted dating, and not at all concerned with coupling. Notably, he also differs from Kevin in terms of professional aspiration. Although work is rarely depicted in this series, Kevin is shown as a competent and professional lawyer, while Pete is most often depicted adjusting his fantasy team at work and having little professional commitment or ambition.

In contrast, Ruxin, who also displays confidence, is often critiqued for being overly invested in trying to win, too obsessed with all aspects of league participation, and possessing a win-at-any-cost mentality. The group repeatedly sanctions Ruxin for this behavior, which suggests that "good men" enjoy competition but maintain perspective on its significance. Even more than Ruxin, Andre and Taco are consistently rendered the sites of mocking and as embodying undesirable masculinities. Notably, Andre is the most professionally successful of the men, but his transgression comes from trying too hard to earn acceptance and for not knowing how, or not being able, to confidently embody his masculinity; instead, he quickly tries on and overly embraces each new fad. Andre continually tries to overcome the constant mocking, apparently with no sense that these very efforts to remake himself—instead of standing his ground—lead to much of the teasing and diminution in status. For example, one episode charts Andre's efforts to replace Kevin in the alpha dyad in a weekend getaway with Pete. Pete seems to affirm Andre, but in time this is revealed as a ruse to reduce Andre's suspicion when Pete asks to trade a key player from his roster.[24] Andre's desperate desire to feel included makes him a compliant mark, and this undesirable aspect of masculinity is easily exploited. In contrast, Taco is depicted as unemployed, dimwitted, a stoner, and unknowledgeable about football, although the most capable of heterosexual prowess. The other characters generally dismiss him as being flaky, and he functions primarily to make already comic situations absurd.

Kevin's wife, Jenny, often intrudes upon the homosocial enclave and she joins the league's competition in the series' second season. Where the other series depict the homosocial enclave disrupted and threatened by women—for example, when the *Rescue Me* firehouse has a woman added to its crew or when Vince takes a serious girlfriend in *Entourage*—Jenny's presence does not have this effect. Little changes in the characters' comportment when Jenny joins them, and her inclusion seems to at least tacitly require that she accept the terms of the homosocial enclave—that the men will behave as they would if she were not present—in order to participate in it.[25] Jenny's acceptance presumably results from an effective neutering of her sexual identity because of her status as Kevin's wife.[26]

In contrast to the complexity created by *Entourage*'s use of characters who embody distinct and consistent performances of masculinity and its obvious elevation of Vince to the top of the hierarchy as a result of his star status and role as financial provider, relations among the men in *The League* are fairly straightforward. *The League* prioritizes the masculinities embodied by Kevin and Pete over Ruxin, Taco, and Andre; however, it is subtler in indicating why Kevin and Pete are affirmed. Jockeying for status is explicit here; the show's premise as a fantasy football competition indicates one dimension of the men's competition for dominance within the group, and maintenance of the group is not presented as a concern, as in *Entourage*. Instead, *The League* features jockeying within the interpersonal relationships that is very much related to the masculinities the series constructs as hegemonic. *The League*'s lack of substantial character development and avoidance of any melodramatic narrative also prevent it from featuring the same kind of complicated interpersonal negotiation of the homosocial space that occurs in *Entourage*.

Befuddled Brotherhood Confronting Changing Masculinities

Rescue Me differs from the other series in that its homosocial enclave is created in the workplace and features men of various ages and ethnicities—although age proves far more relevant to characterization than ethnicity. *Rescue Me* blends many generic attributes. It is foremost about Tommy Gavin (Denis Leary) and similar to the male-centered serials examined in chapters 2 and 3; however, it also consistently utilizes the space of the firehouse as an all-male domestic space in which the firehouse family of men provides the characters' most stable "family."[27] Each episode spends significant narrative time following the firefighters in their personal lives through narrative arcs that offer extensive character development as well as numerous "firehouse scenes"—the focus of this chapter—that take place between fires or other work duties. The only narrative purpose of these scenes is the exchange of dialogue that explores the men's relationships, commonly by interrogating the men's personal issues and concerns. These scenes often appear as non sequiturs, introducing a topic—such as anxiety regarding gay identity, a problem with a wife or girlfriend, or uncertainty about a physical malady—unrelated to previous and ongoing plot action that creates an opportunity for the men to explore opinions, perspectives, and knowledge of some aspect of men's lives. The broader ensemble of the series often gets its most significant development in these scenes.

The central ensemble includes Lieutenant Kenny Shay (known as Lieu) (John Scurti), who, with Tommy, composes the senior leadership of the crew. Audiences first meet Lieu secretly writing poetry to deal with 9/11 grief. He's Tommy's closest friend and is steadily a "good guy" in that he is fair and decent to others, although he struggles with divorce and being conned by a young woman who steals his savings. Though often the nearest the series offers to a moral center, he is shown to have little that makes life worth living outside of the job and his love of food. Franco (Daniel Sunjata) is part of the crew's younger cohort, but is presented as an established and skilled firefighter from the outset. Franco is Puerto Rican and the series' Lothario, although he is depicted over the run of the series as being willing, but unable, to develop more meaningful relationships with women. Sean Garrity (Steven Pasquale) is also an established member of the crew and primarily offers comic relief. Garrity is an attractive, young, and able firefighter, but is presented as shockingly dumb and unable to comprehend complexity or nuance. Significant humor comes at Garrity's expense. Garrity is often paired in plotlines with Mike Silletti (Michael Lombardi), who is introduced first as "Probie" because he is the crew's probationary firefighter when the series begins. Mike too lacks much worldliness and is depicted as fairly simple. Mike struggles with his sexual identity throughout the series and eventually determines that he is bisexual. "Black Shawn"—named as such because he is African American and the crew already has a Sean— (Larenz Tate) joins the crew in its fourth season, and like Mike, joins the profession post-9/11. Black Shawn couples with Tommy's daughter Colleen, which leads to an awkward negotiation of his contribution to the tales of sexual exploits and "broads" common in firehouse banter.

Rescue Me may offer one of the most varied and unconventional narrative structures on television. Episodes often follow as many as six or seven different plotlines so that it could be described as a multiprotagonist, male-centered serial that also features a homosocial enclave.

In addition to the melodrama of the firefighters' personal lives and the comedy within the firehouse, *Rescue Me* includes depiction of firefighting scenes—arguably a third narrative feature. These action scenes do not occur in every episode and may be most significant for creating dramatic tensions that the dark humor of the firehouse scenes counters.

The series depicts its characters negotiating their identities in complex ways by blending this deeper character building with contexts of group male bantering and dyadic conversations. Viewers are privy to the rich melodramatic depth of the firefighters' personal lives in the scenes that portray their individual lives and issues. The characters often then seek out one other firefighter to whom they reveal their dilemmas or concerns about their personal lives. A version of this information then often becomes fodder for discussion by the whole group. For example, during a shower, Mike identifies a growth on a testicle.[28] He emerges from the firehouse shower visibly concerned and finds Sean in the locker room. He tells Sean of his concern, and in a scene made quite comic in its portrayal of the characters' uncertainty about the boundary between homosocial and homosexual behavior, solicits a second opinion from Sean, who confirms that he should get it checked out. The episode then follows Mike on his trip to the urologist and explores his discomfort with the experience, including concern about the implications of having an erection when checked by a male doctor. He recounts the experience to Sean in a dyadic conversation, and then returns to the doctor for the results. Mike again reports the experience only to Sean, including his worry that his lack of erection during the follow-up exam by an attractive female doctor might be further indication that he is gay. However, Sean has set him up, and when Mike opens his locker, it reveals dildos and gay pornography, and all the other firefighters enter with dildos to tease Mike about being "gay"; this is before he determines that he is bisexual and his mere deviation from the patriarchal masculinity hegemonic in the station earns him teasing. The combination of these different types of scenes exposes the viewer to Mike's shifting embodiment of his masculinity and allows them to see Mike at his most vulnerable, what he's willing to share with the entire brotherhood, and how he voices his anxieties using both humor and sincerity.

Different from the context of a group of friends in *Entourage* and *The League*, the workplace of *Rescue Me* requires that the hierarchy of masculinities embodied by the men be negotiated with the hierarchy of the command structure. Here, explicit rank of employment—such as that of chief or lieutenant or, in contrast, probie—imposes a ranking that does not completely correlate with the hierarchy of masculinities the show constructs. In terms of this homosocial group, the primary measure of a man is his job ability because of the danger weakness poses to the others. This command hierarchy is often consistent with the hierarchy constructed by the men's jockeying within the homosocial group, but deviates at times too. For example, the second part of the first season shows an emotionally unstable Tommy making increasingly bold rescues that end well and are consequently deemed heroic, but a growing sense among the crew that his actions are dangerous causes his status in the group to waver despite his seniority in the command hierarchy and guise of tough, patriarchal masculinity. Similarly, when Lieu grows increasingly overweight and out of shape in the last season, Franco challenges his authority on the ground that it presents a danger to the others. Notably, Tommy's recklessness occurs at the same time the crew is forced to accept a woman into the firehouse, and while they all assume she will be unable to do the job, it is Tommy who proves the weaker link and causes substantial injury to Franco.

For the most part, however, all the men of the firehouse are affirmed as adequate firefighters. Within the homosocial space, Franco's ladies' man masculinity and sexual prowess is affirmed, but otherwise, it is difficult to separate command hierarchy or respect for experience from the affirmation of certain masculinities, as here, too, disavowal of certain traits and behaviors most effectively regulates *Rescue Me*'s hegemonic masculinities. Disavowal commonly occurs through mocking; for example, both Sean and Mike are consistently the source of humor because of the general stupidity they express, and this plainly decreases their stature in the hierarchy. *Rescue Me* also disavows gay identity, both through jocular mocking and through material homophobia exhibited particularly by the chief and Franco, which is explored in conversation with the strategies other series use to address, defuse, and enforce gay anxiety in the chapter's final section.

Comfortable Camaraderie in the Maturity of Middle Age

Men of a Certain Age blends features of the other series. On some level, it is an hour-long, more dramatic version of a series such as *Entourage* and also consistent with *Rescue Me* in being a multiprotagonist, male-centered serial; however, relocating its attention to men nearing fifty provides markedly different subject matter and masculinities. Generationally, the men are contemporaries of *Rescue Me*'s Tommy and Lieu and share relationships that date back to childhood. The series' opening credit sequence, set to the Beach Boys' "When I Grow Up (to Be a Man)," follows three boys from preschool through their teens, leaving the audience to assume that the following narrative tells their story as adults.

The series foremost explores the stories of the men individually: Joe (Ray Romano) begins the series in the process of a divorce, has two teenaged children, and owns and runs a small party supply store. Joe once aspired to a career as a professional golfer, a dream he continues to pursue when he can, but his life seems largely to have been derailed by a gambling problem that precedes the start of the series and is suggested to be the root of his marital discord. Owen (Andre Braugher) finds himself at the height of family life with sons roughly ten and eight and a new, unplanned baby. Much of Owen's story traces his complicated relationship with his father, a one-time professional basketball star and the owner of the auto dealership where Owen works. With his flabby, diabetic body and engaged involvement with his family and wife's needs, Owen seems a disappointment to his father, who is often more supportive of the young, single, fast-talking lead salesman who embodies a masculinity more consistent with his own. In many ways Terry (Scott Bakula) seems a conventional character, a never-married, out-of-work actor who has never committed to a job or another person—easily *Entourage*'s Johnny ten years later. Yet the telling of his tale at middle age presents a rarely seen version of this character—commonly only shown in his youth—as we see Terry longing for the familial relationships of his friends and recognizing that he's probably never going to make it as an actor. For the most part, each episode of the series follows a plot complication in each man's life, but brings them together one or two times per episode for a "diner scene" in which the men converse over breakfast and share conversation in a manner reminiscent of *Sex and the City*'s brunches. The series also occasionally depicts the characters hiking together, and one episode chronicles a weekend retreat they share, but the diner scenes are the primary space of interaction among the men and provide the homosocial enclave focused upon here.

Unlike the strategy of establishing a series' hegemonic masculinity through disavowal, as in *Entourage* and *The League*, *Men of a Certain Age* neither clearly affirms nor denigrates any of its characters. All clearly have flaws and are teased for them—Owen for his appetite and poor physique, Joe for his neuroticism and gambling, and Terry for his lack of dependability and commitment. All are presented as "good," though very different, men, offering a range of masculinities that the narrative supports. They are contrasted with the patriarchal masculinity of Owen's father—a man unwilling to negotiate or hear others out and depicted as having little involvement with his family. The series most consistently affirms being a good dad as a critical part of its hegemonic masculinity, yet doesn't suggest that Terry is any less of a man for not being a father. Here, hegemonic masculinity also requires—particularly of these men of a certain age—a degree of dependability and steadfastness. It remains possible that the men of *Entourage* and *The League* could embody this masculinity later in life, but the whimsy and selfishness allowed for in the masculinities of younger characters such as Vince and Pete is absent in this series, except for Terry's initial story, which explicitly critiques this aspect of his identity and requires that he reform.

Men of a Certain Age consequently does not depict jockeying for status within the homosocial enclave. Perhaps because of the smaller group or the maturity of their relationship, this series offers up a more intimate homosocial environment in which all are secure about their apparently equivalent role in the relationship. This series also supports all three of its characters equally, allowing each flaws and a different, but nonprioritized masculinity. This is a decidedly distinctive strategy from the other series that tie a character's rank in the homosocial enclave to the degree of value afforded variant performances of masculinity.

Policing the Homosocial

In addition to exploring how the series affirm and disavow different masculinities within the groups of friends and coworkers, the homosocial enclave provides a particularly rich site for analyzing the status of gay anxiety in a context Sedgwick has identified as particularly fraught. The male-centered serials provide scant consideration of non-heterosexual identities and rarely even interrogate heterosexuality's assumed presence within series that otherwise affirm masculinities notably divergent from patriarchal norms of the past; however, the context of the homosocial enclave examined here and the hetero intimacy of friendship explored in the next chapter do provide contexts for more readily assessing homophobia and heteronormativity within the straight masculinities these shows present. The four series featuring homosocial enclaves utilize remarkably different strategies for affirming the heterosexuality of characters—or, put another way, of naturalizing the heterosexuality of their characters. Apprehension that might be labeled as "anxiety" about the boundary between homosocial and homosexual behavior and identity really only emerges in one of the series *Rescue Me*; rather, the policing of this boundary plays out much more explicitly in the context of the intimate heterosexual dyadic relationships explored in the next chapter, particularly in *Scrubs*. The characters in *The League* and *Entourage* are securely heterosexual and certain of the heterosexuality of those in the enclave. Consequently, they do not invoke gay identity and uncertainty about its detection as a site of panic. These two series speak minimally of gay identity, but invoke the "threat" of gay sex acts as a feature of their verbal jockeying and one-up-manship. Finally, *Men of a Certain Age* does not engage in use of homophobic speech, name calling, or reflection on gay identity.

The variation among the series in characters' attitudes toward gay identity and handling of anxiety toward homosexuality—particularly given the homosocial enclave—provides an opportunity to probe how these series regard gay identity relative to their hegemonic masculinities regardless of the uniform heterosexuality of main characters. On the surface, there may seem great similarity: *Rescue Me*, *The League*, and to a lesser extent *Entourage* incorporate taboo homophobic speech in a manner that seems consistent with what would be expected of locker room talk affirming patriarchal masculinities. But closer analysis of this speech in *Rescue Me* reveals a complicated, though "politically incorrect," engagement with anxiety regarding detecting gay identity and the increasing inclusion of aspects of gay identity into the hegemonic masculinity of the world in which its characters live. The uncertainty about hetero- and homosexual boundaries in *Rescue Me* is also inflected with what Becker terms "straight panic," which is characterized by changing cultural politics that make it difficult to simply disavow homosexual identity.[29] The more extended dramatic storylines and character development of *Rescue Me* make clear that a fair amount of material homophobia underlies the comments of the firehouse crew, and disavowal of gay identity functions as the overriding and somewhat obsessively observed determinant of acceptable masculinity among the crew. The correlation of anything negative with being "gay" is a constant feature of the firehouse banter. *Rescue Me* attends so extensively to gay identity that it could arguably be categorized as a theme of the first few seasons; the title of the second episode of the series is "Gay," an episode that introduces an extended plotline tracing the chief's homophobia. The chief—who has an out gay son who is a firefighter in Boston—openly struggles with homophobia that threatens his relationship with his son and his ability to be a firefighter. He physically attacks a gay firefighter who informed a newspaper article on the extent of gay members of the NYFD force, and the resulting legal and NYFD adjudication nearly ends his career, but forces him to share his son's sexuality with the crew, which arguably begins a process of coming to accept his son.

Others in the crew are clearly homophobic, but their hatred seems to come more from a place of fear and uncertainty over what acceptance of gay identity could mean to the privilege of heteronormativity. Much of the anxiety about gay identity in *Rescue Me*—particularly among the older characters—is related to their growing recognition of the prevalence of gay men and their inability to identify them. This uncertainty is experienced as a threat to the homosociality central to the firefighting experience, and can be seen as nostalgia for a time when they perceived that heterosexuality could be assumed in the firehouse. Finally, the first three seasons clumsily depict Mike's discovery of his bisexuality. All these storylines allow the series to explore attitudes about gay identity in depth, though the series also commonly invokes gay identity by using it as a slur in the course of banter. *Rescue Me* includes and discusses actual gay characters, which makes clear that not only do these men disavow sexual behavior different from their own, but they also possess a level of condemnation for those whose sexual identity differs. The show occasionally goes so far as to use the still-taboo reference to gays as "fags," although because of the context and character development that the series' broader interrogation of sexual identity provides, it is difficult to claim that this indicates an escalated homophobia.[30]

The central question here, however, is how gay identity is regarded relative to the hegemonic masculinity of the show. Ultimately, when considered in context and relative to characterization, *Rescue Me*'s hegemonic masculinity seems more befuddled by gay identity and concerned about its detection than threatened by it—a thematic Becker categorizes as consistent with "post-closet TV." Despite the correlation between being gay and being weak that is implied in the use of gay name calling, the series seems nevertheless capable of imagining a gay person as a heroic firefighter, and in this narrative universe, firefighting ability serves as the primary arbiter of hegemonic masculinity. For example, Tommy encourages the crew to accept Mike after he reveals his bisexuality in a speech in which he ties acceptance of Mike to his proven abilities as a firefighter.[31] Despite the vitriol of talk, an actual gay—or, more precisely, bisexual—man who is a proven member of the homosocial enclave is presented as more desirable than an unknown, assumedly heterosexual, replacement to the unit. This acceptance certainly doesn't compensate for the series' frequent homophobic slurs, but it calls into question the sincerity of the regular and consistent association of anything negative with being "gay" in firehouse banter. The chief is arguably the most homophobic member of the crew, but the series does not affirm his hatred; it depicts his struggle with changing norms of masculinity and his process of becoming comfortable enough with gay identity to speak at his son's marriage.

The League regularly, and *Entourage* far more sparingly, use the suggestion of their friends engaging in gay sex acts as a tactic in verbal jockeying. This jockeying addresses gay sex acts rather than disparages gay individuals.[32] For example, in *Entourage*, this exchange occurs:

JOHNNY: I think he looks bloated. I begged him to see my colonic guy.
TURTLE: Unlike you, I don't like guys sticking stuff up my ass.[33]

Or Eric, to Ari: "Yeah, I can shove it up your ass. I bet you'd like that."[34] *The League* is absent any serious consideration of gay identity, but overflows with deprecation and verbal jousting consistently phrased in language suggesting gay sexual relations; Andre's general deviation from the masculinities of Kevin, Pete, and Ruxin is repeatedly described as "gay"; and Ruxin often suggests that Kevin and Pete are a gay couple because they have the closest friendship among the men—though all clearly perceive the other men's sexuality as undoubtedly heterosexual. This type of homophobic banter, which *Entourage* also uses less frequently, does not mock or disparage gay *identity*—men who are gay—so much as sex acts generally associated with gay identity. Placing their dialogue in context, their words aren't expressions of hatred or fear toward gay men, but a juvenile obsession with their seemingly "taboo" sex acts.[35]

My point here is not to argue that this makes their disparagement of gay sex acts acceptable or any more or less problematic than the tactics of *Rescue Me*, as it certainly can be argued that you can't hate or fear sex acts without hating or fearing those who engage in them. The relevant point here is to acknowledge this as a distinct strategy and to consider its consequences for including or repudiating gay identity from the series' hegemonic masculinities. The banter "threatening" gay sex acts on each other is disconnected from actual gay men; unlike the case in *Rescue Me*, the men of *The League* do not appear concerned with detecting homosexual identity. It also doesn't seem to register to the characters that their banter disparages gay people. Despite their overdetermined language, they are completely nonchalant regarding the identity of the gay men they encounter, and in most cases the humor of such situations ends up being at the main characters' expense rather than suggestive of hatred or intolerance. The foreignness of and their discomfort with the idea of gay sex—and notably sexual behaviors not exclusively the purview of gay sex—makes the "threat" of "gay" sex acts seem a menacing assault in their verbal jousting, which is sophomoric and not related to a valuation about being gay.

The League enforces a hegemonic masculinity that eschews gay identity through teasing consistent with homophobia and the lack of gay men among the core cast, but doesn't engage in de rigueur gay bashing. Despite this, the series seems more ambivalent toward gay identity than concerned with maintaining the heteronormativity of patriarchal masculinities. In comparison, *Entourage*, which includes a gay character, Lloyd—Ari's assistant, who becomes Johnny's agent—makes such a reading more evident because the inclusion of a gay character allows illustration of how gay men might not concern characters who disparage gay sex in their verbal jockeying. In both series, it is not the sex act that threatens their straight masculinities so much as the foreignness of types of sexual intimacy, and this leads to a quite rigid construct of heterosexuality for these characters. These series affirm a heterosexuality that allows for close camaraderie among men but no physical intimacy, though, notably, these shows do not openly assert heterosexuality as a condition of hegemonic masculinity.

Another way to read the obsession with using "gay" as the most common denigration in these series is to view it as an indication of the men's anxiety with the intimacy of the homosocial space, following Sedgwick. The characters arguably distance themselves from the possibility of being gay by constantly constructing gay as other. In this way, the repeated disavowal of gay identity works to circumvent easy queer reading of their intimacy. Both *Rescue Me* and *The League* construct homosocial enclaves that allow for uncommon frankness in the men's conversations rather than depict intimacy that readily lends itself to the assertion of a queer subtext. So while this reading is available—as it might always be—the repeated disavowal of gay identity disables such a reading from being particularly obvious or compelling.

The relationship among the characters in *Entourage*, however, presents an intimacy that more freely can be read queerly, which makes it further noteworthy that the series does not engage in the same level of intergroup jockeying through threatening gay sex acts or gay bashing, especially given the ribald escapades and more juvenile hegemonic masculinity of this series. Here, taunts regarding each other's masculinity are instead more commonly focused on heterosexual prowess, though occasional references to gay sex acts do occur. Further, the most explicit gay bashing is not part of the homosocial enclave of the friends; the type of homophobic rhetoric spewed by the characters of *Rescue Me* and *The League* is most commonly introduced by Vince's agent, Ari Gold (Jeremy Piven), who, Nancy Lee argues, is an ironic characterization of the extremes of "aggressive masculinity."[36] Assessing the significance and intention of Ari's slurs is made complicated by the fact that this speech is introduced by a man who exists outside the homosocial enclave, by Ari's general outrageousness as a character who engages in a wide variety of hateful talk that is not mirrored in his behavior, and by *Entourage's* inclusion of openly gay men in its cast. Ari's perspectives are not affirmed in the homosocial enclave and the friends embrace and often support Lloyd. The series sets up Ari's performance of masculinity as consistent

with disavowed patriarchal masculinities, though even Ari's true identity seems to disavow this masculinity as well. Within the universe of
Entourage, Hollywood power remains characterized as held by men who
continue to adhere to a bombastic patriarchal masculinity—though the
series does not idealize this masculinity and often vilifies it. Of the series
considered here, *Entourage* arguably presents the most intimate brotherhood within the homosocial enclave, yet presents the men as being
secure in the acceptability of heterosexual male intimacy and does not
require repeated disavowal of gay identity as a way to diffuse the intimacy of their friendships.[37] At the same time, this does make the show
most open to queering the relationships among the friends, although I
still would not characterize this reading as readily available.

   Men of a Certain Age avoids these complicated assessments by offering
no mention of gay identity or gay sex. Though this strategy may be less controversial, the absence of any mention of homosexuality arguably enforces
heterosexuality as "natural" in much the same way as occurs in the male-
centered dramas. The series does probe different aspects of heterosexuality through storylines of Joe's uncertain reentry to the world of dating and
negotiation of changed sexual norms and through Terry's coming to accept
that he can find greater intimacy with a woman his own age than by pursu-
ing much younger women, despite social affirmation of the latter.

Conclusion

The particular industrial context of cable is most certainly significant
to contextualizing the jocular homosocial enclave. *Rescue Me* and *The
League*—both aired by FX—clearly transcend broadcast standards and
practices in language and feature an edgy sensibility far from that likely
to appeal to the broad audiences sought by broadcast networks. The
banter featured in *Rescue Me*, *The League*, and *Entourage* is not for the
easily offended; series' dialogue makes extensive use of taboo words
and seems to revel in language deemed unacceptable in terms of the
norms of politically correct speech. However, this type of frank talk
unencumbered by social norms is precisely what makes the conversations in these spaces so relevant to examining the construction and
policing of masculinities. Although offered with bluster and swagger,
the conversations in the homosocial enclave give voice to insecurities

and uncertainties. It is through jocularity that the men can talk about penis size, discoloring of the scrotum, infrequency of sexual interactions, or other realities that suggest they aren't the masters of their universes that they project themselves to be. *Men of a Certain Age* also offers this type of talk, but neuters the crass juvenile masculinity found in the other shows to an extent that it might be consistent with "broadcast" standards. *Men of a Certain Age* sees the world through the eyes of characters who are facing fifty and have been humbled by experience; the bravado of the banter among these men is more humane, but the speech acts are consistent.[38]

As Greven asserts, the homosocial space is key for the safety it provides, and in the case of the series considered here, this sense of safety allows for intimacy and trust that enables the men to share perspectives and outlooks they would not otherwise make public. Of course, no matter the topic introduced in this space, the man opens himself to ridicule and mocking. This is performed as a means to diffuse the seriousness of some topics and the intimacy involved in its negotiation; but the reliance on teasing is not purely an act of policing acceptable boundaries. Through their good-natured ribbing, the men do engage in discussion of meaningful matters that reveal them to have anxieties regarding their masculinity. The joking that dominates communication in the enclave offers the men a supportive context, affirming that each is not alone in his struggles, but simultaneously polices boundaries of acceptable masculinity.

The homosocial enclave is such a significant component to the broader consideration of the negotiation of masculinities because it makes public what are otherwise private acts of uncensored speech that allow a different vantage point on male anxieties and vulnerabilities. This peek into the inner world among men may reveal outlooks beyond the bounds of "proper" norms, but rather than inspire concern that they are evidence of new intolerance, it seems more likely that these sentiments are not new; they've just been hidden.

In a way, these spaces and their discourse present an inversion of what James C. Scott terms as "public" versus "hidden" transcripts. In Scott's use, the public transcript describes the open interactions among subordinates and those who dominate them, while the hidden transcript characterizes "discourse that takes place 'offstage,' beyond direct observation of power holders."[39] Relevant to the examination here, Scott acknowledges that the powerful too have hidden transcripts and a stake in maintaining the public transcript, although the stakes in its maintenance differ. The homosocial enclaves of these series make public transcripts that straight, white men have had to take into hiding in a culture that outlawed the *appearance* of sexism, racism, and other intolerance, ostensibly in an effort to eradicate them. Analysis of the politics of these hidden discourses reveals that though the enclave may create an opportunity for "inappropriateness," it does not consistently nurture patriarchal masculinities, nor is it a space for their perpetuation. In *Rescue Me* and *Men of a Certain Age*, viewers are made privy to men working through contentious social issues or baring vulnerabilities in spaces made safe for negotiation. The fact that men say inappropriate things in these enclaves does not indicate a uniform longing for a time when these utterances were acceptable. In comparison with the construction of masculinities identified in other sections of this book, the homosocial enclave elicits different performances of masculinity because of the intimacy of this space, though the policing of masculinities persists even among friends.

5

Dynamic Duos

Hetero Intimacy and the New Male Friendship

The eponymous Starsky and Hutch. *I Spy*. That *Odd Couple* of Oscar and Felix. *Miami Vice*'s Crockett and Tubs. John and Ponch of *CHiPS*. *Bosom Buddies*' Henry and Kip. *thirtysomething*'s Michael and Elliot. Beavis and Butthead. Certainly, male buddies—and particularly crime-fighting teams—are nothing new to television screens. Consistent with the developments explored in other chapters of this book, however, new dimensions of the male buddy relationship emerge in twenty-first-century fictional series. Expanding the previous chapters' consideration of interiority and the male psyche found in the male-centered serials or the anxieties revealed by the uncensored speech and jockeying for status within all-male homosocial enclaves, this chapter examines series that emphasize the friendship among two male characters and depict considerable intimacy within this relationship.

Unlike many of the buddy/cop-type teams listed above that persist today in series such as *White Collar* (USA, 2009–), *Suits* (USA, 2011–), or the short-lived *Common Law* (USA, 2012), these dyadic relationships are not merely the relationships of occupational happenstance that coworkers commonly inhabit; nor are they occasional dyadic relationships among two of a larger group, such as the relationship between Chandler and Joey in *Friends*. Rather, this chapter examines depictions of male friendship in *Scrubs* (2001–2009), *Nip/Tuck* (2003–2010), *Boston Legal* (2004–2008), and *Psych* (2006–). These series feature dyadic hetero intimacy often utilizing narrative tropes of and attention to relationship maintenance typically reserved for heterosexual coupling. Analysis of these relationships considers how the men negotiate anxieties of homosexuality and push boundaries of homosocial masculinities in these friendships. In some cases, the narratives ultimately enforce heteronormativity by juxtaposing the straight friendship against gay love, which is consequently disavowed, while other series meaningfully disrupt heteronormativity by positing a nonsexual basis for relationships of greatest intimacy.

Although the series may not be explicitly about male friendship to the extent that the male-centered serials impart the broad interpersonal and professional struggles of their protagonists, they indicate extreme self-awareness of the novelty of their depictions of male friendship and the histories of representation and absence in which they operate. These examinations of male friendship can be found in both comedic and dramatic storytelling, and unlike the fraternal environment of the firehouse or a gang of friends, these series move beyond the comfortable jocularity of familiar teasing to depict men engaging in intimate heterosexual relationships with other men. These friendships are built on trust, loyalty, and shared history, albeit with a fair amount of jocular banter as well. The familiarity of these relationships provides the men with an opportunity to express concerns and anxieties and to otherwise bare themselves without the constant need to jokingly diffuse anxiety created by the closeness that occurs in these relationships. The friendships also lack the dimensions of jockeying for status that characterize the homosocial enclave, which deters these series from consistently affirming certain masculinities over others. Series featuring hetero male dyads depict male characters as often somewhat uncertain about the intimacy of platonic relationships but ultimately present deeper and more complex relationships than have been common.

Some of these series make explicit what might, in another time or context, have been considered as a "queer subtext" or cloaked queerness, while others present the men's intimacy openly without calling attention to its queer possibilities and still others attempt to explicitly discourage this reading.[1] In discussing some of these series, Ron Becker describes these characters as embodying a "queer straight masculinity," in which heterosexual men embody what have been identified as "queer" masculinities because they diverge from hegemonic norms.[2] Becker argues that the textual affirmation of queer straight masculinities and the coterminous increase of openly gay characters has "destabilized heteronormativity," an assertion supported by the depictions in several of the shows considered here.[3] The depictions of male friendships in these series—some of which Becker briefly discusses—also challenge patriarchal masculinities that have refused to depict intimacy among men, and even go so far as to contest heteronormativity.[4]

The series use various strategies to ease the potential gay panic instigated by the intimacy they depict: *Scrubs* uses a strategy of disavowal, identifying the relationship between JD and Turk as "Guy Love"—famously addressed in a musical performance—and the characters explicitly and repeatedly affirm their relationship as "not gay";[5] *Boston Legal* alternates between moments of farce and great seriousness to allow Denny and Alan to speak earnestly and with conviction of their love for each other while posing their nonsexual relationship as of greater intimacy than the sexual relationships they experience with women; *Psych* requires imposing a more traditional queer reading strategy through which occasional "knowing glances" in Gus and Shawn's camaraderie encourage intimate readings of the relationship, but the series also refutes explicit expression of intimacy through its playful and flippant tone; and *Nip/Tuck*'s six seasons implicitly tell a story of love, envy, and various betrayals that stress the professional partnership and friendship of plastic surgeons Christian and Sean, who themselves seem uncertain about the implications of their shared hetero intimacy.

Although *Nip/Tuck* (FX) and *Psych* (USA) are cable series, this chapter expands beyond the book's cable focus to include the broadcast series *Boston Legal* (ABC) and *Scrubs* (NBC/ABC) because an examination of dyadic male friendships in the television of this era would be so impoverished if these series were disregarded. Confining this examination to cable may offer a more elegant book construction, but it is more beneficial to avoid being overly dogmatic in the pursuit of neat explanations for inclusion and at times to embrace the inconsistencies. As I explain in the introduction, I did not set out to write a book about cable masculinities; rather, it just happened that the phenomena of interest appeared predominantly in cable series—that is, except for the presentation of dyadic hetero intimacy. The inclusion of both broadcast and cable series introduces new dimensions of analysis such as the questions of why emergent masculinities that embrace intimate heterosexual male friendships flourish in broadcast storytelling that otherwise has been resistant to adjustments in male character types and storytelling and whether distinctions between the storytelling about dyadic male friendships can be linked to their different industrial origins.

This chapter considers televised depictions of male friendship in an era Becker characterizes as one of "post-closet TV," a designation that acknowledges the complicated and contradictory nature of men's portrayals at this time.[6] Shifting cultural attitudes toward gay identity contribute an explanation for the emergence of depictions of deeper intimacy between heterosexual friends evident in these series. These friendships—and the stories about them—contest the previously common, and arguably patriarchal, strategy of portraying male friendships as lacking personal intimacy and as deemphasized in the heteronormative regime that encompasses the many practices, assumptions, and privileges that construct hegemonic male identity as heterosexual.[7] Although the depictions of friendship in these series hardly obliterate the hetero-homo binary Eve Kosofksy Sedgwick posits as a defining tension in the negotiation of male identity,[8] some of the series do begin to disrupt this norm and make considerable strides toward allowing for intimate friendships among men. Such depictions sanction a wider array of straight male relationships and deconstruct heteronormativity, allowing the creation of male relationships built on something other than patriarchal masculinities that often have emphasized bonding rituals that exploit women (e.g., the stereotypical stag party trip to a strip club) and remain common in television series privileging a more juvenile and patriarchal masculinity (*Blue Mountain State* [Spike, 2010–2011], *Workaholics* [Comedy Central, 2011–], *Men at Work* [TBS, 2012–]). The chapter's analytic focus examines the friendships, rather than the individual identities, of the male characters and the way they indicate aspects of patriarchal or feminist masculinities. Relative to this conceptual schema, contestation of heteronormativity and depictions of meaningful hetero intimacy illustrate feminist reconstruction of patriarchal norms that have otherwise relegated hetero intimacy to a structuring absence in men's lives or depicted considerable anxiety over potential homosexuality in these relationships.

Television's Twenty-First-Century Bromances

Although much of this chapter explores the commonalities among the friendships central to the four series explored here, it is important to begin by acknowledging and mapping their dissimilarities. One way to organize the series and their varied presentations of male friendship is along axes based on *how openly the series speak of intimacy* and *how central the process of relationship maintenance* is to the series narrative.

Both *Boston Legal* and *Scrubs* fit in the High/Explicit quadrant of figure 5.1 despite generic differences as workplace drama and comedy, respectively. These shows attend regularly to the issue of relationship maintenance, albeit in different ways. By episode nine of its first season, *Boston Legal* began carving out a coda scene in each episode in which lawyers Denny Crane (William Shatner) and Alan Shore (James Spader) share a drink or cigar on Denny's office veranda and discuss the events of the episode. This created an opportunity to bring the characters together even when they were involved in unrelated plotlines and situated amidst a much larger ensemble of characters, as was often the case. Interactions between the two in plots throughout the episode became increasingly common in later seasons as the role of the friendship and its negotiation in the workplace became a narrative focus of the series. Although the men often referenced after-hours time spent together, the series primarily depicted only their workplace encounters.

Scrubs too featured a friendship primarily observed in the workplace as it followed the travails of Christopher Turk (Turk) (Donald Faison) and John Dorian (JD) (Zach Braff)—friends since college—through their medical residencies and early years working in the same hospital. Most series' action is set in the workplace of the hospital, but the men share an apartment at the beginning of series, which created opportunities to view their relationship outside of work. *Scrubs* also utilized fantasy and flashback sequences that occasionally offered glimpses of the earlier days of their relationship. *Scrubs* never developed a tool like *Boston Legal*'s balcony sequence to regularly address this central relationship, and many episodes did not feature relationship maintenance. More commonly, the series devoted a central episodic plot in order to offer more extensive, though irregular, examination of the challenges to their relationship that the men faced.[9]

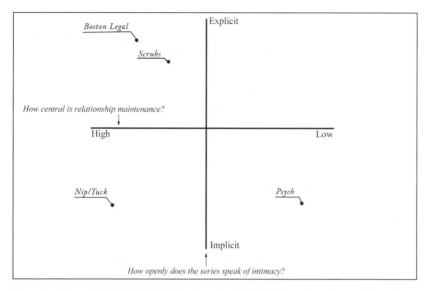

Figure 5.1. Matrix of Friendship Intimacy and Explicitness. This figure depicts the relative importance of friendship maintenance in the narrative and the explicitness with which the series discuss friendship intimacy.

Nip/Tuck is characteristic of a show in the High/Implicit quadrant. The plastic surgery practice shared by college lab partners Christian Troy (Julian McMahon) and Sean McNamara (Dylan Walsh) featured nearly all the plot action, and the two men were intricately involved in each other's personal lives as well. The lines between surgical partner and friend were exceedingly amorphous, making it difficult to categorize any medical interaction as unrelated to the relationship tensions the two struggled through. Unlike *Boston Legal* and *Scrubs, Nip/Tuck* rarely acknowledged that the maintenance of Sean and Christian's relationship in many ways provided the series' primary narrative arc; *Nip/Tuck* appeared to be a series about a plastic surgery practice, but it was as much—if not more—about the relationship of Christian and Sean. Moments of extreme crisis—as when Sean learned that Christian fathered the adult son Sean believed to be his own, or when usually hyperheterosexual Christian spends multiple episodes questioning whether his affections for Sean are more homosexual than homosocial—drew attention to the relationship, but it was more commonly unmentioned—always there, but unspoken.

Finally, *Psych* occupies the Low/Implicit quadrant and operates most like a conventional buddy film narrative. The history of the men's relationship—which begins in their youth—and occasional focus on relationship issues, however, allow greater depth than common in buddy films. *Psych* is primarily an episodic "who done it" featuring "psychic detective" Shawn Spencer (James Roday) and his sidekick Burton (Gus) Guster (Dule Hill). Shawn is not psychic, just uncommonly observant, but has convinced the Santa Barbara police department to employ him and Gus as consultants. *Psych* emphasized the deep roots of Shawn and Gus's childhood friendship by beginning many episodes with a flashback to an event in their childhood that bears some relevance to the contemporary events the episode presents, although plot action otherwise largely mirrors that in other buddy detective teams that I would not categorize as intimate enough to be relevant to this chapter. The series does not work at relationship maintenance in the manner common to *Boston Legal* or *Scrubs*, nor is a story about their friendship an underlying narrative arc, as is the case of *Nip/Tuck*. *Psych* occasionally and haphazardly presents Shawn and Gus negotiating their relationship and provides them opportunities to speak of its importance to each other, although in a manner tonally very different from the earnestness of *Boston Legal*.

The comparison along the two axes of the importance of relationship maintenance to the series and the openness with which the characters express their intimacy may be of limited utility at this point of relatively few series. It will prove a more helpful organizing, and eventual analytic, tool if the depiction of intimate male friendships continues. At this nascent point of development, the chart maps the range of strategies the series offer, but provides little meaningful ground for analysis given the paucity of series to consider. A notable point—although admittedly made minimally significant by the few series considered here—is that the two series developed for broadcast networks are both more explicit in their attention to intimacy within the friendship than the two series developed for cable channels. This is counterintuitive given the depth of attention to men's interior struggles with masculinity in cable series discussed to this point. Broadcast series—with their need for larger, more heterogeneous audiences—have otherwise avoided or failed in their efforts to engage in meaningful probing of male identity, making it surprising that two broadcast series would present male friendship in this way.

Admittedly, other series that aired at the same time as these also featured a central male friendship or professional relationship: *House, Franklin & Bash, White Collar, It's Always Sunny in Philadelphia, Bored to Death, Suits,* and *Common Law* are among the most prominent. The buddy detective teams at the core of many of these series led journalist June Thomas to term them "brocedurals" in acknowledgment of the trend of episodic procedurals driven by a male team.[10] In determining the scope of this chapter I considered these other series, but ultimately concluded that they did not include the level of intimacy and attention to relationship maintenance achieved by those series included.[11]

Out of the Closet: Guy Love and Its Challenge to Heteronormativity

What I categorize as dyadic hetero intimacy draws most closely on the so-called buddy film that has been an occasional object of analysis of film scholars, particularly when the dyad of focus involves an interracial friendship. These analyses provide a broad, but only tangentially relevant, framework for the analysis here that otherwise has little scholarship from which to draw. Although I might informally refer to the series considered in this chapter as "buddy" shows, the categorization of "buddy" identifies a markedly less intimate relationship than is evident in these series. The television relationships are explicitly characterized as of high interpersonal value and are more significant than the casual pairing of characters common to film buddies.

Before interracial buddy pairings became common in the 1980s, Robin Wood identified six characteristics in the 1970s buddy film, a cycle including such films as *Easy Rider* (1969), *Butch Cassidy and the Sundance Kid* (1969), and *Midnight Cowboy* (1969): the journey, the marginalization of women, the absence of home, the male love story, the presence of an explicitly homosexual character, and death.[12] Wood argues that these buddy films develop in response to the feminist activism of the late 1960s and indicate an ideologically regressive strategy that marginalizes women.[13] More recently, David Greven has offered a new angle by considering films centering on a dyadic male relationship as the "double protagonist" film, a form that features two men who "double" each other in a "battle over narrative dominance, sexual objects and audience sympathy."[14] Films of this subgenre, which include *Seven* (1995), *Face/Off* (1997), *Fight Club* (1999), *The Talented Mr. Ripley* (1999), and *Brokeback Mountain* (2005), either pit the protagonists against each other or "demonstrate the merging of the two central males into one."[15] Greven argues that the double protagonist film "simultaneously literalizes the metaphorical split within the tortured psyche of the divided, lonely noir protagonist and re-imagines the male-male relationships of the western and the later buddy-film genres as it represents not so much a response to feminism and queer sexuality as it does the next stage in cinematic manhood after those challenges were raised."[16] Although these narratives are quite distinct from the ones I consider, Greven's project of teasing apart the way new gender scripts might be a response to feminist activism and queer sexuality and a "next stage" bears considerable commonality.

The interracial buddy film became increasingly common following the 1970s cycle Wood writes about. Melvin Donalson traces this format throughout film history in a largely descriptive account, and scholars such as Cynthia Fuchs and Ed Guerrero provide detailed analysis of interracial buddy films such as *Silver Streak* (1976), *Brewster's Millions* (1987), *Beverly Hills Cop I* (1984) and *II* (1987), and the *Lethal Weapon* series.[17] Guerrero argues that the interracial buddy film becomes prevalent as a way to capitalize on the largest possible audience for stars such as Richard Pryor and Eddie Murphy by teaming them with white partners to suggest a politics of integration. He argues that these films ultimately offer "escapist fantasy narratives and resolutions" that commonly isolate the black lead within an entirely white environment.[18] Fuchs similarly identifies the conservative impulse of these films but focuses on arguing that they "efface the intimacy and vulnerability associated with homosexuality by the 'marriage' of racial others."[19] In other words, the assumed transgressiveness of featuring an interracial couple is used to displace the homosocial anxiety created by the intimacy of the buddy relationship.

Although this film scholarship assessing buddies and interracial buddies is persuasive and well argued in the cases it presents, it is of limited utility to the considerations of the buddy relationships emerging on television in the first decade of the twenty-first century. Foremost, these films consider "buddies"—a term denoting a more casual relationship than the intimate friendships of *Boston Legal, Scrubs, Nip/Tuck,* and *Psych.* The films also have a contained narrative arc that enforces conclusion, while the television series are able to play out ongoing relationship negotiation and evolution, a strategy perhaps utilized most extensively in *Nip/Tuck.* These television series consequently highlight the continuous process of being in a relationship. Some of the points regarding interracial buddy structures made by Guerrero and Fuchs are relevant to the television series utilizing interracial dyads (*Scrubs, Psych*), and I'll return to those in considering this dynamic of these series later in the chapter.

I include this brief acknowledgment of film studies' buddy literature because men's friendships and intimacy have otherwise been rarely considered in television or film scholarship. Scholarship on series featuring dyads, such as *Miami Vice,* attended to other foci and lines of analysis.[20] Lynn Spangler offers a descriptive history in her 1992 article examining "Buddies and Pals: A History of Male Friendships on Prime-Time Television."[21] Organized by decade, her account notes the loose camaraderie of western heroes and sidekicks in the 1950s, relationships between *Star Trek*'s Spock and Kirk and *I Spy*'s Kelly and Robinson in the 1960s, the families of friends in 1970s shows such as *M*A*S*H, Barney Miller, WKRP in Cincinnati,* and *The Mary Tyler Moore Show,* as well as those in *The A-Team* and *Magnum, P.I.* in the 1980s, but concludes by noting, "There have been intimate male friendships depicted on television for more than four decades, but never in abundance. The majority of men on TV are seen doing together, not being together."[22] Margo Miller treads near the topic in her provocative analysis of how the male characters in *Seinfeld* are portrayed as engaging in a comfortable intimacy that does not utilize an "ironic dismissal" when other characters wrongly assume this intimacy to suggest homosexuality, which she argues is the common comedic strategy of other 1990s comedies.[23] Miller contends that the tendency to play the identity confusion for laughs is evidence of "new hostility toward queerness in straight male characters" and is a reinforcement of heteronormativity, while Becker conceives of the politics of the mistaken identity plotlines somewhat differently.[24] Becker explains the mistaken sexual identity plot in the comedies of the 1990s as a result of the uncloseting of gay identity creating a "new semiotic landscape—one where more and more same-sex interactions were read as seemingly self-evident signs of gayness."[25] The confusion isn't a wholesale indictment of heteronormativity; Becker notes that "[p]roducers also played up the illegibility of sexual identity by casting, dressing, and directing actors who played gay characters in ways that challenged preconceived notions about the supposed differences between gay and straight men's mannerisms, speech patterns, or other markers of difference."[26] Becker argues that series depicting characters as "gay-friendly straight-men" placed them in a double bind in which they sought to not degrade gay identity in the process of disavowing it for themselves: *Seinfeld*'s often quoted, "We're not gay! Not that there's anything wrong with that" expresses this succinctly. A trajectory of gay inclusion could be argued that begins with the ironic dismissal, in which the suggestion of gay identity is played for humor, which gives way to characters who do not distance themselves from gay identity when mistaken for gay, and then to a significant reduction in mistaken-identity storylines altogether.

This paucity of research about depictions of male friendships or male intimacy probably relates to the fact that there was not much to analyze in previous male relationships such as those that introduce the chapter. Many of these dyads were indeed buddies in the most superficial sense—they were men who worked together and maybe knew of each other's personal lives, but the narratives of these series did not present their relationships with each other as dynamic or central to the storytelling. The comedies featured a lighthearted tone and presumed relationships that were established and not in need of maintenance, while dyads created by workplace necessity—such as those of crime fighting and detection partners—ventured into the realm of the personal only in the case of the exceptional episode. The narrative centrality of the dyadic relationships distinguishes the series considered here and invites, if not requires, analysis of the terms by which the texts negotiate such relationships.

Acknowledging the popular emergence of the term "bromance" to describe male intimacy is a necessary part of contextualizing the relationships considered in this chapter. Although it was a widely used slang term by the late 2008 debut of the MTV show *Bromance*, Ron

Becker valuably explores "bromance" as a cultural discourse, as "a way of talking and thinking about male friendships that helps produce specific ways of feeling and experiencing homosocial intimacy and masculinity," which he connects with the increase of gay and lesbian visibility in the 1990s.[27] Becker argues that "male bonding no longer serves to foreground straight men's anxieties about being misread as gay" in the bromantic discourse emerging in the 2000s. Since then, the mistaken-gay-identity plot—and the negotiation of masculinity's hegemonic sexual identity that was at stake in it—has largely disappeared and been replaced by bromantic portrayals that self-consciously announce the intimacy and heterosexuality of their characters.[28]

The series considered here emerge after this cycle of "mistaken gay identity" plots but a little before the term "bromance" emerges to identify narratives that self-consciously attend to male bonding and related negotiation of masculinity and heteronormativity. Becker argues that the bromance "relies on the cultural awareness of and general positive associations connected to gay love to reframe straight masculinity and male homosocial relations,"[29] noting, "Homosexual relationships become an elucidating analogy or reference point that helps identify and, in many instances, validate the genuine affection and deep friendship that can exist between two (typically straight) men."[30] Bromance discourse extends beyond the series considered here and is also evident in a cycle of films, often in some way connected to Judd Apatow, that likewise openly explore the bounds of heterosexual expressions of male intimacy.[31] Despite Becker's preliminary work, "bromance" remains too nascent and characteristic of jargon to warrant using it here. This chapter examines how the varied depictions of dyadic male hetero intimacy challenge heteronormativity and the strategies by which they do so.

Hetero Intimacy in an Ironic Age

In an exploration of comedic male duos and the implications of their intimacy, Mark Simpson presents a brief history that juxtaposes the displays of affection between men that have been possible relative to societal acknowledgment and acceptance of gay identities.[32] Beginning with the bed shared by comedians Laurel and Hardy and traced haphazardly through that shared by the animated Ren and Stimpy, Simpson explores how such sleeping arrangements and the relationships of those occupying the beds have evolved from presumed homosocial "innocence" to "'knowing' displays" in which series acknowledge "'I know you know I know what this means'" so that "'irony' replaces 'innocence' and there is no longer any subtext."[33] It is such irony that Miller then identifies as a common comedic strategy in the mid-1990s and terms the "ironic dismissal": a "standard method for sitcom characters to maintain their heterosexuality when their masculinity or male friendships were questioned."[34]

In evaluating the ideological politics of ironic play with the potential homosexual dimensions of these dyadic hetero relationships, Simpson acknowledges a "strange contradiction": as contemporary attitudes toward queerness and gay identity have deemed these relationships more culturally acceptable, the gag of deriving humor from mistaken gay identity has become less humorous and required greater "*excess*" and campiness.[35] An ideological examination thus requires assessing how the "spectacle of two men behaving toward one another in the very way homophobia forbids" is presented in the text and determining whether gay love gets constructed, in Simpson's terms, as the "*wrong kind* of manly love" or is made an allowable part of hegemonic masculinities.[36]

The friendships depicted particularly in *Boston Legal*, *Scrubs*, and *Nip/Tuck* exemplify the changing trajectory of male-male relationships that Simpson, Becker, and Miller consider and illustrate different strategies in their presentation of intimacy among male friends that proffer varied challenges to heteronormative ideologies. All of the series present relationships of uncommon intimacy between two men, yet feature distinct strategies for dealing with their "knowing displays" of intimate heterosexuality. *Scrubs* uses joking that is buoyed by the tone of the series. *Nip/Tuck* presents characters confused by male intimacy: at one point Christian wonders whether he might be gay because he lacks a script for such hetero intimacy. This confusion is not played for laughs but is offered as a "working through" of how men might differently understand and perform their friendships in a post-closet era. *Psych* develops its intimacy even less, and the relative immaturity of its characters makes it seem as though they are simply not aware of or equipped to deal with intimacy with each other or anyone else. The series teases viewers with knowing glances that suggest intimacy, but features characters unable to express affection without immediately retreating to jokes and humor. *Psych*'s depiction of relational intimacy is most consistent with the cycle of bromance films that feature more superficial relationships, pose women as a threat to the male bond, and conclude in hetero coupling.

But *Boston Legal* presents a male friendship that suggests no fear of or concern about a possible homosexual basis for the relationship. The series emphatically asserts the relationship as extremely intimate, yet not at all sexual, and consequently does not consider that there might be "confusion" over the men's sexuality or the nature of the relationship. The relationship between Alan and Denny radically suggests that sex is not a prerequisite of the most intimate relationship two people might share, a profound challenge to the heteronormative organization of society that affords greatest privilege—socially and legally—to the coupling of a man and woman. Some gay activists and queer theorists have attempted to disrupt heteronormativity by trying to access that same privilege for same-sex couples who similarly have relationships defined by intimacy achieved through sex acts.[37] The disruption suggested by *Boston Legal* more markedly challenges heteronormative constructions, which, as Becker notes, "work to obscure the complexity of sexuality" by posing that the greatest relational intimacy can be achieved without sexual intimacy in a manner that might disarticulate the differentiation of gay and straight from sex acts.[38] In its contestation of heteronormativity, *Boston Legal* allows for a feminist reconstruction of patriarchal masculinity absent from any other series considered here.

Buddy Love? Friendly Fun and Farce

Psych is probably the most disputable inclusion in this chapter given that it features the most conventional portrayal of a male dyad and a depiction of hetero intimacy least disruptive of heteronormativity. Although a male friendship is certainly present, there is little that sets *Psych* apart from the male friendships depicted in *Suits* or *Common Law*—so much so that this is arguably part of the USA original series "formula" at this time.[39] The series is episodically structured around solving a case-of-the-week with minimal serial storyline plotting. Little changes in the relationships among the characters throughout the series, giving it a more traditional organization than many of the series considered throughout this book. Many of the series contemporary with *Psych*—especially on cable—make character and relationships more dynamic in order to provide a serial narrative dimension to the series. Shawn's romantic interest in officer Juliet O'Hara (Maggie Lawson) eventually performs this function most minimally, and their relationship does not begin until the midpoint of the fifth season. Further, the series willfully avoids even the most basic incorporation of relational melodrama. Gus and Shawn's relationship thus becomes the most central of the series, but it too fails to offer even incremental change. It remains the running gag of the series that Shawn is irresponsible and often leaves Gus culpable for his mistakes even though he has great fondness for him.

The series' reliance on the characters' back story as childhood friends helps *Psych* exceed the basic buddy relationship and achieve hints of intimacy that allow it relevance here. The series, especially in early seasons, frequently begins with a flashback to the late 1980s–early 1990s childhood of the friends, with young actors depicting the characters as boys. These episode epigraphs underscore the personality differences of the men—ten-year-old Gus already displays considerably more maturity than ten-year-old Shawn—and often identify a theme or character trait that comes to be relevant in the present-day part of the episode. Such scenes reinforce the duration of the relationship between the characters, but may do the most to illuminate Shawn's retarded maturation: the present-day character seems little different from, and perhaps even more immature than, his ten-year-old doppelganger.[40]

Given the lack of character and relationship development, Shawn and Gus exist in an odd stasis in which they are best friends, though it is somewhat unclear why Gus maintains the relationship. They have the same types of conflicts in most episodes, typically related to Gus feeling taken advantage of or frustrated with Shawn's lack of consideration. Their contrasting personalities—Gus is serious, careful, reliable—perhaps balance each other, pulling each back from his opposing extreme nature. But this too points to the fact that the focus of this series is episodic detective work, not sophisticated character growth.

Despite the series' relatively superficial relationship development, it is possible to read Shawn and Gus's friendship queerly, as have some fan fiction writers.[41] The characters in *Psych* do not have heart-to-heart conversations about the status of their friendship in the manner of those in *Scrubs* and *Boston Legal*, which makes it possible to read them as lovers instead of friends. Paradoxically, then, in under-exploring the hetero intimacy between the two men, *Psych* allows audiences to read gay coupling onto the relationship precisely because it does not enforce its status as friendship.

The greatest support for a queer reading develops through uncharacteristic tension between the friends that emerges as Shawn's relationship with Juliet advances. Shawn tries to tell Gus about his intention to propose before taking Juliet away for a spa weekend, but Shawn's plans are derailed when their room is burgled and they become involved in a murder investigation.[42] Gus finds the ring that Shawn intended to use to propose to Juliet and is overcome with an expression of hurt, disbelief, and anger (fig. 5.2). The episode ends without addressing his discovery, but the next one begins with the men back in the Psych office with Gus holding out the ring and asking, "You want to explain this?"[43] Shawn is clearly relieved to have the ring returned and uncomfortable regarding Gus's awareness of it. Gus's earlier expression of hurt and anger persists, and is reinforced by his tone as he asks Shawn, "You're actually ready to be married?" In a scene that uncharacteristically does not break dramatic tension with humor, Shawn mutters, "No, someday, maybe, not anytime soon." The scene ends with Shawn trying to repair the situation by saying, "Just know if I ever pop the question, I want you on one side, Jules on the other." Gus maintains his expression of hurt and anger and denies Shawn's offer of a fist bump (fig. 5.3). The scene is ambiguous regarding precisely what upsets Gus so significantly—is it hurt over a friend's lack of disclosure or a betrayal and sense of being replaced?—but the point is less to make an argument particularly for a queer reading than to acknowledge the series' openings, even if limited, relative to the strategies used in the other series to present hetero intimacy.

In a well-argued article exploring the racial politics of *Psych*, Davi Johnson Thornton argues that the series tonally encourages a "lighthearted, breezy attitude toward race and racism."[44] Thornton skillfully pulls apart the series' comedic strategies to argue the limits of the series' depiction of a biracial friendship in a manner more detailed than any comment on this component of the show I could include in the brief

Figure 5.2. Gus learns of Shawn's intention to propose to Juliet.

Figure 5.3. Gus remains wary of Shawn's proposal plan.

space available here. Many of the arguments Guerrero and Fuchs make regarding the depoliticized tendencies of the interracial buddy film hold here, although Thornton addresses this case as emblematic of a "post-race" context. In casting black lead actors, both *Psych* and *Scrubs* do contrast the otherwise monolithic whiteness of the series considered here, but arguably do so simply by casting black actors as characters rather than by constructing characters that meaningfully address the ways racial difference might be experienced by two male friends in early-twenty-first-century American culture. Both black characters are overwhelmingly excerpted from black culture and isolated within white worlds.

Irreconcilable Man Love

The six-season run of *Nip/Tuck* traces the melodramatic turmoil of the professional partnership and ostensible friendship of Sean McNamera and Christian Troy, whose lives are complicatedly intertwined both professionally and personally. Series creator and writer Ryan Murphy described "the core" of *Nip/Tuck* as "a love story between two hetero-sexual men," although those writing about the show have rarely empha-sized this central relationship, nor have interviewers pushed Murphy to speak in greater detail about his assumptions or intentions regarding their relationship.[45] Instead, most address the show's graphic and vio-lent depictions of plastic surgery and excessive attention to and depic-tion of sex acts. Although an uncommon depiction of dyadic hetero intimacy is central to the narrative, its atypicality gets lost in this pro-vocative series.

Nevertheless, the relationship between Christian and Sean is an important aspect of the show, and it is distinctive from the others explored here. *Nip/Tuck's* plastic surgery–related plotlines are often quite satirical and presented in a manner that critiques aspects of van-ity in culture, but its moments of comedy are quite dark and overall tone more melodramatic, so that it never playfully diffuses moments of intimacy between Christian and Sean in the manner used by *Psych* and *Scrubs*. As Murphy's description suggests, the series strongly insists upon the heterosexuality of Christian and Sean. It also discourages—though certainly does not disable—the type of queer reading feasible in *Psych*. *Nip/Tuck* features an intensely melodramatic tension between Sean and Christian that results from their shared love for Sean's wife, Julia, although it is sometimes unclear whether it is just Julia that Christian desires or the conventional familial experience that characterized Sean's life before the series begins. The conflict over Julia foregrounds their heterosexuality as does the thoughtful examination of homosexual desire the series poses in the fourth season. The series sincerely interrogates the nature of the men's relationship as it explores the cumulative narrative of Sean determining who he is as a man and detangling this identity from the personal and professional fusion with Christian in the years prior to the series start. Retrospectively, it is the story of how Sean comes to eventually leave the partnership, or rather, how Christian comes to finally let him go.

From the first scenes of the series, Sean is driven by midlife dissatisfaction, much of which results from his disdain for the superficiality and vanity that much of his work as a plastic surgeon is based upon. We learn in a final-season flashback to the men's first meeting in college that Christian pushed the specialization in plastic surgery, which he undoubtedly sold to Sean on the grounds of the meaningful work that can be done in this area.[46] Yet when the series begins, Sean has grown disinterested by the overwhelming amount of elective cosmetic procedures they perform. His quest for professional fulfillment—which leads him to pursue pro bono work, go to work for the federal witness protection program, and, in the final episode, leave the practice to pursue work with Doctors Without Borders—is frequently sidelined by familial crises. He and wife Julia separate and reconcile repeatedly, often reunited by an issue with their children, but ultimately split amicably in the fourth season. Although the series is unquestionably about both men, Sean is arguably the primary protagonist; he has more people in his life to introduce crises, and the series, perhaps unwittingly, traces his journey to professional fulfillment. Christian has occasional plotlines of his own, but unlike Sean is content with stasis and is not actively driven to pursue a life different from the one with which he begins the series. Christian is commonly a foil or impediment to Sean's journey and is regularly implicated in Sean's familial discord, most notably when Julia reveals that Christian fathered Matt.

Like Shawn and Gus of *Psych*, the two men are presented as near opposites. Sean is steady and predictable, tightly wound, and the master surgeon. He is a family man, having married a college sweetheart, and begins the series with a teenage son and a preteen daughter. In contrast, Christian is a playboy and focused primarily on satiating his appetite for sexual satisfaction and all manner of luxury goods. Christian's choices— both in whom he sleeps with and in managing practice finances—often contribute to the perpetual crisis of the practice's economic stability and are constructed as poor choices within the moral universe of the series. Christian struggles with intimacy and the series depicts him as made unhappy by his inability to develop close bonds with anyone other than Sean. The series depicts each man possessing a bit of envy toward the life of the other and insecurity about the manhood he embodies, but ultimately Sean's dutiful masculinity is presented as more heroic. Sean's journey is often difficult and he's depicted as making the wrong decisions at times, but the series presents his motives as noble. In contrast, Christian is the sad rake who lacks the reflexivity to interrogate his discontent and is thus destined to remain the same man in the final episode as he was at the beginning of the series—even unchanged from the college version of Christian seen in flashbacks.

In many ways, *Nip/Tuck* is the story of the ultimate undoing of Christian and Sean's relationship, with repeated moments of relationship maintenance over the course of the series being required to delay the split that occurs in the end.[47] The series begins with Sean trying to leave the practice due to his lack of fulfillment with the type of surgeries they must rely upon to maintain appearances and the standard of living they have come to enjoy. Sean threatens to leave the practice in the pilot, reiterates this intention throughout the series, and finally does so in the finale. His final departure is enabled by the fact that Christian, after Julia and others insist that staying will ultimately destroy Sean, forces him to go by dissolving the partnership and handing him one-way plane tickets to Romania.[48] Though it is clear from the beginning that Sean will never be happy in the partnership, his sense of duty to Christian, as well as happenstance and Christian's manipulations, lead him to subordinate his own knowledge of what he needs until Christian releases him.

Relative to the other series considered here, the central relationship in *Nip/Tuck* is better described as one of partners than one of friends. Certainly the partnership produces a friendship, but the intimacy the men share is more forced by the duties of their venture and the connections the partnership creates than by a mutually rewarding experience of friendship. Partnership and brotherhood—a description of the relationship Jennifer Stoy uses in a close analysis of Sean's character—are similar, yet both are different from friendship in the sense that friendship is more readily chosen.[49] The intimacy developed between Sean and Christian is ultimately far more a matter of duty than choice—at least on Sean's part—substantially differentiating it from the other series. Given this chapter's exploration of how television series depict men "being" friends, *Nip/Tuck* is important because the series' melodrama makes the intimacy explicit and intensely experienced in an uncommon manner. Though the partnership fails in the end, the narrative affirms the importance of the men in each other's lives in a way that presents the intimacy as acceptable and desirable.

Guy Love—Silly, but Sincere

Relative to the other series considered here, *Scrubs* plays at challenging heteronormativity. It doesn't go as far as *Boston Legal* to seriously pose dyadic male hetero intimacy as an alternative to heterosexual coupling, but it does acknowledge male friendship more explicitly and presents it as more significant to the characters than does *Psych*. The relationship between JD and Turk is unquestionably a central aspect of *Scrubs*—most so in the early seasons—with less attention devoted to it later in the eight-season run of the series, which spans the two men's transition from being roommates through Turk's marriage to the birth of his daughter. The series takes the men's friendship seriously; it isn't just an assumed feature of the series, but is negotiated in plotlines depicting meaningful efforts toward relationship maintenance. The narrative significance of the friendship thus surpasses that of most other series in that it is explicitly spoken of and the men sincerely express the importance of the intimacy—even referred to at times as love—they share with each other. Within its narratives, the series clearly supports the role JD and Turk play in each other's lives, but it also presents it as less important than their heterosexual partnerships and consistently undercuts moments of meaningful negotiation of the relationship and displays of intimacy with joking and pratfalls. The playful tone of the series and its undermining of moments of sincerity with tonal shifts clearly diminishes its slight efforts at challenging heteronormativity and makes the sincerity of the relationship difficult to sustain. Beyond the heteronormativity, both JD and Turk embody masculinities that defy most norms of patriarchal masculinities.

Understanding the tone of *Scrubs* is crucial to appreciating the possibilities and limitations of its challenge to heteronormative ideologies. The series bears considerable similarity to *M*A*S*H* in its exploration of the simultaneously silly and serious that can be found among those dealing with life-and-death scenarios. Unlike *M*A*S*H*, which adopted a realist film style, *Scrubs* makes use of a broad range of televisual and narrative devices, the most prominent of which are scenes that JD imagines that consistently present a farcical connection to the action at hand. The frequency of these scenes creates an inherent textual instability because the viewer is often uncertain whether the action on screen is "real" or part of JD's imagination. The series' tendency to abruptly shift tonal registers adds to the complexity of analyzing the series. *Scrubs* can be quite serious and frequently pulls twenty minutes of silliness into a thoughtful concluding point through JD's narration that knits together what might otherwise seem unrelated plot points.[50]

Scrubs presents an uncommon level of intimacy in Turk and JD's friendship and does become serious on matters such as work/life balance and the psychological toll of dealing with life and death for doctors, but undercuts the potential challenge of its displays of dyadic hetero intimacy by embedding these expressions in otherwise humorous moments or by minimizing the sincerity through tonal shifts. A good illustration of these tonal shifts can be found in episode 103, "My Best Friend's Mistake," in which JD feels as though he and Turk are growing apart because Turk's budding romantic interest in Carla and his new surgery friends seem to leave him no time for JD. Early in the episode JD is working through his interpersonal crisis while talking about it to a patient when the scene depicts Donald Faison, the actor who plays Turk, as the patient, who tells JD, "Look man, I'm surgery and you're medicine, this isn't college anymore, things have to change," and JD responding, "I know relationships have to change, I guess I thought yours and mine never would." The scene switches back to the original actor as the patient, flummoxing JD, who then turns to find Turk approaching the patient's bed asking, "What's going on with you, man?" JD continues to express his disappointment about the growing distance between them: "We always used to look out for each other, but I guess I don't feel like you've got my back anymore." We see Turk respond, nodding, and saying, "You really feel that way," then the reverse shot of JD saying, "Yeah, I really do," but when the scene cuts back to "Turk," it isn't Turk at all, and never was; it is a nurse, obviously confused by JD's expression. The surprise shots, where "Turk" is replaced by the patient and the nurse, include a nondiegetic sound cue that suggests the audience is to read this as humorous.

Near the conclusion of this episode, JD realizes that Turk caught an error JD made and begins to thank him when Turk—who, inexplicably aware of JD's earlier conversation with "him"—says, "Come on, man, you know I've always got your back." As he walks away, JD's voice-over encourages him to summon the courage to tell Turk how he feels, and he loudly announces, "I miss you so much it hurts sometimes," which he immediately registers as an overdisclosure of intimacy. Turk walks back to him and acknowledges, "OK, you've had a rough day, so I'm going to let that go for now. We're going to find time to hang man, it's just that we're both really swamped right now and I'm hanging out with Carla a lot, I know. But tell me, if there was someone you were into you wouldn't be doing the same thing." The episode then ties up other plotlines and concludes with JD and Turk back in their apartment. JD complains that Turk misplaced the bottle opener and Turk teases, "I miss it so much it hurts sometimes." Here the series polices a thin line between acceptable and unacceptable disclosures of masculine intimacy. Notably, JD isn't ridiculed so much for having these feelings, but because of his inability to properly manage their expression.

These two scenes illustrate the opportunities for sincere expression of intimacy that *Scrubs* allows, but also the way it contains them through tonal shifts or humor. In the first scene, JD expresses his hurt, but the gag of it being a false conversation positions the viewer to laugh at the discomfort he experiences after realizing the false disclosure. The final scene allows sincere expression and meaningful relationship negotiation between the men, but Turk then polices JD's bald utterance, using its sincerity to mock him. JD's utterance is not rendered entirely illegitimate by Turk's mocking; as the previous chapter argues, the bantering among male friends is a crucial part of homosocial maintenance. Yet it is important to acknowledge that the episode does come back to the utterance in this way for one last laugh.

In addition to its use of humor to undercut the sincerity of moments of serious relationship negotiation, the series regularly features joking disavowal that anticipates the need for "ironic dismissal" of JD and Turk's relationship as a homosexual coupling in a manner that further erodes its challenge to heteronormativity. For example, in the series' "Guy Love" musical number the men openly categorize their relationship as "guy love" and sing that "[w]e're closer than the average man and wife" and "I'll stick by you for the rest of my life" to make clear the significance of their relationship. The song continues, "It's like I married my best friend, but in a totally manly way." Though, when JD sings, "You're the only man who's ever been inside of me," Turk appears panicked and clarifies, "Whoa, whoa, I just took out his appendix,"[51] indicating how the series acknowledges the homosexual anxiety triggered by JD and Turk's intimacy and expressions of love.

The discussion of Turk being "in" JD recalls the language used in the episode in which Turk removes JD's appendix, which provided another of the series' more sincere moments of relationship negotiation.[52] JD, only able to see Turk as the joking friend he's had since college, hurts Turk's feelings by requesting another surgeon for his appendectomy. But when his appendix bursts, Turk is the on-call surgeon and performs the surgery, after which they discuss JD's need to distinguish the fun they have together away from the hospital from the seriousness with which Turk approaches his vocation. JD apologizes and tells Turk, "If I ever need surgery again, I want you to be the one inside of me," and Turk's response, "I'm gonna be the one inside you, man." Throughout this episode, humorous scenes cut to a gang of actors meant to be Fat Albert and the Cosby Kids as a comedic chorus, but at this moment the cut to the gang has them just looking baffled (fig. 5.4). This has the effect of making the queer subtext of Turk being "in" JD as a sex act more, though not quite, explicit in the text. Such a joke illustrates Simpson's argument of the "knowing display" signaling "I know you know I know

Figure 5.4. *Scrubs'* "Cosby Kids" chorus is befuddled by confessions of intimacy.

what this means."[53] In the original episode, the sincerity of the moment holds even though the men transition into more joking banter supporting the importance of their intimacy. Despite this, the series more often disavows the potential queerness of the relationship through humor in the manner of the "Guy Love" musical scene.[54]

Consequently, *Scrubs* may present dyadic hetero intimacy, but it does so in a way that diminishes gay intimacy and arguably forecloses the possibility of intimate friendships between gay and straight men by so consistently enforcing the opposition. In a quick reference to the "Guy Love" scene, Becker suggests that its use of irony enables viewers not to take the expression of intimacy too seriously, but also acknowledges that "moments of homosociality aren't established in any simple homophobic opposition to homosexuality. . . . [G]ay love helps give meaning to this guy love by being amiably acknowledged even as it is being disavowed."[55] Becker's reading appropriately acknowledges the ideological nuance of *Scrubs'* play, but is focused on a broader look at the emergence of what he terms "queer straight masculinity" on US television, which *Scrubs* clearly illustrates. The sustained focus of this chapter on dyadic male hetero intimacy needs to assess the implications of this strategy of acknowledging homosociality while disavowing homosexuality relative to the other depictions of male intimacy considered.

The series' recurrent attention to the panic JD and Turk articulate about their intimacy being construed as gay love constructs it as, in Simpson's terms, the "wrong kind" of male intimacy, and the consistent positioning of their friendship as something to laugh at severely undermines the challenge the series might present to heteronormativity. *Scrubs* does offer a male friendship of uncommon intimacy, but clearly supports hetero coupling as of greater importance than their friendship. When friendship impedes on hetero coupling, the "good" friend defers to coupling. Becker is correct to describe *Scrubs* as not homophobic; however, the degree to which the series falls short of contesting heteronormativity becomes clear in comparing it with *Boston Legal*'s presentation of a male friendship, which seems to have no need to repeatedly define that relationship as "not gay." On its own, JD and Turk's relationship does contrast the type of underlying anxiety about mistaken gay identity through the ironic dismissal that Miller notes as common previously, but its inching toward a presentation of nonanxious male intimacy is made minuscule by the comparative leap of *Boston Legal*.[56] Yet other aspects of Turk and JD's masculinities are far more feminist than that of Alan and especially the patriarchal, if somewhat parodically so, Denny.

Man Love: Challenging Heteronormativity through Earnest Intimacy

HBO's gal pal stories of *Sex and the City* (1998–2004) offered an initial template of how hetero friendships might challenge heteronormativity. By the end of this series, which unquestionably emphasized women's quest to find a heterosexual life partner, the series' greatest adherent to ideologies of romantic heteronormativity, Charlotte, proposes that the answer to the dissatisfaction the women find in their romantic relationships should be that they "be each other's soul mates," while relegating their husbands and boyfriends to the status of "great, nice, guys to have fun with."[57] Although this and related dialogue open up readings of *Sex and the City* that contradict its otherwise determinedly hetero-normative emphases (which are enforced even more in its subsequent films), it meaningfully suggests the possibility of consequential, non-sexual intimacy. *Boston Legal* expands upon such fleeting suggestions and develops what begins as a casual coda in which Alan and Denny share a drink and ponder the events of the episode to the point that their friendship becomes a key narrative component of the show.

Boston Legal was not apparently meant to be even tangentially the story of a friendship between two men. The series was created as a spin-off of the legal drama *The Practice* (1997–2004) to feature the exploits of Alan Shore after his firing from a brief, disruptive tenure at *The Practice*'s Young, Frutt, and Berlutti.[58] *Boston Legal* is based in the law firm of Crane, Poole, and Schmidt, and begins after Alan has joined the firm. He and Denny initially appear as colleagues, but they build a perceptible bond and their relationship becomes a substantial com-ponent of the series. The men's balcony discussions expand in length and significance and their relationship comes to be featured in plot-lines throughout entire episodes, including episodes in which they go fishing and to a dude ranch as well as to try a case before the Supreme Court—all of which provide greater narrative time for the fostering of the relationship.

Relative to the way the other series frequently deflect the hetero-normative challenge of male intimacy though humor, it is necessary to begin by addressing *Boston Legal*'s tone. The series and the depiction of Denny and Alan's relationship are often silly and absurd. Unlike the dour seriousness of *The Practice*, *Boston Legal*'s tone from the outset was flighty and preposterous: it opened its pilot with a senior partner attending a meeting pantless—indicating that he was experiencing a psychotic break that required hospitalization, though the scenario was played for humor. The series, more consistent with Kelley's fanciful *Ally McBeal* than with *The Practice*, commonly toyed with the absurdity of the potential extremes of law in a manner that introduced considerable levity.

Given the series' frequent lack of seriousness, some might wrongly presume that Denny and Alan's uncommonly explicit friendship is similarly offered up jokingly. Indeed, the series featured a running gag of office costume parties that created an opportunity for Denny and

Alan to dress as matching flamingos, to cross-dress as the Lennon sisters, or for Alan to costume himself as Denny's unrequited love: firm partner Shirley Schmidt (Candace Bergen). Such visual gags were playful, though largely separate from the moments of sincerity in which the series established and negotiated the intimacy of Alan and Denny's relationship. The series' tone unquestionably fluctuated: many of the nonlegal situations that drew Denny and Alan together were used for humor, such as Denny's erratic behavior and his explanation of it as a result of "mad cow" (though really the initial onset of Alzheimer's disease); Alan's bouts with "word salad" in which he speaks gibberish; or Alan's experience of night terrors that begin Denny and Alan's "sleepovers." But despite the levity of these moments, the series consistently treated the men's relationship maintenance with sincerity.

I acknowledge these components of comedy and silliness to make clear that the subsequent analysis that focuses on the men's relationship is indeed aware of their existence. It is my argument, nonetheless, that the series quite carefully moderated its tone and did not fall back on absurd humor in a manner that could undercut the sincerity of truly intimate moments between Denny and Alan. With the exception of an incident in which Denny encourages Alan to drink from the Stanley Cup and then inadvertently drops it over the ledge of the balcony, the silliness just recounted does not extend onto Denny's balcony. Even in scenes in which they are dressed as the Lennon sisters, the tone is earnest and the conversation sincere. As Becker recounts in relation to one of the most intense moments in Alan and Denny's relationship, in which Denny is hurt by Alan's growing affection for another male lawyer, Jerry Espenson, whom Denny finds on the balcony with Alan, seemingly sharing the intimacy of their relationship, the men work through Denny's feelings of jealously in a scene encompassing dialogue such as "I love you, Denny. *You* are my best friend," which, Becker notes, "is done 'straight' . . . without the playful tone or ironic winking."[59] *Boston Legal*'s presentation of Denny and Alan's relationship may at times depict two friends having fun together in a ridiculous manner, but it never suggests that the intimacy they share or their importance to each other is in any way frivolous or less than centrally significant to each man. That said, as characters, they do inhabit more patriarchal masculinities than many of the other characters considered in the book. Denny clearly was not acculturated with the post-second-wave norms characteristic of other protagonists, and even Alan displays boorish attitudes toward women uncommon in the male-centered serials.

Although it has been recounted in other writing about the series, it is nonetheless necessary to illustrate the intimacy of the speech shared by the men.[60] As the previous dialogue suggests, they do speak openly about loving each other, and the moments of levity are contrasted with serious interpersonal negotiation related to matters of differing politics, jealousy, and concerns about Denny's mental abilities. Alan accompanies Denny as he undergoes MRI scans measuring the progression of his Alzheimer's disease and is the confidant Denny speaks with regarding his fears. Late in the series, Alan discloses his first sexual experience to Denny—an encounter with a much older neighbor woman that would be regarded by most as scandalous—acknowledging that he had never told anyone else about it, and this is typical of their conversation and sharing. Moments of sentimentality or vulnerable honesty are not undermined by quick jokes, but offered with bald intimacy.

Various love interests enter and exit the lives of Denny and Alan throughout the series, but their relationship remains unthreatened or unencumbered by such developments, which supports the series' suggestion that sexual intimacy may not be the paramount connection between two people. Notably, neither man ever endeavors upon a long-term relationship. Alan holds an imagined love in such regard that no real woman ever achieves his expectations. Denny loves women as a glutton does food, fully and obsessively, but tires quickly, moving on to the next; a running joke in the series is Alan's inability to remember whether Denny has had five or six divorces. While other series present the de rigueur plotline in which one friend feels slighted by the other when "replaced" by a heterosexual interest, *Boston Legal* never suggests that the men consider women as suitable replacements. When Alan expresses concern over Denny's brief courtship and sudden engagement, it is because the marriage would require Denny to move to Montana, and shortly after realizing the marriage would mean moving away from Alan, Denny ends the engagement. *Boston Legal* instead explores jealousy in the context of Alan's budding friendship with Jerry. In the previously mentioned scene in which the men negotiate Denny's

jealousy, the episode initially constructs it as comical, given its unex-
pectedness, and as knowingly played through the conventions of heterosexual jealousy. The episode then turns quite sincere with no suggestion of humor.

The series takes its heteronormative challenge farther yet in its final
two episodes, proposing and then depicting the legal marriage of Denny
and Alan. After experiences that suggest the advance of his Alzheimer's,
Denny proposes marriage to Alan in order to secure the right of medical decision making, spousal privilege, and property transfer. Alan initially takes this as joking, but Denny continues to push it in all seriousness. Denny entreats Alan by noting, "Cleanest, simplest, most efficient
transfer of property is marriage. . . . I've always wanted to remarry before
I die . . . , and like it or not, you are the man I love. . . . Take my hand,
Alan, take my money." Alan responds by noting, "I always thought if I
were to get married again it would be for love and romance," to which
Denny pleads, "You love me, romance never lasts, money can." Recognizing Denny's slipping cognitive state, Alan assents.

Through this marriage, which occurs in the series' penultimate
scene, the series challenges the proposition that sexual intimacy should
provide the basis for the institution of marriage. It does this explicitly
through a court scene necessitated when a gay rights group attempts an
injunction against the marriage because the men are not sexual partners. The group argues that allowing such a union uses gay marriage to
"make a mockery" of marriage, just as the religious right had contended
would be the outcome of extending the privilege of marriage to gay
couples. The series is somewhat ambiguous about why it is necessary
for the men to marry, as the true advantage is primarily the avoidance
of estate tax. Alan's central defense when pushed on why they should be
wed is that Denny has the right to privacy for his reasons. In his impas-
sioned court speech, Alan argues,

> Before I see Mr. Crane's money go to fund immoral wars or less moral
> government bailouts I'd rather see it go to me. The plans I have for it are
> far more philanthropic and, by the way, I love him, okay. I love the man;
> he loves me; we're partners. To say that we cannot get married because
> we don't have sex is just as preposterous and bigoted as banning mar-
> riage based on who a person chooses to have sex with.[61]

The controversy highlights how gay marriage laws provide a limited challenge to heteronormative privilege and the absurdity that sexual intimacy should be so relevant to the institution of marriage—whether the sex is between gay or straight people. Denny and Alan's marriage is presented as logistically advantageous in terms of the end-of-life dilemmas Denny faces and the tax advantages it affords to Alan's desire to open a legal aid firm in the wake of Crane, Schmidt, and Poole being taken over by new management. But it is equally predicated on the men's clear affection for each other. Their marriage—and the injunction hearing explicitly—challenges the primacy of sexual intimacy in a meaningful way that only seems absurd to the degree that this priority has remained so unconsidered throughout the last decade of contentious cultural negotiation of the politics of marriage.

Conclusion

It may be the case that only *Boston Legal* provides substantive challenge to heteronormativity revolutionary for television in its depiction of serious, loving intimacy among male friends. The extent it achieves is most uncommon, and all these series succeed in subverting prevalent depictions of men's friendships rooted in patriarchal masculinities. The writing of this conclusion finds me holed up in my office the day after President Obama went on record in support of gay marriage and less than a week after Vice President Joe Biden publicly reaffirmed his support for gay marriage while explaining, "I think *Will & Grace* probably did more to educate the American public than almost anything anybody's ever done so far."[62] Such moments speak to the curious and uncertain ways media texts may be involved in public opinion. Notably, the majority of academic analysis of *Will & Grace* is more critical than supportive. Similar to my own treatment of *Scrubs* here, much of it argues something like this: "Yes, it is good to depict gay characters, but look at how it undercuts. . . . "[63] And while Biden's assertion of *Will & Grace*'s role in the cultural reassessment of gay marriage is unproven, it certainly resonates and poses a plausible hypothesis for what public opinion pollsters have recounted as a change in public opinion data profound in terms of both the reversal of opinion and the pace at which it has occurred.

Fragmentation of the television audience was significant by the early 2000s, even more so than for *Will & Grace*, which in its prime reached over eleven million households. *Boston Legal* came close to this figure and *Scrubs* even surpassed it in its early seasons, while *Nip/Tuck* and *Psych* at best reached half that many viewers. I note this for context, but my point is that few among the varied audiences of any of these shows may have thought extensively about the depictions of male friendship they observed. Nevertheless, they may have filed away these interactions as illustrations of how male friends behave toward one another, allowing them to become part of normalized scripts of male friendship. As Kimmel notes, "images of gender in the media become texts on normative behavior, one of many cultural shards we use to construct notions of masculinity."[64]

Unquestionably, one of the most fascinating aspects of this chapter is the conundrum posed by channel of origin. It is utterly counterintuitive that the depictions of the most intimate friendships originated from broadcast networks that have been excluded from analysis up to this point for lacking the novel masculinities examined here. Any effort I make to explain this quickly becomes convoluted: *Boston Legal* could do this because of Kelley's status and the show was ostensibly about other things; *Scrubs* flew under the radar in an era of increasing programming abundance; shows about friendship are generally uncommon so this wasn't perceived as controversial; *Will & Grace*, with its friendship between two gay men, was already on the air—but the bottom line is that I don't think a fully defensible explanation can be derived.

I remain on the watch for other examples of dyadic hetero intimacy. The short-lived HBO series *Luck* offered a preliminary glimpse of a long-term relationship of great intimacy between Dustin Hoffman's Chester Bernstein and Dennis Farina's Gus Demitriou, particularly for men of their generation, but production problems led to an early end for the show. In its final episodes, the broadly popular *House, MD* made central the friendship between House and Wilson that had been implicit for many preceding seasons. Though in some ways depicting a homosocial enclave, *Sons of Anarchy* also created several opportunities for intimate dyadic relationships, perhaps most particularly between Jax and Opie, who grew up together as sons of club members. Even these relationships that are a small part of a series are important in posing different models of male friendship that might contribute to normalizing greater intimacy as an "acceptable" part of male friendship.

The depiction of heterosexual intimacy between men in these series and others counters a long history of representations of men as partners in jobs who abided by patriarchal norms of separating the personal from the professional. At the same time, the expanding oeuvre of "brocedurals" reaffirms the more common flippant relations between men in buddy films. Given their relative newness, it remains to be seen whether greater intimacy develops among men in series such as *White Collar* and *Franklin and Bash* since television's ongoing narratives can allow for character and relationship change. The series discussed here raise new possibilities for imagining the intimate bonds among men, and notably depict men across the spectrum of generations doing so.

Conclusion

Is It the End of Men as We Know Them?

I experienced a series of panic attacks as the fall 2011 television season debuted. I was embedded somewhat in the middle of the book-writing process—too far along to go back, but still a good distance to go—and suddenly it seemed the rest of the free world had figured out that something interesting was happening with men on television. Most of the hullabaloo centered on the fact that one of the most apparent "trends" in new television shows for that fall was that stories about men and issues related to their being men seemed central. No less than the *Atlantic*'s Hanna Rosin, whose analysis of changing graduation, employment, and earning data had announced "The End of Men" in July 2010, now declared "Primetime's Looming Male Identity Crisis."[1] A few weeks earlier, the *Wall Street Journal* gave Amy Chozick an astounding seventeen hundred words with which to detail "A New Generation of TV Wimps";[2] and these authors were not alone in noting some curious trends in the depiction of masculinity on television.[3]

The articles previewed new broadcast comedies set to debut that fall, such as CBS's *How to Be a Gentleman*, ABC's *Man Up!*, *Work It*, and *Last Man Standing*, and NBC's *Up All Night*. Chozick reported that network executives recounted hearing pitches referencing Rosin's "End of Men" article at least twenty times, and thus it seemed some sort of apocalypse of male crisis was now upon the country. In case you missed them, *How to Be a Gentlemen* briefly explored the hilarity that might be found if a *GQ* columnist found himself instead writing for *Maxim* and had to learn about his audience from an old high school classmate who now owns a gym; *Work It* depicted two laid-off car salesmen who cross-dress as women to secure employment in pharmaceutical sales; and *Man Up!* explored three men in their thirties acting more like teenagers.

Though the media attention to the new shows initially incited panic that a project-disrupting cultural phenomenon might occur, a few weeks into the fall season revealed that television comedies based on a high-concept version of a hyperbolically titled *Atlantic* article do not make for good television. Mercifully, *Work It* lasted only two episodes, while *How to Be a Gentleman* survived for three, and *Man Up!*, inexplicably, for eight. I won't offer detailed analysis here as these shows have already received far more attention than they were due; I hope it will suffice to say that their swift failures can be explained as a result of being poorly conceived and executed more than as a matter of their topics.

The other two shows turned out to be interesting in other ways. *Up All Night* shouldn't have been included in the trend pieces. Its lead male character—like those of *Man Up!*—played a video game in an early episode, and apparently that was adequate to justify the assumption that the characterizations were similar. But in fact, *Up All Night* offered the story of the tribulations a couple faces with a newborn, a story made less typical in this case because dad Chris (Will Arnett) chooses to give up his job as a lawyer to care for the baby while his wife, Regan (Christina Applegate), continues her job as a television talk show producer.[4]

Unlike the routine "Mr. Mom" trope that shows men struggling to figure out how to use a vacuum or the hilarity that ensues when they handle situations commonly the purview of women, *Up All Night* rarely drew attention to the fact that it was exceptional for a man to choose to stay home with an infant, and instead mined the challenges of a couple experiencing new parenthood for its laughs. Of course Regan and Chris experienced these crises in gendered ways, but the humor wasn't based on the incongruity of their disruption of gender norms. The series offered a considerably different model of paternity than common on television, with Chris completely invested and satisfied with his role as stay-at-home dad, while also voicing the challenges likely to be experienced by parents of either gender who step off the career track and feel the world has gone on without them, who struggle to explain their choice to friends and coworkers, or who feel their spouse has no understanding of the stresses they face.

In its first season, *Up All Night* provided a glimpse of Generation X marriage and parenting that was a remarkable blueprint of gender scripts enabled by second-wave feminism and thirty years of its gradual incorporation, though a model that remained rarely represented in fictional media. *Up All Night* somehow seemed unburdened from the history of the domestic comedy and offered a fresh look at a perennial situation. Unlike its failed competition, the series said quite a lot about the challenges of balancing work, parenthood, and marriage without making this its central premise. Unfortunately, the show never quite found the sizable audience required by broadcast sitcoms and was canceled eleven episodes into the second season after considerable creative turmoil and various efforts to broaden its appeal.

In terms of prestige, though, the most potential of the new crop of shows attending to men was riding on the return of comedian Tim Allen to prime-time television in *Last Man Standing*. Allen's Tim "the Toolman" Taylor had provided a significant embodiment of early post-second-wave masculinity in the family comedy *Home Improvement* (ABC, 1991–1999). As father to three sons and host of the *Tool Time* home improvement show, Allen's character embodied what Robert Hanke describes as a "mock macho" masculinity through which signs of masculinity "are expressed and played off one another within the parodic mode of US television situation comedy."[5] Hanke carefully dissects how Allen's humor—rooted in his stand-up career before the series—makes light of masculine stereotypes and engages in self-disparagement in a way that draws attention to the construction of masculinity. The mock macho humor provides a light critique of patriarchy, though it is difficult to unpack the series' use of parody without audience research. Hanke's skilled textual analysis illustrates how the series mocks "soft males" —like Tim's assistant, Al—who embody a version of the 1980s sensitive new man, though also frequently shows the fallibility of Tim's efforts to solve domestic problems or properly use tools.

The evolution of Allen's character, who is now called Mike Baxter, in the twenty years between the 1991 premiere of *Home Improvement* and that of 2011's *Last Man Standing* indicates some of the differences between the early and late post-second-wave contexts. *Last Man Standing* does not simply return to Tim Taylor two decades later. The series opens with Baxter downscaling his career as a marketer for "Outdoor Man" sporting good outfitters as his wife's career as a college professor grows more demanding. He is needed to help look after their three mostly grown daughters, one of whom is a single mom raising her own son in her parents' home.[6] The series is split between Mike's time in the Outdoor Man store and offices, where he negotiates his outlook on masculinity with those of his boss and longtime friend Ed Alzate (Hector Elizando), who has a failed marriage and distant relationship with his adult daughter, and Kyle (Christoph Sanders), a young new employee. Ed generally embodies a more patriarchal masculinity than Mike's, while Kyle, a somewhat hapless stock boy, dates Mike's oldest daughter throughout the first season and seems to have lacked a male role model. The result of Mike's middle ground on this continuum is to critique the masculinities of both the patriarchal Boomer, Ed, and the flighty Millennial, Kyle.[7]

At home, the Baxter's relationship appears more evenly balanced than was the case on *Home Improvement*, as both husband and wife negotiate work and home situations rather than foregrounding battle-of-the-sexes/"men-are-from-Mars"–type conflicts. Tim Taylor's guttural, simian grunting is gone, though the promotional web videos Mike makes for Outdoor Man provide a venue for ranting about the failures of modern masculinity and society. Like the objects of Tim Taylor's derision, Baxter takes aim at the loss of traditional masculine spirit and endeavors evident in such things as prioritizing "stress reduction" instead of engaging the stress of white water rafting; overreliance on modern gadgetry; fantasy football; baby proofing; miniature dog breeding; and the parenting culture of extreme self-esteem building. Baxter's masculinity has been reconstructed enough to share authority in the home and to seek for and believe in his daughter's achievements, yet he openly longs for an era in which survival skills and physical ability were more valued. Baxter's diatribes about modern men not knowing how to change a tire critique contemporary masculinity without being nostalgic for a more entrenched patriarchy; indeed, he makes sure that all of his daughters know how to change tires as well.

Baxter's characterization reveals the advantage of an analytic tool that allows for placing a character on a continuum between patriarchal and feminist masculinities. His characterization reveals the possibly problematic conflation of all things "traditional" with patriarchal ideology and the ways class status and gender scripts intersect. Baxter admonishes Kyle for lacking knowledge about how engines work or how to hunt—activities and knowledge that, like the prefeminist association of canning and other domestic arts with women, aren't inherently patriarchal but are identified with patriarchy or more "patriarchal times" because they were characteristic of gender embodiments when patriarchal outlooks were less contested. Mike values aspects of more traditional masculinities without being nostalgic for the patriarchal ideologies also commonly associated with such masculinities.

Both *Up All Night* and *Last Man Standing* returned in the fall of 2012 for a second season, and both also underwent significant revisions in an effort to improve their ratings—though they remained the same at their core. *Last Man Standing* became more overtly political and constructed Mike more in the model of Archie Bunker; the series' fall premiere featured an explicit discussion of Mike's support for Mitt Romney, while his oldest daughter adamantly supported Obama and both lobbied for the vote of middle daughter Mandy. These comedies exploring contemporary masculinity were joined in 2012 with the dad-centered comedies *Guys with Kids* on NBC and *See Dad Run* on Nick at Nite. Though the new shows debuted without the fanfare of the previous year, both feature fathers in primary caretaker roles: *Guys with Kids* followed three friends living in the same apartment building while *See Dad Run* depicts Scott Baio (once the teen actor who was *Charles in Charge*) as a former sitcom actor who becomes the primary caretaker so his soap opera actress wife can return to work. While *Guys with Kids* diligently avoided clichéd "Mr. Mom" humor, instead basing its comedy on the peculiarities of the characters and the inevitably absurd situations parents of young children experience, *See Dad Run* is built on the premise that being a dad isn't as easy as playing one on TV, and thus trafficked heavily in banal gendered parenting jokes. Though the audience for *See Dad Run* was far smaller than that for *Guys with Kids*, the latter wasn't able to attract the broadcast-size audience needed for NBC and was canceled after a single season.

The imagined masculinity crisis in fall 2011 and the noteworthy characters launched nevertheless create an opportunity to address some of the comedic portrayals of men that remain difficult to organize—as illustrated by the contradictory offerings of Barney Stinson, Charlie Harper, and Sheldon Cooper that open the book. The breadth of contemporary television comedy—in sheer quantity as well as the diversity of comedic sensibilities now addressed—allows for a vast range of masculinities and requires careful parsing of the complicated uses of parody, satire, and sincere representation.

In several cases, the return of actors, like Allen, to television in the 2010s after notable roles in the 1980s and 1990s underscores the transitions in masculinity evident in the texts considered throughout the book. Hanke's analysis of the mock macho masculinity pairs *Home Improvement* with *Coach* (ABC, 1989–1997), which starred Craig T. Nelson, who is now the patriarch—in every sense of the term—of the Braverman family in NBC's *Parenthood* (2010–). Though the ensemble structure of *Parenthood* distinguishes it from the male-centered serials, the series' depiction of brothers Adam (Peter Krause) and Crosby (Dax Shepard) struggling with contemporary masculinity and familial expectations is very much related. Generation X Adam, Crosby, and brother-in-law Joel (Sam Jaeger) are all quite different from each other as men, yet uniformly contrast starkly with father Zeek's patriarchal masculinity. Zeek is perpetually befuddled by the actions of his sons—whether it be Adam's involvement in caring for his autistic son or Crosby's willingness to defer to his son's mother. In a telling scene, Zeek tries to offer advice to Crosby about needing to take control of a parenting situation and asks, "Who wears the pants in the family?" Crosby, every bit as perplexed by Zeek's reality as Zeek is by Crosby's, stammers, "What year do you think this is, the 1950s? There's no one wearing the pants or not wearing the pants. You know, it's a partnership."[8] Zeek responds to this exchange by noting, "God, that sounds dreadful." Though at times he risks being utterly unsympathetic as a unidimensional patriarchal type, the constant presence of multiple generations of men in this series allows it to explore these generational tensions—particularly through the relationships of Adam and Crosby with their father and those they seek with their sons. *Parenthood*'s family ensemble enables deeper probing of father/son relations than many of the male-centered serials that feature similar relationships, but do not regularly include the patriarch.

In contrast to seeing Allen and Nelson playing similar characters in different contexts, actor Corbin Bernsen's transition from legal playboy Arnie Becker in *L.A. Law* (1986–1994) to retired detective Henry Spencer, father of Shawn, in *Psych*, illustrates a notable evolution of a past character and the world surrounding him. As Becker, Bernsen was a smooth divorce lawyer who embodied a prefeminist masculinity and could be expected to bed a succession of beautiful women. As Henry Spencer, Bernsen is no longer the ladies' man, but is long divorced—by a character played by no less than 1980s icon Cybill Shepherd—enjoys things like fishing and grilling, and is generally bewildered by his son.[9] A much briefer span marks the departure of Kiefer Sutherland as the iconic Jack Bauer of *24* (2001–2010) and his return in 2012–2013 as Martin Bohm in *Touch*, in which he plays the single father to a boy so profoundly emotionally challenged that he does not speak, yet has savant-like mathematical and perceptual capabilities. As Bohm, Sutherland displays a masculinity stunningly different from Bauer's; he is a man overwhelmed by his circumstances and struggling with the most mundane aspects of life. After his wife's death in the World Trade Center on 9/11, he quits his job as a journalist to care for the boy and is working as a baggage handler in the series' pilot. As in the male-centered drama, we see a father who prioritizes familial care over all else.

Obviously, actors often play many roles in their lifetimes, but the connection among similar roles inhabited decades apart, such as Allen's in *Home Improvement* and *Last Man Standing* and Nelson's in *Coach* and *Parenthood*, and the disjuncture between such roles, as in the cases of Bernsen and Sutherland, illuminate changing televisual and cultural norms. In the 1980s, there weren't television roles like those seen in the last few years. By this strategy, the next installment of this analysis will have to catch up with Peter Krause and Charlie Hunnam in a decade or so. Krause established himself as the Generation X every man as Nate Fisher, the son who reluctantly returns to the family mortuary after his father's death in *Six Feet Under*, a character who could have believably become Adam Braverman by 2010. Hunnam, who followed his breakout role as fifteen-year-old gay teen Nathan Maloney in the British *Queer as Folk* by playing motorcycle club outlaw Jax Teller, suggests the range of masculinities available to those in this generation. It is difficult to imagine who these characters might be in their fifties and sixties, what kind of family relationships they will share, and what points will prove contentious between the masculinities they come to inhabit and those of their progeny.

* * *

In the decade or so considered here, it was largely the case that a key element in the formula for critically acclaimed television was, as Amanda Marcotte describes it, "a powerful man grappling with the limits of traditional masculinity."[10] Citing *The Sopranos, Mad Men, The Wire, Breaking Bad, Friday Night Lights, True Blood, The Walking Dead,* and *Justified,* she argues, "If you want to make a critically acclaimed drama, you need to build up a patriarch, preferably in a highly masculine environment, and then start to peel away his certainty about the way the world works and what it means to be a man in this world." Brian McGreevy similarly noted that a recent "competition" to determine the greatest television show of the last twenty-five years produced four finalists—*The Sopranos, Breaking Bad, Mad Men,* and *The Wire*—and that all feature "a protagonist who is an aggressive, morally ambivalent male navigating a complex power hierarchy," and, of course, that all four originated from basic or premium cable.[11]

Rather than search too extensively for the answer to why these series about morally ambivalent characters appear at this time, this book has endeavored to more systematically think through what these series and characters have contributed to cultural negotiations among patriarchal and feminist masculinities. As chapter 3 illustrates, it is an easy assertion to note thematic preponderance, as Marcotte and McGreevy do, but identifying why these men find themselves in the predicaments that they do requires closer examination. As noted from the outset of the book, the characters and stories examined in these series do not present role models for emulation, but something more like a range of cautionary tales, each posing the conundrum of finding the balance among aspects of patriarchal and feminist masculinities.

This book can only really tell us anything about television characterizations, but the analysis here offers a foundation from which research on men might build. Sociological surveys such as the research of the Work and Families Institute and interviews of men, such as those collected in Donald Unger's recent book, *Men Can: The Changing Image and Reality of Fatherhood in America,* query men's satisfactions and dissatisfactions and provide data with which to think through the connections between these protagonists and their real-world counterparts.[12] Though the textual evidence from this project suggests that balancing a sense of duty of family provision with marriages reflecting equitable gender relations is particularly challenging for male characters, other stressors, less easily narrativized or depicted in television storytelling, may be more central in the lives of men.

Knitting the varied series and situations considered in this book together are the questions of what is the status of patriarchal masculinities, what aspects persist most strongly, and what aspects have been dismantled. In answering these questions, I continue to find the absences even more profound than those aspects present. The lack of contention between men and women and consistent avoidance of placing blame on the women in the male protagonists' lives or on changing structures of gender that have empowered women substantially distinguishes these men and the masculinities supported in their series from the preliminarily reconstructed masculinities of the new men. The sociocultural context of the 1980s that created a hyperconsciousness that imprinted "women's lib" through signifiers such as women wearing power suits and shoulder pads—even when it was unspoken—has now dissipated. Revisiting the pilot of *thirtysomething* twenty years after either one of them had last viewed it, in commentary accompanying the DVD release, creators Marshall Herskovitz and Edward Zwick reflected on how the issue of women working became a lightning rod for the series that was polarizing because it appeared in the context of US culture having just come through the "radical" feminist movement.[13]

Thirtysomething garnered particular attention for its negotiation of post-second-wave gender scripts for women, but also proposed that feminism would have as significant an effect on men—an effect more conjecture than reality in the 1980s. In their DVD commentary, Herskovitz and Zwick also discuss the departure Michael Steadman presented as a lead male character and recalled the difficulty actor Ken Olin initially experienced performing as a "leading man" in moments of intimate conversation in which the character acknowledged uncertainty and openly complained about aspects of his life, work, and marriage—all atypical of television's previous leading men. In their monograph on the series, Albert Auster and Leonard Quart describe *thirtysomething* as presenting a "massive shift" in "men's relationship to domestic life and fatherhood" in which "all that men could be assured of in this freer, less prescriptive environment was that they would have to live with the constant juggling of guilt and good intentions," a reality borne out in several series considered here.[14]

The protagonists of the male-centered serials are likewise products of their era and indicate a significant departure from the new men *thirtysomething* came to epitomize. Creators of the shows examined in this book, such as Vince Gilligan, Kurt Sutter, and David E. Kelley, did not face the challenge of crafting gender relations under the specter of a defining cultural event that would so inevitably imprint unavoidable meaning on the dilemmas of their characters in the manner of the second-wave feminist movement. Certainly, the 9/11 attacks had the potential to impose additional meaning—anticipated and deliberate in the case of *Rescue Me*'s Tommy Gavin, and more coincidental in the case of a character such as Jack Bauer—but the struggles with masculinity experienced by the protagonists are not related to changes in society initiated by the 9/11 attacks. Indeed, it is the lack of a catalyzing event that makes the concurrent emergence of the characters of the male-centered serial so unexpected and all the more remarkable.

Aspects of patriarchal masculinities have not been eradicated from the men considered here, but some aspects have been made uninhabitable. If I were to try to condense and generalize the themes and characterizations of the series examined in *Cable Guys*, the series reveal the following about the masculinity of "good men":

- Men should be involved and interested in the lives of their children. Long gone are men who hide behind newspapers at the breakfast table before slipping out to work and returning after their children have gone to bed.
- To paraphrase Crosby Braverman: there are no pants. Good marriages are collaborations in which men negotiate family decisions with their wives. Sometimes narratives show couples following paths preferred by female characters, while at other times couples follow the path preferred by male characters. Both can and do make choices that don't turn out well. Couples who weather those challenges cooperatively stay intact, while male characters who endeavor to fix things on their own often lose their families. Male characters trying to invoke patriarchal authority inspire laughter rather than reverence. Decisions made without consulting wives consistently prove flawed.
- Some men still cannot control their sexual desires and cheat on their wives, though this is now presented as a character weakness. This choice

has consequences and reduces others' esteem of the character. The "good man" can control his sexual desires, and disrespecting his wife diminishes the regard others hold of him.[15]

- Though it is often depicted as foolhardy, many male characters still feel considerable duty to "provide" for their family.
- Absent, however, are feelings of guilt. Reviewing 1980s films about men's relationships, Neil Rattigan and Thomas P. McManus identified a central thematic of the "guilt of inadequacy" commonly experienced by characters positioned as new men who feel a "burden of being or believing themselves to be, inadequate sons, of not measuring up to their respective fathers' requirements."[16] Television's 1980s new men presented similar guilt over not being the "men" of their fathers' generation, but the characters of male-centered serials display not guilt but rather anger with their fathers for not offering a sustainable legacy and not recognizing that that is the case.[17]
- Authentically sexist men are the butt of jokes, while ironic sexism remains okay; the same holds true, in most cases, for heterosexism.

The depictions and characterizations that produce these dictums of good manhood are necessarily limited by their context and the life stage depicted for the protagonists. It remains to be seen, for example, how these male characters might cope as they become empty nesters and arrive at middle age. They too may be shown to have midlife crises or as tempted to leave their wives for younger women, as have been common conventions in times where more patriarchal masculinities reigned. Likewise, we'll only know in time whether the involved parenting by fathers yields different relationships with adult children than these characters are depicted as having with their own fathers.

* * *

As I endeavored to write this conclusion in the summer of 2012, a flurry of political punditry emerged that left me—I thought—with a concluding angle. A number of significant pieces of scholarship on men and media frame the periodization of their studies through the contemporary presidency: consider Susan Jeffords's *Hard Bodies: Hollywood Masculinity in the Reagan Era*, David Greven's *Manhood in Hollywood from Bush to Bush*, or Brenton Malin's *American Masculinity under Clinton:*

Popular Media and the Nineties "Crisis of Masculinity."[18] In an opinion piece about the developing presidential race between incumbent Barack Obama and Mitt Romney, *New York Times* pundit David Brooks explained Obama's continued popularity despite the dismal economy as related to his display of an "ESPN masculinity—postfeminist in his values, but also thoroughly traditional in style—hypercompetitive, restrained, not given to self-doubt, rarely self-indulgent."[19] In this incisive sentence Brooks tapped into evidence within the broader culture of this negotiation among patriarchal and feminist masculinities and identified the gulf between the masculinity of a Boomer such as Romney (born in 1947) and that of Obama (born in 1961), which was made even more expansive by the different class and ethnic privileges of the men. While it is unclear and inexplicable why Brooks chose "ESPN" as the modifier of the emergent, more feminist masculinity he identifies, his instinct to categorize Obama and the masculinity he displays in this way briefly brought to popular attention the struggle with transitions in masculinity that this book explores. Obama unquestionably embodies a masculinity different from that of his predecessors and challengers, and his years in office will contribute to changing cultural expectations of what a man does and how a man leads.

Throughout this book I've sated my own concerns about shortcomings of my project by noting myriad sites requiring others' more careful and focused analysis. Some of these projects are complementary to mine, such as expanding the largely imagined universe in which this book fits, and in other cases, augmentation of the themes, topics, and series considered here is needed. Complementary work includes nuanced analysis of the cultural transformations of the 1990s that more precisely traces how and when the "backlash" receded and poses vocabulary that speaks of this era through terminology more relevant than "post-9/11." Also, development of other continua than the one I pose of patriarchal and feminist masculinities and examination of other facets of the dynamic post-second-wave period in the masculinities of real men and other media would help fine tune discussions. There certainly is an "ESPN masculinity," though I wouldn't characterize it in the manner offered by Brooks, and developing multifaceted and clearly distinguished masculinities can only add sophistication to the thinking in this area. I suppose this is a backward way of suggesting less reliance on broad, macro modifiers such as "hegemonic" and "dominant" that seem pointlessly vague in the current climate, though I suspect this has always been the case.

In terms of augmenting the work here, more sustained investigation of the relationships between protagonists and their fathers and in relation to new-men narratives outside of the films Rattigan and McManus consider would help build insight into this transition from guilt to anger with patriarchal fathers and build more extensive arguments about the other relationships in which shifts in hegemonic masculinities are evident. Some very different trends than those noted here can be identified in narrative and representational forms such as comedy and reality that require greater attention. Likewise, male characters in ensemble, episodic, workplace series also compose a significant number of the televised roles for men and have gone largely unconsidered here. These other forms may include a broader range of ethnicities and sexualities among their male characters that might be useful in identifying discrepancies in representational trends that are unclear due to the paucity of nonwhite, gay men considered in this book. Very different trends are evident in the masculinities of Millennial characters and those younger than Generation X that Michael Kimmel identifies in *Guyland* as exhibiting a delayed maturation process.[20] Although they also have inhabited a post-second-wave world from birth, those among the generations born after the early 1980s have still other defining experiences and will need their own contextualized story of televised representation. The storytelling of subsequent series—and the conclusion of some discussed here that remain incomplete—will suggest yet other topics and foci.

As I have chronicled the challenges characters depict in negotiating competing aspects of masculinities, I must admit sharing some of the hesitation voiced by Marcotte, who writes,

> The irony is that these new shows about men mine territory familiar to feminism, and could even be described in many cases as explicitly feminist. But for all the feminism on TV, high quality dramas about *women* haven't taken off. Women get plenty of meaty, complex roles in these top tier shows, but only as supporting characters in shows centered around men's gender drama.[21]

Curiously, while a broader context of successful experiments with female-centered series across television in the 1990s to some degree predicts the arrival of male-centered serials, it is more difficult to answer the question of why female-centered shows fail to feature the narrative and character depth of the male-centered serials. By 2010 few, if any, female-centered dramas remained, especially those offering significant character development or complexity. The few that might be noted were of the more episodic variety—*The Closer, Saving Grace,* and *Hawthorne* on cable; *Desperate Housewives* and *The Good Wife* on broadcast; or the dark comedies of *Weeds, Nurse Jackie, United States of Tara,* and *The C Word,* all found on Showtime. As is often the case with industrially produced art forms, the explanation of industrial reliance on formula seems as good an explanation as any other. *The Sopranos* succeeded on premium cable and then *The Shield* succeeded in creating a basic cable version. The subsequent series then varied the formula enough to remain original while capitalizing on the rough balance of features that proved successful in the original. Although I share Marcotte's concern, I remain optimistic that the form will come to include female characters, as somewhat evident in *Damages* (FX/DirecTV, 2007–2012) and *The Killing* (AMC, 2011–). That said, I still wonder whether television critics and scholars—and audiences, for that matter—are ready to see female characters that are as deeply flawed as Walter White and Dexter Morgan as individuals and not as indictments of feminism, contemporary career women, and mothers.[22]

A key part of better understanding the men and masculinities on display in these series and theorizing about what they might tell us about their real-world doppelgangers is letting go of some of the old explanatory narratives and considering the status of men and masculinity on their own trajectories, without the zero-sum assumption that men's gains are women's losses and the reverse. I am most certainly not calling for a celebration of the emergent feminist masculinities or disregard of the continued patriarchal currents, but rather for nuanced consideration of men and the stories told about their lives. Analysis must begin somewhere other than the assumption that crisis narratives are symptomatic of a mourning of entitlement thwarted, and instead, the type of holistic contextualized analysis that has characterized thirty years of feminist media scholarship examining female characters is needed to better understand changing norms among males.

Evidence of contestation of patriarchal norms can be found across the television dial and in the homes tuning in to them. As Kimmel notes in the epilogue to his 2012 updated edition of *Manhood in America*,

> The biggest shift in American masculinity has taken place quietly, with little fanfare and even less media coverage. As women have become increasingly equal, most men have simply accepted these changes. American men have quietly and relatively easily accommodated to the dual-career couple model that now characterizes most marriages. . . . This acceptance isn't the result of some grand ideological transformation in the meaning of manhood. Rather, it is the inevitable result of countless micro-level decisions made by families every day: about their daughters' and sons' education, a growing unwillingness to tolerate bullying or harassment, a sense of fairness about reducing wage inequality and discrimination. It's not that men woke up one morning and decided to scrap their traditional definition of masculinity. Rather, they gradually, and without fanfare or struggle, drifted into more egalitarian relationships because they love their wives, partners, and children.[23]

Though misogyny espoused by Rush Limbaugh or sexist rantings offered by Howard Stern continue to blast perspectives consistent with patriarchal masculinities into the nation's homes like hurricanes coming to shore, we mustn't let them drown out the subdued but steady tide that has already dismantled much of their foundation. Though incomplete, phenomenal changes in American gender roles have occurred in the post-second-wave era. Continued battles may remain, but valuable lessons can be found about how revolutions secure meaningful gains not at the height of the conflict, but over decades of steady erosion. Attending only to flashpoints can obscure evidence of process. These adjustments have been quiet, but some sectors of US television offer a dim beacon suggesting a way forward.

INTRODUCTION

1. The same viewer could find Barney hilarious because of the text's repudiation of this masculinity and acknowledgment of its artifice and find Charlie tedious and dirty.

2. The pervasiveness of "Jack Bauer" as shorthand for a particular masculinity and American attitude was clear in the nomination of Bauer to a series that sought essays on favorite fictional characters by National Public Radio's *All Things Considered*. Of Bauer, contributor Mike McCabe notes, "If someone were to ask me what I think of when someone says America, I would say red meat, power tools and Jack Bauer. Jack Bauer has struck a chord with die-hard patriots in our country along with people who love explosions and firefights." This encapsulates the meaning "Bauer" took on entirely separate from the travails of the actual character. See *All Things Considered*, 28 Jan. 2008, *http://www.npr.org/templates/story/story.php?storyId=18491526* (accessed 17 July 2011).

3. Derek Johnson, "That Other Jack," *Antenna*, 25 May 2010, http://blog.commarts.wisc.edu/2010/05/25/that-other-jack (accessed 25 Aug. 2010).

4. Michael S. Kimmel, *Manhood in America: A Cultural History*, 2nd ed. (New York: Oxford University Press, 2006), 1.

5. Ibid., 1.

6. See Gaye Tuchman, Arlene Kaplan Daniels, and James Benet, eds., *Hearth and Home: Images of Women in the Mass Media* (New York: Oxford University Press, 1978). Also Fred Fejes, "Images of Men in Media Research," *Critical Studies in Mass Communication*, June 1989: 215–21, summarizes the limited early work focused on men.

7. Admittedly, commonality in portrayals in particular genres at particular times have led to arguments about stereotypes in segments of television, such as Spigel's argument about buffoon fathers in domestic comedies of the 1950s and 1960s, but those stereotypes were never prevalent across genres in the manner common to depictions of women. See Lynn Spigel, *Make Room for TV: Television and the Family Ideal in Post-War America* (Chicago: University of Chicago Press, 1992).

8. *The Dick Van Dyke Show* is one such example of a series that offered greater balance of both private and professional life.

9. Ginia Bellafante, "Thomas Jane on *Hung*, Symbol of the Recession," *New York Times*, 6 Aug. 2010, http://www.nytimes.com/2010/08/06/arts/television/06hung.htm (accessed 18 Aug. 2010).

10. Stephanie Coontz, "Sharing the Load," *The Shriver Report: A Woman's Nation*, edited by Heather Boushey and Ann O'Leary (New York: Free Press, 2009); *Fresh Air with Terry Gross*. "Social Historian Stephanie Coontz 'Stirs' Up *The Feminine Mystique* 47 Years Later." NPR, http://www.npr.org/templates/transcript/transcript.php?storyId=132931581 (accessed 20 Dec. 2012).

11. Hanna Rosin, "The End of Men," *Atlantic* (July/Aug 2010), http://www.theatlantic.com/magazine/archive/2010/07/the-end-of-men/8135 (accessed 3 Nov. 2010); *The End of Men: And the Rise of Women* (New York: Riverhead Books, 2012).

12. Susan Murray, "Lessons from Uncle Miltie," in *Hitch Your Antenna to the Stars: Early Television and Broadcast Stardom*, 65–92 (New York: Routledge, 2005); Mary Desjardins, "Lucy and Desi: Sexuality, Ethnicity, and TV's First Family," in *Television, History, and American Culture: Feminist Critical Essays*, edited by Mary Beth Haralovich and Lauren Rabinovitz, 56–73 (Durham, NC: Duke University Press, 1999); George Lipsitz, "The Meaning of Memory: Family, Class, and Ethnicity in Early Network Television Programs," in *Private Screenings: Television and the Female Consumer*, edited by Lynn Spigel and Denise Mann, 71–108 (Minneapolis: University of Minnesota Press, 1992); James Gilbert, "The Ozzie Show: Learning Companionate Fatherhood," in *Men in the Middle: Searching for Masculinity in the 1950s*, 135–63 (Chicago: University of Chicago Press, 2005); Martin Pumphrey, "The Games We Play(ed): TV Westerns, Memory, and Masculinity," in *Action TV: Tough Guys, Smooth Operators, and Foxy Chicks*, edited by Bill Osgerby and Anna Gough-Yates, 145–58 (London: Routledge, 2001); Bill Osgerby, "'So *You're* the Famous Simon Templar': *The Saint*, Masculinity, and Consumption in the Early 1960s," in ibid., 32–52 (London: Routledge, 2001); Paul Cobley, "'Who Loves Ya, Baby?': *Kojak*, Action, and the Great Society," in ibid., 53–68 (London: Routledge, 2001); Robert F. Gross, "Driving in Circles: *The Rockford Files*," in *Considering David Chase: Essays on* The Rockford Files, Northern Exposure, *and* The Sopranos, edited by Thomas Fahy, 29–45 (Jefferson, NC: McFarland, 2008); Nickianne Moody, "'A Lone Crusader in the Dangerous World': Heroics of Science and Technology in *Knight Rider*," in *Action TV: Tough Guys, Smooth Operators, and Foxy Chicks*, edited by Bill Osgerby and Anna Gough-Yates, 69–80 (London: Routledge, 2001); Steve Cohan, "Queer Eye for the Straight Guise: Camp, Postfeminism, and the Fab Five's Makeovers of Masculinity," in *Interrogating Postfeminism: Gender and the Politics of Popular Culture*, edited by Yvonne Tasker and Diane Negra, 176–200 (Durham, NC: Duke University Press, 2007); Dennis W. Allen, "Making Over Masculinity: A Queer 'I' for the Straight Guy," *Genders* 44 (2006), www.genders.org/g44/g44_allen.html (accessed 19 Mar. 2009); Brenda R. Weber, "What Makes the Man: Masculinity and the Self-Made (Over) Man," in *Makeover TV: Selfhood, Citizenship, and Celebrity*, 171–212 (Durham, NC: Duke University Press, 2009); Rachel Moseley, "'Real Lads Do Cook . . . but Some Things are Still

Hard to Talk About': The Gendering of 8–9," *European Journal of Cultural Studies* 4, no. 1 (2001): 32–39; Joanne Hollows, "Oliver's Twist: Leisure, Labour, and Domestic Masculinity in *The Naked Chef*," *International Journal of Cultural Studies* 6, no. 2 (2003): 229–48; Hamilton Carroll, "Men's Soaps: Automotive Television Programming and Contemporary Working-Class Masculinities," *Television & New Media* 9, no. 4 (July 2008): 263–83; Elaine Pennicott, "'Who's the Cat That Won't Cop Out?': Black Masculinity in American Action Series of the Sixties and Seventies," in *Action TV: Tough Guys, Smooth Operators, and Foxy Chicks*, edited by Bill Osgerby and Anna Gough-Yates, 100–114 (London: Routledge, 2001); Yvonne Tasker, "*Kung-Fu*: Re-Orienting the Television Western," in ibid., 115–26 (London: Routledge, 2001).

13. Michael S. Kimmel, *Manhood in America: A Cultural History*, 3rd ed. (New York: Oxford University Press, 2012), 288.

CHAPTER 1

1. A characteristic expression of this sentiment, though in this case more focused on the loss of racial rather than gender privilege, can be found in Anna Quindlen, "The Great White Myth," *New York Times*, 15 Jan. 1992, A21.

2. Hanna Rosin, "The End of Men," *Atlantic* (July/Aug 2010); *Newsweek*'s cover article "Man Up," 20 Sept. 2010.

3. Michael Kimmel, *Guyland: The Perilous World Where Boys Become Men* (New York: Harper, 2009); Leonard Sax, *Boys Adrift* (New York: Basic Books, 2009).

4. Kay Hymowitz, *Manning Up: How the Rise of Women Has Turned Men into Boys* (New York: Basic Books, 2011).

5. Eric Klinenberg, *Going Solo: The Extraordinary Rise and Surprising Appeal of Living Alone* (New York: Penguin, 2012).

6. Readers familiar with my other scholarship will appreciate the deliberateness with which I made this decision and understand that my scholarship has a trajectory of meaningful engagement with both postfeminism and third-wave feminism. This choice was carefully considered and not simply dismissive of emerging feminist ideologies. I consider it illustrative of a use of Chela Sandoval's operationalization of oppositional consciousness as manual car transmission, and that the theoretical and activist formation of second-wave feminism is the "gear" most relevant for the analysis here. Chela Sandoval, "U.S. Third World Feminism: The Theory and Method of Oppositional Consciousness in a Postmodern World," *Genders* 10 (1991): 1–24.

7. This discourse is pervasive in conservative media, where it masquerades as fact; see, for illustration, Rosie Boycott, "Feminism Has Turned Men into Second-Class Citizens, but Have Women's Victories Come at a Price?" *Daily Mail* (London), 7 Feb. 2008, http://www.dailymail.co.uk/femail/article-512550/Feminism-turned-men-second-class-citizens-womens-victories-come-price.html (accessed 26 Apr. 2012).

8. Importantly, complicated conversations about the utility and damage of organizing US feminist history through the wave metaphor exist and I don't mean to dismiss these concerns here.

9. Susan Faludi, *Backlash: The Undeclared War against American Women* (New York: Crown, 1991).

10. Nancy Whittier speaks carefully about the "micro-cohorts" raised in the wake of second-wave feminism that allows sophisticated analysis of the complexity of feminist politics in the 1980s–2000s. Nancy Whittier, *Feminist Generations: The Persistence of the Radical Women's Movement* (Philadelphia: Temple University Press, 1995), 228.

11. Related scholarship dealing with masculinity in popular media has connected shifting masculinities evidenced in films to political periods of various US presidents: consider Susan Jeffords, *Hard Bodies: Hollywood Masculinity in the Reagan Era* (New Brunswick, NJ: Rutgers University Press, 1994); David Greven, *Manhood in Hollywood from Bush to Bush* (Austin: University of Texas Press, 2009). Greven also uses "masculine identity in post-Clinton America" as the context signifier in an essay on another set of films. Indeed, the study at hand can be properly described as "post-Clinton" by chronological measures, though such a naming does not capture the phenomenon as well as "post-second-wave." We are now post-Clinton by more than a decade, but the topics and themes examined here don't seem to have much to do with Clinton—or Bush or Obama for that matter. Such descriptors may work better for the typical scope or evidentiary needs of film analysis than those of television; or the connection between the phenomenon of study and presidential persona were more centrally linked—as in the case Jeffords argues—than they are here. The period of study may indeed be post-Clinton, but Clinton had little to do with creating this context.

12. Some might suggest "post-9/11" as an appropriate designator of the era, and a decade ago most would have reasonably presumed that "post-9/11" would become the defining descriptor of this age. Indeed, in the weeks and months after the attacks, a discernable return of patriarchal masculinities was on display in the hero narratives of rescue workers and the frontier-justice rhetoric of seeking vengeance that emanated from White House spokespersons and 24-hour news channel talking heads (see Susan Faludi, *The Terror Dream: Myth and Misogyny in an Insecure America* [New York: Picador, 2008]). The events of the day are important in some of the stories examined here, yet, with the passage of time, this immediate late-2001 moment appears more a brief aberration in broader cultural struggles over masculinity and has proven surprisingly fleeting. Perhaps as a result of the decade of delayed gratification in the quest for vengeance on Osama bin Laden, the sense that the Iraq and Afghanistan wars were also initially failed efforts, and the broader economic crisis gripping the nation and the globe by the end of the decade, the construct of more patriarchal masculinities that had been embodied in the World Trade Center rescue workers and immediate post-9/11 longing for John Wayne types faded from view as the anxiety of the events faded in memory.

13. A key exception here is the abortion debate. Although the right to legal abortion was legally threatened at the federal level and substantially curtailed at the state level in this period, it too, took second place to the economy and issues

of international policy in much of the mid-00s. Notably, I'm not suggesting this gain was a result of feminists' work alone. Shifts in the US economy, for example, that made dual-income families a prerequisite for middle-class life were crucial to acceptance of this shift in gender norms.

14. Denny Crane of *Boston Legal* and to some degree Denis Leary of *Rescue Me* provide exceptions. Most who have offered generational subgroupings categorize two post-Boomer generations—commonly Generation X and Generation Y/Millennials—although this generational terminology is rarely used to make central distinctions about attitudes toward gender politics to such an extent that we might presume significant commonality among these generations.

15. Ron Becker terms these audiences "slumpies"—socially liberal, urban minded professionals—and argues that the broadcast networks' desire to attract this audience in the 1990s considerably contributed to the increasing presence of gay characters. Ron Becker, *Gay TV and Straight America* (New Brunswick, NJ: Rutgers University Press, 2006).

16. See Amanda D. Lotz, *The Television Will Be Revolutionized* (New York: New York University Press, 2007).

17. As broadcast economies shifted, many broadcast stations began requiring payment from the cable systems that carried their signals.

18. It would be an exaggeration to say that all cable content is edgy or edgier than broadcast content. It is true that the "edgiest" content is uniformly on cable, but many cable channels offer programming quite similar to broadcasters.

19. See Amanda Lotz, *Redesigning Women: Television after the Network Era* (Urbana-Champaign: University of Illinois Press, 2006), 39–42.

20. For example, *Remember WENN* (AMC), *Pacific Blue* (USA), *Linc's* (Showtime), *Rude Awakening* (Showtime), *First Wave* (SciFi).

21. See Amanda D. Lotz, "If It's Not TV, What Is It? The Case of U.S. Subscription Television," in *Cable Visions: Television beyond Broadcasting,* edited by Sarah Banet-Weiser, Cynthia Chris, and Anthony Freitas, 85–102 (New York: New York University Press, 2007). Notably, Lifetime and USA achieved moderate success in developing original narrative series alongside HBO in the late 1990s, but followed a somewhat different strategy. By the late 2000s, USA, TNT, FX, and AMC dominated in the production of original narrative series for cable and followed fairly similar competitive strategies.

22. See Lotz, *Redesigning Women*, 27, for a discussion of edge and narrowcasting as competitive techniques.

23. Michael S. Kimmel, *Manhood in America: A Cultural History*, 3rd ed. (New York: Oxford University Press, 2012), 238–43.

24. This is notably different from the way women were targeted in this era through programming that did not hail heterosexual male companions.

25. This anxiety was particularly high in fall of 2004, a period analyzed in Max Dawson, "Network Television's 'Lost Boys': TV, New Media, and the 'Elusive' Male Viewer," Society of Cinema and Media Studies, March 2008, Philadelphia, PA.

26. John Consoli, "What Are Men Watching Other Than Sports in Broadcast TV Primetime?" *Broadcasting & Cable*, 14 Dec. 2012, http://www.broadcastingcable.com/article/490878–What_Are_Men_Watching_Other_Than_Sports_in_Broadcast_TV_Primetime_.php?rssid=20065 (accessed 20 Dec. 2012).

27. Horace Newcomb and Paul Hirsh, "Television as a Cultural Forum," in *Television: The Critical View*, 5th ed., edited by Horace Newcomb, 505–13 (New York: Oxford University Press, 1994).

28. bell hooks, *Ain't I a Woman: Black Women and Feminism* (New York: South End Press, 1981).

29. This plurality of patriarchal depictions distinguishes representations of men from those of women. While Stuart Hall and others countered the pervading theory at the time that "good" representations could combat "negative" ones by arguing that a preponderance of images was necessary, this strategy has less purchase in the case of white, heterosexual men. This group was portrayed in an array of ways, but consistently in accord with patriarchal power. Whereas Hall's theories were about empowering subordinated groups, it is trickier to use these tools for empowering those who are subordinated within the empowered group. Stuart Hall, *Representation and the Media*. Sut Jhally, dir. Media Education Foundation, 1997.

30. R. W. Connell, "An Iron Man: The Body and Some Contradictions of Hegemonic Masculinity," in *Sport, Men, and the Gender Order: Critical Feminist Perspectives*, edited by Michael Messner and Don Sabo, 83–95 (Champaign, IL: Human Kinetics Books, 1990), 83.

31. Notably, the concept of a masculinity that dominates women that I demarcate as patriarchal masculinity is encompassed by the notion of hegemonic masculinity Connell initially offered. R. W. Connell, *Masculinities*, 2nd ed. (Berkeley: University of California Press, 2005), 76.

32. The concept of the performative aspects of gender introduced by critical theorists such as Judith Butler also adds sophistication to understandings of masculinity (see Judith Butler, *Gender Trouble: Feminism and the Subversion of Identity* [New York: Routledge, 1990]). As in the case of conceiving of a plurality of masculinities, the idea that individuals are acculturated into performance of gender—and may even be so in strategically consonant or dissonant ways—further breaks old conflations of sex and gender and thinking that presumed the existence of a set of traits inherent to being a man. Such theoretical refinements require nuanced vocabulary, such as that distinguishing "masculinity"—the characteristics, traits, and qualities one performs that are gendered male—from "manhood"—the "inner life of being, becoming, and performing maleness" (distinctions made by Celine Parrenas Shimizu, *Straightjacket Sexualities: Unbinding Asian American Manhoods in the Movies* [Palo Alto, CA: Stanford University Press, 2012], 9). This expanding nuance in conceptualization of gender has allowed for the acknowledgment of gender categories such as Judith Halberstam's "female masculinity" that indicates how masculinity is not the terrain of men alone (Judith Halberstam, *Female Masculinity* [Durham, NC: Duke University Press, 1998]). As is the case

with theories about masculinity developed by sociologists, many of the ideas about the performativity of gender are theorized to speak of the experience of gender and real people, rather than that of fictional television characters that have always been more readily conceived of as "performing" identity or as deploying gender through characterizations in particular and intentional ways (see Judith Butler, *Bodies That Matter: On the Discursive Limits of "Sex"* [New York: Routledge, 1993], 95). Conceptually, performativity provides a language for speaking of how gender is constructed within and by cultures rather than originating in sex designation and speaks to how performance is an inseparable part of identity. My invocation of Butler is intended not to meaningfully engage with the nuance of her theoretical offerings but to acknowledge that the analysis here is certainly influenced by her work and aims to use this insight as a tool in the analysis of popular television. Though these theories expand our language for speaking of gender construction, they were developed to assess the performative aspects of gender by "real" individuals, and consequently may proffer greater utility to sociologists studying real people than to media analysts who at times explore the mediation of real individuals such as sports figures, musical performers, or politicians and very deliberately constructed fictional characters at others.

33. Raymond Williams, "Base and Superstructure in Marxist Cultural Theory," *New Left Review* 82 (1973): 3–16; R. W. Connell and James W. Messerschmidt, "Hegemonic Masculinity: Rethinking the Concept," *Gender & Society* 19, no. 6 (December 2005): 829–59.

34. And I should note that I too borrowed exactly this definition in previous, less carefully considered work. Nick Trujillo, "Hegemonic Masculinity on the Mound: Media Representations of Nolan Ryan and American Sports Culture," *Critical Studies in Mass Communication* 8 (1994): 290–308, 291–92.

35. Robert Hanke, "On Masculinity: Theorizing Masculinity with/in the Media," *Communication Theory* 8, no. 2 (1998): 183–203, 186–87. Hanke does an excellent job in this article of bringing together communication studies, film studies, and critical theorists such as Foucault and Butler to argue for an approach to studying masculinity in the media that I draw from extensively.

36. Robert Hanke, "Hegemonic Masculinity in *thirtysomething*," *Critical Studies in Mass Communication* 7 (1990): 231–48; Robert Hanke, "The 'Mock-Macho' Situation Comedy: Hegemonic Masculinity and Its Reiteration," *Western Journal of Communication* 62, no. 1 (1998): 74–93; Mary Douglas Vavrus, "Domesticating Patriarchy: Hegemonic Masculinity and Television's 'Mr. Mom,'" *Critical Studies in Media Communication* 19, no. 3 (2002): 352–75; Lori Henson and Radhika E. Parameswaran, "Getting Real with 'Tell It Like It Is' Talk Therapy: Hegemonic Masculinity and the *Dr. Phil* Show," *Communication, Culture & Critique* 1 (2008): 287–310.

37. John Fiske, *Television Culture* (London: Routledge, 1987), 186. Fiske uses his distinction of "feminine television" instead of melodrama in the original material, but this is a complicated classification, and at this point seems a dubious distinction.

38. Importantly, this is not to critique *Mad Men* as advancing patriarchal ideologies. I find its representational strategy aims to critique the more patriarchal norms of 1960s culture; the historical distance it provides merely allows a clear example.

39. Louis Althusser, "Ideology and Ideological State Apparatuses," in *Lenin and Philosophy and Other Essays*, translated by Ben Brewster (London: Monthly Review Press, 1971).

40. Nickianne Moody, "'A Lone Crusader in the Dangerous World': Heroics of Science and Technology in *Knight Rider*," in *Action TV: Tough Guys, Smooth Operators, and Foxy Chicks*, edited by Bill Osgerby and Anna Gough-Yates, 69–80 (London: Routledge, 2001), 78.

41. Constance Penley and Sharon Willis, eds., *Male Trouble* (Minneapolis: University of Minnesota Press, 1993); Steve Cohan, ed., *Screening the Male: Exploring Masculinities in the Hollywood Cinema* (New York: Routledge, 1993); Jeffords, *Hard Bodies*; Peter Lehman, ed., *Masculinity: Bodies, Movies, Culture* (New York: Routledge, 2001); Murray Pomerance and Frances Gateward, eds., *Where the Boys Are: Cinemas of Masculinity and Youth* (Detroit, MI: Wayne State University Press, 2005); Stella Bruzzi, *Bringing Up Daddy: Fatherhood and Masculinity in Post-War Hollywood* (London: British Film Institute, 2005).

42. Hanke, "Hegemonic Masculinity in *thirtysomething*," 245.

43. Sasha Torres, "Melodrama, Masculinity, and the Family: *thirtysomething* as Therapy," *Camera Obscura* 19 (1989): 86–107.

44. Peter J. Boyer, "TV Turns to the Hard-Boiled Male," *New York Times*, 16 Feb. 1986, http://www.nytimes.com/1986/02/16/arts/tv-turns-to-the-hard-boiled-male.html?sec=&spon=&&scp=1&sq=TV%20turns%20to%20the%20hard-boiled%20male&st=cse (accessed 10 June 2009).

45. Jonathan David Tankel and Barbara Jane Banks, "The Boys of Prime Time: An Analysis of 'New' Male Roles in Television," in *Studies in Communication*, vol. 4, edited by Sari Thomas, 285–90 (Norwood, NJ: Ablex, 1986).

46. Ibid., 289.

47. See H. G. Brown, "How to Outfox TV's New Breed of Macho Man," *TV Guide* 34, no. 31 (1986): 10–12; Amitai Etzioni, "Nice Guys Finish First," *Public Opinion* 7, no. 14 (1984): 16–18; Tom Shales, "The Tough Guy Makes a Come Back," *Washington Post*, 29 Jan. 1984: C1, C9.

48. Susan Douglas argues that a similar tactic occurred earlier in the women's movement as shows such as *Bewitched* presented contradictory femininities to address women's changing attitudes toward gender roles. Susan Douglas, *Where the Girls Are: Growing Up Female with the Mass Media* (New York: Times Books, 1994).

49. As reported in Tim Brooks and Earle Marsh, *The Complete Directory to Prime Time Network and Cable TV Shows, 1946–Present*, 9th ed. (New York: Ballantine Books, 2007), 1690–91.

50. A close reading of *Dallas* might argue Bobby Ewing as a version of the new man relative to JR and others.

51. Again, these shows "dominate" more in the writing about television than necessarily in viewership—with the exception of *L.A. Law*, which remained a mainstream hit throughout its run.

52. Ron Becker, *Gay TV and Straight America*, 3.

53. Ron Becker, "Guy Love: A Queer Straight Masculinity for a Post-Closet Era?" in *Queer TV: Theories, Histories, Politics*, edited by Glyn Davis and Gary Needham, 121–40 (New York: Routledge, 2009).

54. LOGO's *Noah's Ark*, for example.

55. Though these shows are ensemble series and therefore attend in less detail to the circumstances of particular characters.

56. Peter Alilunas, "Male Masculinity as the Celebration of Failure: The Frat Pack, Women, and the Trauma of Victimization in the 'Dude Flick,'" *Mediascape* (Spring 2008), http://www.tft.ucla.edu/mediascape/Spring08_MaleMasculinity. html (accessed 18 July 2011).

57. Heather Havrilesky, "*Men of a Certain Age, Community*: The Meek Inherit Your TV," *Salon.com*, 20 Dec. 2009, http://mobile.salon.com/ent/tv/iltw/2009/12/19/ men_of_a_certain_age_community (accessed 18 July 2011); Jessica Grose, "Omega Males and the Women Who Hate Them," *Slate*, 18 Mar. 2010, http:// www.slate.com/id/2248156 (accessed 18 July 2011). David Greven, "Fears of Millennial: *Scream*'s Queer Killers in *Bromance*," in *Rad Bromance: Male Homosociality in Film and Television*, edited by Michael DeAngelis (Detroit, MI: Wayne State University Press, forthcoming).

58. David Greven, "Dude, Where's My Gender? Contemporary Teen Comedies and New Forms of American Masculinity," *Cineaste* 27, no. 3 (June 2002).

59. J. Jack Halberstam, *Gaga Feminism: Sex, Gender, and the End of Normal* (Boston: Beacon, 2012).

CHAPTER 2

1. Diane Holloway, "Tortured Souls Are the New Breed of Antihero," Cox News Service, 24 Oct. 2006, http://www.thestar.com/entertainment/article/107075- -cold-blooded-villains-now-tv-heroes (accessed 20 July 2011); Janice Rhoshalle Littlejohn, "Sensitive Men Take TV by Storm," *Florida Today*, 22 Aug. 2007; Tim Goodman, "They Steal, They Cheat, They Lie, and We Wouldn't Have It Any Other Way: The Timeless Appeal of the Anti-Hero," *San Francisco Chronicle*, 22 June 2005, E1; Lynn Smith, "TV's Role: Produce Male Leads; Shows Shift Attention to More Mature Complex Characters," *Ann Arbor News*, 19 Dec. 2007: C5.

2. Alessandra Stanley, "Men with a Message: Help Wanted," *New York Times*, 3 Jan. 2010, http://www.nytimes.com/2010/01/03/arts/television/03alpha. html?sq=men%20with%20a%20message&st=nyt&adxnnl=1&scp=1&adxn nlx=1311185095-yTx3XZY/Yr7y7fBD4Q2ddg (accessed 20 July 2011).

3. Ibid.

4. See Roberta Pearson, "Anatomizing Gilbert Grissom: The Structure and Function of the Televisual Character," in *Reading CSI: Crime TV under the Microscope*,
edited by Michael Allen, 39–56 (London: Tauris, 2007).

5. The distinction between the characters in the male-centered serial and those in
episodically organized shows such as *Burn Notice, Leverage*, or *Monk* is that the
male-centered serials depict the way the choices and situations the protagonists
face redefine them as men in an ongoing manner and to such a degree as to
become the central problematic of the series—not just a preliminary explanation of character circumstance. The episodic cable shows of the 2000s use this
back story primarily to explain or create the conditions of the series premise:
the death of Nate Ford's (Timothy Hutton) son after his insurance provider and
employer refuses to pay for experimental treatment on *Leverage* leads to his
pursuit of avenging the underdog; the murder of Monk's wife, Trudy, explains
his idiosyncrasies and the occasional pursuit of a perpetrator of her death; the
circumstances of Michael Weston's "burn notice" explain his serial storyline
of uncovering who "burned" him and why he is available to solve a pro bono
case each week. Yet, this back story is often only relevant to weekly narrative
development as a lens for understanding the premise of the series or the static
motivation of the lead character. Further, several of the episodically organized
shows utilize broad ensembles, while the male-centered serial probes the situation of an individual to allow greater intensity of character exploration than
in ensemble casts that must allocate narrative time to developing a range of
characters.

6. Horace Newcomb, "Magnum: The Champagne of TV?" *Channels* 5, no. 1 (1985):
23–26.

7. Roberta Pearson provides a masterful deconstruction of the Grissom character
and the way *CSI* uses character development to add serial layers to its episodic
organization; see Pearson, "Anatomizing."

8. Matthew Gilbert, "Killer Serial," *Slate*, 12 Dec. 2008, http://www.slate.com/
id/2206519 (accessed 20 July 2011).

9. "The Crusader," *America in Prime Time*, Lloyd Kramer, dir. (2011).

10. Goodman, "They Steal."

11. The 2012 NBC series *Awake* featured a gimmicky concept, but on some level
illustrates this tension between the episodic cases and serial story about which
reality was "real" and the circumstances of Britton's car accident.

12. See Jimmy Draper and Amanda D. Lotz, "Making Sense of Homophobia in
Rescue Me: Working Through as Ideological Intervention," *Television & New
Media* 13, no. 6 (2012): 520–34, for more on working through as an ideological
strategy.

13. This perspective dominates Susan Faludi's account of men and masculinity
in crisis in the eighties and nineties. Susan Faludi, *Stiffed: The Betrayal of the
American Man* (New York: Morrow, 1999).

14. Barbara Ehrenreich, *Hearts of Men: American Dreams and the Flight from Commitment* (Garden City, NY: Anchor Press, 1983); Michael Kimmel, *Manhood in America: A Cultural History*, 2nd ed. (New York: Oxford University Press, 2006).

15. Susan Faludi, *Backlash: The Undeclared War against Women* (New York: Crown, 1991); Faludi, *Stiffed.*

16. The FX series *Justified* is difficult to place in this regard. It initially followed the episodic organization but gradually became more serialized and similar to the male-centered serials. Yet Raylan's status as a single, childless man distinguishes him from the other protagonists of these series.

17. That maxim may have been true, but the competitive logic of television changed enough to make it irrelevant. Maybe men wouldn't watch female leads, but audiences had fragmented so significantly that networks no longer needed men in the audience to have a hit.

18. These shows were well produced and as compelling as those that succeeded in this era. Although centering on a male protagonist, they also featured multiple central female characters, which leads me to doubt that the gender of the protagonist explains the failures. I frankly can offer no good argument that explains their failure. *Citizen Baines* and *Max Bickford* featured major star talents James Cromwell and Richard Dreyfuss, respectively. Perhaps their star power necessitated high production fees that the networks felt warranted more than marginal viewership.

19. *Deadwood* and *Rome* could hardly address contemporary masculinity, yet these series too presented overwhelmingly male protagonists.

20. Film Noir Studies Glossary, http://www.filmnoirstudies.com/glossary/index.asp (accessed 5 July 2012).

21. "The Crusader," *America in Prime Time*, Lloyd Kramer, dir. (2011).

22. Holloway, "Tortured Souls Are the New Breed of Antihero."

23. Earlier cable originals that were successful enough to last a few seasons include *La Femme Nikita* on USA, through an international coproduction deal, and *Any Day Now* on Lifetime, though neither drew the journalistic attention common to the male-centered serials.

24. Many shows required judgment calls on the question of including or excluding rather than a precise math. I don't consider *Six Feet Under* because it is most centrally a family drama despite devoting significant narrative time to stories about Nate and David.

25. Newcomb, quoted in Holloway, "Tortured Souls Are the New Breed of Antihero."

26. See ibid.; Maureen Ryan, "The Watcher: Serial Dramas, Anti-heroes under Scrutiny," *Chicago Tribune*, 16 Jul. 2006, http://articles.chicagotribune.com/2006–07–17/features/0607170160_1_tommy-gavin-heroes-serialized (accessed 20 Jul. 2011).

27. A few words on why not a focus on some of the other series: As a series, *Huff* had limited success, his troubles were more bumbling than the type of negotiation characteristic of the other series, and his problems were more a threat to career than to family. *Brotherhood* was more about the brothers' relationships and their negotiations of their work lives. *Californication* isn't really a drama,

and the shorter narrative time makes it difficult to compare, although it is certainly related. *In Treatment* is narratively distinctive: very little time is spent on Paul; rather, bits come out through his seeing of patients to a degree that it is difficult to say the show is adequately about him. *Nip/Tuck* is centrally about the friendship and is thus better dealt with in chapter 5. The first season of *Justified* (which is all that had aired when I began this chapter) suggested that it would be more episodically oriented, though far more seriality developed in subsequent seasons. Raylan's single status also more exclusively sets the series in the professional realm, though father issues are an important part of Raylan's struggle to figure out how to be a law man. FX's 2011 boxing drama *Lights Out* fit very much with the male-centered serial's themes, but isn't emphasized because it lasted only a season. Many will note that I don't consider *Mad Men*, which is primarily based on a decision to only include shows set in the present because of the thematic attention to men's negotiation of post-second-wave America. *Ray Donovan* had just debuted on Showtime as I finished the manuscript though it very much followed the formula of many other series.

28. Official employment is at best informal in *The Sopranos* and *Sons of Anarchy*, as the "work" of characters in these series exists outside common legal classifications, but the activity of participating in the Mafia and the gun running of the motorcycle club, respectively, is responsible for producing the characters' livelihoods. Admittedly, one might have a college education and go into a career that doesn't require one, but on the basis of the character information presented, this does not seem the case.

29. The figure was 27.7 percent in 2008; http: www.census.gov/compendia/statab/cats/education/educational_attainment.html (accessed 10 May 2011).

30. Notably, this examination of men's lives outside highly professionalized fields was also present in a few broadcast television series that featured male breadwinners as coaches/teachers in *Friday Night Lights* and *Glee*.

31. The only woman at the center of a drama during this time who doesn't have a highly professionalized career is *Desperate Housewives'* Susan. *Desperate Housewives'* Gabrielle spends much of the series unemployed, but ends the series as a successful entrepreneur. *Weeds'* Nancy Botwin and the *United States of Tara's* Tara Gregson might also be considered as unemployed female cable protagonists, but these shows are better, though uncertainly, classified as comedies in comparison with male-centered serials. While there is a different argument about the unanticipated consequences of feminist intervention in the history of underrepresentation or stereotypical portrayals as wives, love interests, and mothers that is relevant to understanding these female-centered series, the focus here is the occupations male characters inhabit.

32. Christopher Lockett, "Masculinity and Authenticity: Reality TV's Real Men," *Flow* 13, no. 1 (2010), http://flowtv.org/2010/10/masculinity-and-authenticity (accessed 20 July 2011); Andrew King, "The Politics of 'Dirt'" in *Dirty Jobs*," *Flow* 13, no. 1 (2010), http://flowtv.org/2010/10/the-politics-of-%E2%80%98dirt%E2%80%99-in-dirty-jobs (accessed 20 July 2011).

33. *Breaking Bad* was incomplete at the time I finished the manuscript, so I wrote with the presumption that Skyler and Walt would not reconcile, as seemed likely to be the case following the penultimate season.

34. Notably, a similar trend emerges among women depicted in female-centered dramas of the late 1990s—here too, stable marital relationships for the protagonists were lacking. See Amanda D. Lotz, *Redesigning Women: Television after the Network Era* (Urbana: University of Illinois Press, 2006).

35. In his book exploring several of the series considered here (*Breaking Bad, The Shield*), Alan Sepinwall reflects on fan discussion of antihero shows and notes,

    Because the revolutionary dramas were mostly about men, and male antiheroes at that, and because viewers tend to bond most with the main character of a show, there was a side effect to the era, where characters who on paper should be the sympathetic ones become hated by viewers for opposing the protagonist. And the greatest vitriol has been unfortunately saved for wives like Skyler White, Corrine Mackey, Carmela Soprano, and Betty Draper, who are viewed by some viewers as irredeemable bitches, no matter how poorly they're treated by their husbands.

    Alan Sepinwall, *The Revolution Was Televised: The Cops, Crooks, Slingers, and Slayers Who Changed TV Drama Forever* (self-published by Alan Sepinwall, 2012). Though I don't consider audience response here, this tendency is worth noting.

36. This plot point is left hanging as a result of the series' cancellation. After Owen confronts his father, it seems as though he will rescind the sale. There are many parallels between Owen's story and Tony Soprano's struggle with the ghostly legacy of his own father.

37. Both *Californication* and *In Treatment* feature an arc of episodes devoted to paternal death. These series differ from those focused on here, yet also bear some commonality with the male-centered serials and depict their protagonists ultimately unprepared for their father's deaths with sentiments left unsaid and considerable regret. Paul, the therapist at the center of *In Treatment*, only comes to realize the partial truths of his construction of the story of his father leaving and his mother's suicide at his own therapist's urging. He goes to his father before he dies, but long after his Parkinson's, which Paul then fears he has inherited, has left him incommunicative. The death of Hank's father in *Californication* catches Hank by surprise and similarly opens wounds and leads him to assess the man he's become.

38. Becker refers to this psychographic as "slumpies." Ron Becker, *Gay TV and Straight America* (New Brunswick, NJ: Rutgers University Press, 2006). One exception is *The Shield*'s limited storyline about a tertiary character, Julian, who struggles with a gay identity and ultimately "decides" to be straight. Gay identity is a constant topic for *Rescue Me*, but is dealt with primarily through comedic banter, examined in chapter 4, though one of the firefighters has an extended plot arc in which he determines he is bisexual. The series largely drops this plot line after he comes out to the crew. Homosexuality emerges in *The Sopranos* in relation to one of the men in Tony's crew and possibly Ray Drecker's (*Hung*) son.

39. Additionally, series such as *Queer as Folk*, *Oz*, and *Six Feet Under* do emphasize storytelling about male protagonists with greater attention to gay identity and sexuality, but vary considerably from the male-centered serial formula as ensemble dramas.

40. I should also note that Julian is initially presented as gay; however, this aspect of his identity is diminished in subsequent seasons as the character struggles to make himself straight. According to research on the show's production by Kevin Sandler and Daniel Bernardi, this resulted from the actor's aversion to playing a gay character.

41. Also, the leader of the drug ring Walt cooks for and murders, Gus, is of an unclear, but nonwhite, ethnicity.

42. The strike team gets a black member in the third season as the result of a community review. Tavon Garris lasts eleven episodes and ends up comatose after injuries sustained in a car accident he causes after receiving a blow to the head in a fight with Shane.

43. The absence of two shows, *Kevin Hill* (UPN, 2004–2005) and *Lincoln Heights* (ABC Family, 2007–2009), should be acknowledged. Both series feature African American protagonists, and *Lincoln Heights* is firmly grounded in the issues faced by African American families in urban, economically disadvantaged environments. Though the series feature male protagonists, neither meets the distinction of the male-centered serial. *Kevin Hill*, which explores the disruption to the single, professional life of its eponymous protagonist caused by a ten-month-old cousin left to him, attends to many themes of family provision. Its brief run very much chronicled Kevin's coming to understand the importance of family, but the series—with its episodic legal plotlines—was much more an ensemble show and too short lived to include in the analysis here. *Lincoln Heights* targeted a teen and family audience and is best categorized as a family drama that didn't afford its patriarch, Eddie Sutton, the level of attention of the male-centered serials. These shows offer notable examples of black male lead characters, but exist outside of the male-centered serial phenomenon. Also, FX's *Thief* (2006), featuring Andre Braugher, also comes close. *Thief* structurally bears more in common with the male-centered serials, but was ultimately limited to only a season of six episodes and categorized as a miniseries. This short run provides little to compare with the other series.

44. Production incentives may also explain these locations as many of the original cable series aided the economics of production by shooting in and setting series outside of Los Angeles. See analysis in Kathleen Battles, "Low Stakes TV: The Basic Cable Original Series," *Flow* (2008), http://flowtv.org/2008/06/low-stakes-tv-%E2%80%93-the-basic-cable-original-serieskathleen-battlesoakland-university (accessed 20 July 2011).

45. As was the case in *Ed*, *Everwood*, or *October Road*.

46. *Breaking Bad*, "Mas," 305.

47. Interview by Kristopher Tapley, "Interview: 20 Questions with Denis Leary," *Incontention.com*, 3 Jul. 2009, http//incontention.com/?p=9546 (accessed 24 June 2010).

48. Goodman, "They Steal."

CHAPTER 3

1. *Nip/Tuck*'s Sean and Christian murder a drug dealer, although the plot point passes and isn't central to the overall story. Also, *Rescue Me*'s Tommy Gavin is never arrested, but drives drunk, delivers a range of beatings, and fails to stop his uncle's plan to avenge the death of Tommy's son by shooting the drunk driver that ran him down.

2. To some degree, Hamilton Carroll makes this argument in *Affirmative Reaction: New Formations of White Masculinity* (Durham, NC: Duke University Press, 2011). Indeed, the difference in our assessments of how white masculinity is being negotiated in cultural texts at this time has a lot to do with our objects of analysis. I don't disagree with his analyses, but would dispute that his texts are indicative of broad trends in culture and would suggest that his reading of Jack Bauer makes Bauer far more significant, makes the ideology of the series less complicated, and fails entirely to contextualize *24* as produced by particular industrial processes at a particular time.

3. A tradition much different from the outlaw in film; the use of "outlaw" here is not meant to connect with the outlaw hero Ray discusses in film, as drawn from literary characters. Robert B. Ray, *A Certain Tendency of the Hollywood Cinema, 1930–1980* (Oxford: Oxford University Press, 1985).

4. Protagonists: Walter White, Vic Mackey, Dexter Morgan, Jax Teller, Tony Soprano, Ray Drecker, Hank Moody, Tommy Gavin, Joe Tranelli. Prosecutable offenses: White, Mackey, Morgan, Teller, Soprano, Drecker, Moody, Tranelli. Irredeemably selfish in their personal lives: Gavin, Moody. Murder repeatedly: White, Mackey, Morgan, Teller, Soprano.

5. Jeffrey Sconce, "What If? Charting Television's New Textual Boundaries," in *Television after TV*, edited by Lynn Spigel and Jan Olsson, 93–112 (Durham, NC: Duke University Press, 2004), 97.

6. Economists Elizabeth Warren and Amelia Warren Tyagi examine these changes in *The Two-Income Trap: Why Middle-Class Mothers and Fathers Are Going Broke* (New York: Basic Books, 2003). In comparing the costs of family life of a single earner family in the 1970s and a dual-income family in the 1990s (of the median and adjusted for inflation), they identify that the dual-income family has roughly eight hundred dollars less in discretionary income because of the childcare costs, increased price of comparable housing, second car costs, and increased tax rate (50–51).

7. This is also true for "outlaw" Jax Teller.

8. Stephanie Coontz, "Sharing the Load," *The Shriver Report: A Woman's Nation*, edited by Heather Boushey and Ann O'Leary (New York: Free Press, 2009). Indeed, Andrew Kimbrell published *The Masculine Mystique: The Politics of Masculinity* (New York: Ballantine, 1995) nearly fifteen years earlier, but had little influence. Though addressing some similar points, it is an example of an approach to masculinity study in a way that sets men and women in contest and fails to acknowledge the broader structure of patriarchy in his laments about injustices facing men.

9. Betty Friedan, *The Feminine Mystique* (New York: Norton, 1963), 43.

10. Stephanie Coontz, "The Myth of Male Decline," *New York Times*, 29 Sept. 2012, http://www.nytimes.com/2012/09/30/opinion/sunday/the-myth-of-male-decline.html?pagewanted=3&_r=0&ref=general&src=me&pagewanted=print (accessed 2 Oct. 2012).

11. Kerstin Aumann, Ellen Galinsky, and Kenneth Matos, "The New Male Mystique," Families and Work Institute: National Study of the Changing Workforce, 2009, available familiesandwork.org/site/research/reports/main.html (accessed 5 Dec. 2012), 1.

12. Ibid., 1.

13. Ibid., 2.

14. Ibid., 19.

15. Indeed, many of the male characters in Apatow films described as "man boys" feature men embodying a slacker/stoner masculinity. Notably, this masculinity is typically a source of humor rather than affirmed as heroic or desirable. Also relevant, but a distinct phenomenon, is Vavrus's examination of news treatments of stay-at-home dads during the late 1990s, Mary Vavrus, "Domesticating Patriarchy: Hegemonic Masculinity and Television's 'Mr. Mom,'" *Critical Studies in Media Communication* 19, no. 3 (2002): 352–75.

16. Women who entered the workforce in the aftermath of second-wave feminism were found to work a "second shift" upon returning home to do all the domestic duties previously their responsibility. In seeking to remedy some of the second shift situation, men have taken on greater responsibilities at home, but US society has offered little institutional flexibility to aid the work/life balance for men or women. Arlie Hochschild, *The Second Shift: Working Parents and the Revolution at Home* (New York: Viking, 1989).

17. The trajectory of Vic Mackey is tricky on this point. In the second season, the strike team takes down an Armenian "money train," leaving each with a vast fortune, far in excess of what I'm arguing is generally the case. None of the men actually has much opportunity to spend the money, as the threats it causes immediately begin their downward spiral. At one point, Shane and Vic find Lem burning the money in an effort to eliminate the problems it introduces.

18. For example, in *Parenthood*, when Adam Braverman is laid off, his stay-at-home wife goes back to work.

19. *Hung*, 101, Pilot.

20. *Hung*, 101, Pilot.

21. *Hung*, 101, Pilot.

22. *Hung*, 101, Pilot.

23. In season 3 episodes "We're Golden" or "Crooks and Big Beaver," Ray finds out he has been servicing a female police officer. After he suggests they not see each other again, she places him in her police cruiser and threatens to book him. The series does not otherwise suggest fear of arrest as a deterrent to Ray's behavior. Jessica learns of his side career in the series' penultimate episode and responds

minimally—asking only if he's good at what he does. The series' cancellation prevented it from mining this storyline further.

24. In interviews, Gilligan describes his style as one of "subtle storytelling" that requires some work by audiences, and says that he aims to make connections within the series "mysterious versus confusing." Todd VanDerWerff, "Vince Gilligan Walks Us through *Breaking Bad*'s Fourth Season (Part 4 of 4)," *The AV Club*, 13 Oct. 2001, http://www.avclub.com/articles/vince-gilligan-walks-us-through-breaking-bads-four,63288 (accessed 31 May 2012).

25. David Segal, "The Dark Art of *Breaking Bad*," *New York Times*, 6 July 2011, http://www.nytimes.com/2011/07/10/magazine/the-dark-art-of-breaking-bad.html?pagewanted=all (accessed 21 June 2012).

26. Although this book indentifies and focuses upon the aspects of *Breaking Bad* consistent with coterminous male-centered serials, on its own terms, the series primarily deliberates upon good and evil.

27. See Jason Mittell's analysis of the complicated way *Breaking Bad* does this through what he terms "inferred interiority." "Serial Characterization and Inferred Interiority," *In Media Res*, 14 Dec. 2011, http://www.mediacommons.futureofthebook.org/imr/2011/12/14/serial-characterization-and-inferred-interiority (accessed 3 Jan. 2012).

28. This is one plot point where Gilligan's "subtle storytelling" is most unsatisfying. The reason Walt leaves and the origin of his relationship with Skyler are never made clear or suggested. It seems feasible that Walt could have been seeing Skyler after meeting her at the diner and impregnated her and that would have motivated his unexplained departure from the research and Gretchen and Elliot's world, but that is entirely speculation. And why he would have chosen to teach high school chemistry is equally unclear.

29. *Breaking Bad*, 105, "Gray Matter"

30. Notably, narrative time in *Breaking Bad* is much slower than the world of time experienced by viewers waiting weeks between episodes and a year between seasons. Skyler White is visibly pregnant with the same child for the first two seasons of the series so that it takes eighteen months of audience time to cover about six months of the Whites' lives.

31. Todd VanDerWerff, "Vince Gilligan Walks Us through *Breaking Bad*'s Fourth Season (Part 2 of 4)," *The AV Club*, 13 Oct. 2001, http://www.avclub.com/articles/vince-gilligan-walks-us-through-breaking-bads-4th,63113 (accessed 31 May 2012).

32. Gilligan describes Walt by noting, "Walter White is a man who is one of the world's greatest liars . . . he is lying to himself," which lends further credence to viewing Walt's motivation as not rooted in family provision to the extent he claims. Todd VanDerWerff, "Vince Gilligan Walks Us through *Breaking Bad*'s Fourth Season (Part 1 of 4)," *The AV Club*, 13 Oct. 2001, http://www.avclub.com/articles/vince-gilligan-walks-us-through-season-four-of-bre,63013 (accessed 31 May 2012).

33. Notably, Gilligan originally planned that Jesse would die at the end of the first season, suggesting that he was not meant to play such a crucial role in the

long-term narrative. Vince Gilligan, Paleyfest, 10 Mar. 2010, http://www.you-tube.com/watch?v=YqnoJ10HqP0 (accessed 21 June 2012).

34. The mystery of why Walt leaves the company/Elliot/Gretchen might make this more understandable.

35. Gilligan on Walt:

I think Walter is the most prideful character you will ever come upon. . . . He lies to himself more than he does anybody else, and that's saying a lot. . . . We love the irony of the bad guy causing himself a whole lot of grief that he didn't need to suffer, but for the pride that he possesses. . . . Maybe one of the biggest watershed moments in the life of the show was way back in the fourth episode of the first season where Walt essentially had this deus ex machina offer given to him (job and cancer treatment paid for) . . . and Walt, I think because of his pride, says no.

Todd Van Der Werff, "Vince Gilligan Walks Us through *Breaking Bad*'s Fourth Season (Part 4 of 4)," *The AV Club*, 13 Oct. 2001, http://www.avclub.com/articles/vince-gilligan-walks-us-through-breaking-bads-four,63288 (accessed 31 May 2012).

36. *Hung*'s writers did not anticipate cancellation in writing the end of the third season, leaving these matters of conclusion dangling.

37. Alan Sepinwall, "Sons of Anarchy: Kurt Sutter Q&A," *What's Alan Watching*, http://sepinwall.blogspot.com/2008/11/sons-of-anarchy-kurt-sutter-q.html, 26 Nov. 2008 (accessed 8 Sept. 2011).

38. The manifesto is titled "The Life and Death of Sam Crow: How the Sons of Anarchy Lost Their Way."

39. In short, the Mexican cartel they'd been trafficking drugs for turns out to be CIA. The CIA needs the gun trade with the RIRA that only SAMCRO can facilitate, so Jax is given a "choice" between staying and maintaining the line to the RIRA or having the CIA turn evidence over that will lead to the prosecution of him and the club.

40. Episode 401, "Out."

41. Even Gemma, a woman of a generation more rooted in patriarchy, is shown to possess considerable authority despite lacking an official place at the club table.

42. See Amanda D. Lotz, *Redesigning Women: Television after the Network Era* (Urbana: University of Illinois Press, 2006).

43. Ibid., 82. I submitted this book manuscript for publication after the end of the fifth season, which ended at the start of an important storyline for this analysis. In the final moments of the season, Tara tells Jax she has accepted a job in Portland and is taking the boys, asserting to him that he has done what was needed to save the club and that the preceding months had illustrated the danger to the family of remaining involved. Jax is incensed by this but before he can comment, the sheriff arrives with a warrant for Tara's arrest, perhaps enabled by Gemma. The closing image features Gemma figuratively replacing Tara. The way the subsequent seasons deal with Tara's prosecution and the exposure of Gemma's role in her arrest and JT's death have important

implications for the arguments that can be made of *Sons of Anarchy* and the entirety of Jax's story arc.

44. Douglas L. Howard, "An Interview with *Dexter* Writer and Developer James Manos, Jr.," in *Dexter: Investigating Cutting Edge Television*, edited by Douglas L. Howard, 14–26 (London: Tauris, 2010), 21. Notably, *Dexter* is based on a series of novels and the central creative management of the television series has changed repeatedly. Manos is only responsible for the first episode.

45. *Dexter* suffered from many changes in showrunners and some seem to understand Dexter as categorically inhuman, while others present stories that suggest he can be made human.

46. This plays out most extensively in episode 107, "Long Neck," in which AJ's troubles at school lead Tony to reflect on his childhood and parenting, particularly his realization of his father's involvement in the family business and how his work might impact his children.

47. Hanna Rosin, *The End of Men: And the Rise of Women* (New York: Riverhead Books, 2012).

CHAPTER 4

1. Peter Alilunas, "Male Masculinity as the Celebration of Failure: The Frat Pack, Women, and the Trauma of Victimization in the 'Dude Flick,'" *Mediascape*, Spring 2008, http://www.tft.ucla.edu/mediascape/Spring08_MaleMasculinity.html (accessed 22 June 2012).

2. David Greven, "Dude, Where's My Gender? Contemporary Teen Comedies and New Forms of American Masculinity," *Cineaste* 27, no. 23 (June 2002): 14–21, 15.

3. Eve Kosofsky Sedgwick, *Epistemology of the Closet* (Berkeley: University of California Press, 1990).

4. Ron Becker, "Guy Love: A Queer Straight Masculinity for a Post-Closet Era?" in *Queer TV: Theories, Histories, Politics*, edited by Glyn Davis and Gary Needham, 121–40 (New York: Routledge, 2009).

5. Ron Becker, "Becoming Bromosexual: Straight Men, Gay Men, and Male Bonding on U.S. TV," in *Rad Bromance: Male Homosociality in Film and Television*, edited by Michael DeAngelis. (Detroit, MI: Wayne State University Press, forthcoming).

6. Heather Havrilesky, "In Defense of the Aging Frat Boy," *Salon.com*, 29 Oct. 2009, http://www.salon.com/ent/tv/iltw/2009/10/28/aging_frat_boy_the_league_men_of_a_certain_age/print.html (accessed 9 Jan. 2010).

7. Jennifer Coates, *Men Talk: Stories in the Making of Masculinities* (Malden, MA: Blackwell, 2003).

8. Ibid., 35.

9. Ibid., 44.

10. Ibid., 46.

11. Ibid., 53.

12. Ibid., 55.

13. Ibid., 55, 56.
14. See, among others, Patricia Mellencamp, "Situation Comedy, Feminism, and Freud: Discourses of Gracie and Lucy," in *Studies of Entertainment: Critical Approaches to Mass Culture*, edited by Tania Modleski, 80–95 (Bloomington: Indiana University Press, 1986); Darrell Hamamoto, *Nervous Laughter: Television Situation Comedy and Liberal Democratic Ideology* (New York: Praeger, 1989).
15. Brett Mills, *The Sitcom* (Edinburgh: Edinburgh University Press, 2009), 77.
16. See, for example, Kylo-Patrick Hart, "Representing Gay Men on American Television," *Journal of Men's Studies* 9, no. 1 (2000): 59–79. In his book exploring television's dominant narrative comedy form, the sitcom, Brett Mills identifies three main categories that constitute much of the "humor theory" that has developed to explain why humans find things funny: superiority theory, incongruity theory, and relief theory. In addition to the already referenced superiority theory, which "supposes that people laugh when they feel a kind of superiority, particularly over other people," incongruity theory explains humor that comes from the "surprise of confounded expectations," and relief theory posits that "humour has evolved into a valuable tool for 'serving the purpose of exposure,' for it allows people to say rude, offensive and violent things in a manner which renders their force powerless while simultaneously allowing their expression." Mills, *The Sitcom*, 77, 82, 88.
17. Michael V. Tueth, "Breaking and Entering: Transgressive Comedy on Television," in *The Sitcom Reader: American Viewed and Skewed*, edited by Mary M. Dalton and Laura R. Linder, 25–34 (Albany: State University of New York Press, 2005), 27. For the most part, the humor considered here is most consistent with relief theory and transgressive humor, although the particular application varies as it is not the type of humor that leads to the analysis of these four shows, but their creation of the context of the homosocial enclave. Given the topical focus on the construction of masculinity, the following analysis does not belabor the task of categorizing the humor of these series so much as explore how the humor works to support or mock ideas and individuals within the series to police the boundaries of hegemonic masculinities.
18. Ibid.; Jonathan Gray, Jeffrey P. Jones, and Ethan Thompson, *Satire TV: Politics and Comedy in the Post-Network Era* (New York: New York University Press, 2009).
19. David Barker, "Television Production Techniques as Communication," *Critical Studies in Mass Communication* (Sept. 1985): 234–46.
20. Greven, "Dude, Where's My Gender?" 15.
21. Dialogue reproduced in Peter Paterson, "Television Mail: Oldest Sinners in Town," *Daily Mail* (20 Feb. 2002), 61.
22. *Entourage* is not easily classifiable as either a comedy or drama; it doesn't feature the heavier melodramatic aspects of some dramas, but it also isn't a show focused on being funny so much as it's a show exploring the quartet of characters and their relationships.
23. This does not negate the earlier point that Vince's and Eric's performances of masculinity are affirmed as generally more valuable. The distinction is that this does not correlate with status in the homosocial space.

24. *The League*, "Mr. McGibblets," 104.
25. *The League* was created and is written by the husband/wife writing team of Jeff Schaeffer and Jackie Marcus Schaeffer.
26. Notably, the men treat Ruxin's wife quite differently. She has no interest in participating in their group and appears rarely relative to Jenny. She is also presented as a "trophy wife," very much in accord with dominant beauty standards, and it is suggested that she must have married Ruxin for his professional success. Jenny is also conventionally attractive, but presents herself as comfortable being just one of the guys.
27. The *Rescue Me* ladder company is forced to accept a woman into its ranks for a nine-episode plot arc spanning the end of season one and the beginning of season two.
28. *Rescue Me*, "Happy," 212.
29. Ron Becker, *Gay TV and Straight America* (New Brunswick, NJ: Rutgers University Press, 2006).
30. See Jimmy Draper and Amanda D. Lotz, "Making Sense of Homophobia in *Rescue Me*: Working Through as Ideological Intervention," *Television & New Media* 13, no. 6 (2012): 520–34.
31. Admittedly Tommy's support is largely based on his concern about the potential breaking up of the crew, as without support, Mike will probably transfer to a different house. Even in the first season storyline about a gay firefighter who claims that dozens of the firefighters who died on 9/11 were gay, the focus of the men's discussion is on their anxiety over being able to detect those who are gay rather than questioning the ability or heroism of other firefighters. Additionally, the series never proposes that the chief's son lacks any capability because he is gay.
32. Of course, anal penetration is not exclusively a gay sex act; I believe the association with gay sex acts is intended in its use in these shows.
33. Episode 502, "Unlike a Virgin."
34. Episode 701, "Stunted."
35. There is undoubtedly a rich Freudian analysis available for an appropriately trained scholar. Indeed, one could argue that the taboo comes from the men's fear that they too enjoy these sex acts and that, within their construct of these distinctions, that might make them gay—so that they do indeed fear being gay. Though this is a thoroughly plausible reading, I'd suggest that it reads too much into what is minimally considered banter in these particular series.
36. Nancy Lee, "'Let's Hug It Out, Bitch!': The Negotiation of Hegemony and Homosociality through Speech in HBO's *Entourage*," *Culture, Society & Masculinity* 2, no. 2 (2010): 181–98.
37. Likewise, *Men of a Certain Age* completely eschews taunting, and avoids even *Entourage*'s focus on heterosexual prowess. This seems most related to the age, life stage, and maturity of the characters, but the intimacy of decades-old friendships may play a role as well.

38. Heather Havrilesky has two excellent articles on these shows: "In Defense of the Aging Frat Boy," *Salon.com*, 29 Oct. 2009, http://www.salon.com/ent/tv/iltw/2009/10/28/aging_frat_boy_the_league_men_of_a_certain_age/print.html (accessed 9 Jan. 2010); and "*Men of a Certain Age, Community*: The Meek Inherit Your TV," *Salon.com*, 20 Dec. 2009, http://www.salon.com.ent/tv/iltw/2009/12/19/men_of_a_certain_age_community/print.html (accessed 9 Jan. 2010).

39. James C. Scott, *Domination and the Arts of Resistance: Hidden Transcripts* (New Haven, CT: Yale University Press, 1990), 2, 4.

CHAPTER 5

1. Alexander Doty, "Introduction: What Makes Queerness Most?" *Making Things Perfectly Queer: Interpreting Mass Culture*, xi-xix (Minneapolis: University of Minnesota Press, 1993).

2. Ron Becker, "Guy Love: A Queer Straight Masculinity for a Post-Closet Era?" in *Queer TV: Theories, Histories, Politics*, edited by Glyn Davis and Gary Needham, 121–40 (New York: Routledge, 2009), 122.

3. Ibid., 122.

4. Ibid., 121.

5. Also see ibid., 121–22.

6. Ibid., 125.

7. Michael Warner, "Introduction," *Fear of a Queer Planet: Queer Politics and Social Theory*, vii-xxxi (Minneapolis: University of Minnesota Press, 1993), xxi-xxv.

8. Eve Kosofsky Sedgwick, *Epistemology of the Closet* (Berkeley: University of California Press, 1990).

9. Episode 103, "My Best Friend's Mistake"; also 109, "My Day Off."

10. June Thomas, "Television's First Great Brocedural," *Slate*, 13 June 2012, http://www.slate.com/blogs/browbeat/2012/06/13/brocedural_franklin_bash_on_tnt_is_tv_s_first_great_brocedural_.html (accessed 14 June 2012).

11. The friendship between Wilson and House in *House* is less central to the main narrative than these others, yet it too offers a glimpse of the dynamics of meaningful male friendships, albeit as made complicated by House's antisociality. In the series' final episodes, however, it does emphasize the importance of the relationship. This relationship is examined by Murray Pomerance in "The Bromance Stunt in *House*," in *Rad Bromance: Male Homosociality in Film and Television*, edited by Michael DeAngelis (Detroit, MI: Wayne State University Press, forthcoming).

12. Robin Wood, *Hollywood from Vietnam to Reagan* (New York: Columbia University Press, 1986), 227–30.

13. Ibid.

14. David Greven, *Manhood in Hollywood from Bush to Bush* (Austin: University of Texas Press, 2009), 129

15. Ibid., 129.

16. Ibid., 137.

17. Melvin Donalson, *Masculinity in the Interracial Buddy Film* (Jefferson, NC: McFarland, 2006); Cynthia J. Fuchs, "The Buddy Politic," in *Screening the Male: Exploring Masculinities in Hollywood Cinema*, edited by Steven Cohan and Ina Rae Hark, 194–210 (New York: Routledge, 1993); Ed Guerrero, "The Black Image in Protective Custody: Hollywood's Biracial Buddy Films of the Eighties," in *Black American Cinema*, edited by Manthia Diawara, 237–46 (New York: Routledge, 1993).

18. Guerrero, "The Black Image," 240, 244.

19. Fuchs, "The Buddy Politic," 195. More recently, Jillian Sandell examined male intimacy in John Woo films. Jillian Sandell, "Reinventing Masculinity: The Spectacle of Male Intimacy in the Films of John Woo," *Film Quarterly* 49, no. 4 (1996): 23–34.

20. Andrew Ross, "Masculinity and *Miami Vice*: Selling In," *Oxford Literary Review* 8 (1986): 143–54; Douglas Kellner, *Media Culture: Cultural Studies, Identity, and Politics between the Modern and the Postmodern* (London: Routledge, 1995); Scott Benjamin King, "Sonny's Virtues: The Gender Negotiations of *Miami Vice*," *Screen* 31, no. 3 (1990): 281–95, 293.

21. Lynn C. Spangler, "Buddies and Pals: A History of Male Friendships on Prime-Time Television," in *Men, Masculinity, and the Media*, edited by Steve Craig, 93–110 (Newbury Park, CA: Sage, 1992).

22. Ibid., 110.

23. Margo Miller, "Masculinity and Male Intimacy in Nineties Sitcoms: *Seinfeld* and the Ironic Dismissal," in *The New Queer Aesthetic on Television*, edited by James R. Keller and Leslie Stratyner, 147–59 (Jefferson, NC: McFarland, 2006).

24. Ibid., 148.

25. Ron Becker, "Becoming Bromosexual: Straight Men, Gay Men, and Male Bonding on U.S. TV," in *Rad Bromance: Male Homosociality in Film and Television*, edited by Michael DeAngelis. (Detroit, MI: Wayne State University Press, forthcoming).

26. Ibid., 7.

27. Ibid., 3.

28. Ibid., 4.

29. Ibid., 9.

30. Ibid., 10.

31. Greven deals slightly with these films in David Greven, "Fears of a Millennial Masculinity: *Scream*'s Queer Killers," in *Rad Bromance: Male Homosociality in Film and Television*, edited by Michael DeAngelis (Detroit, MI: Wayne State University Press, forthcoming).

32. Mark Simpson, "The Straight Men of Comedy," in *Because I Tell a Joke or Two: Comedy, Politics, and Social Difference*, edited by Stephen Wagg, 137–45 (London: Routledge, 1998).

33. Ibid., 140.

34. Miller, "Masculinity and Male Intimacy," 148.

35. Simpson, "The Straight Men of Comedy," 140.

36. Ibid., 142. Emphasis original.

37. While others have pushed for the dissolution of marriage's privileged status in society.
38. Becker, "Guy Love," 133, 136.
39. USA series *Common Law*, *Psych*, *White Collar*, *Suits*, and *Royal Pains* all feature a male dyad solving a medical/mystery/legal case of the week.
40. If there is a serial question driving *Psych*—which perhaps only the most serially compelled viewer might seek—it is the question of what happened in the break-up of Shawn's parents and in the college years the men seem to have spent apart that might explain why Shawn remains a veritable man-boy.
41. "At the Gay Bar," by transcendenza, http://trascendenza.livejournal.com/377798. html (accessed 4 Apr. 2012).
42. Episode 609, "Neil Simon's Lover's Retreat."
43. Episode 610, "Indiana Shawn and the Temple of the Kinda Crappy, Rusty Old Dagger."
44. Davi Johnson Thornton, "*Psych*'s Comedic Tale of Black-White Friendship and the Lighthearted Affect of 'Post-Race' America," *Critical Studies in Media Communication* 28, no. 5 (2011): 424–49, 427.
45. Murphy is clear in interviews that he intended the series as a satiric examination of the excesses in early-twenty-first-century culture. *Nip/Tuck* Paley Festival, 2/7, 8 Mar. 2007, http://www.youtube.com/watch?v=RrqTCB1tlow (accessed 11 Apr. 2012); Ryan Murphy, "Interview," *Fresh Air with Terry Gross*, 18 May 2009.
46. Episode 611, "Dan Daly."
47. Nearly every season features some sort of crisis that nearly destroys the partnership. The revelation of Matt's paternity gives Sean legal cause to dissolve the partnership without penalty and leads to one of the richest episodes (209, "Rose and Raven Rosenberg") in which the doctors join a team that attempts to separate conjoined twins at the same time Sean ostensibly is dissolving the practice. Learning of the twins' love for each other and the emotionality of the deaths lead Sean to reconsider. In other seasons, the men are threatened by a serial killer and by financial problems that force them to sell the partnership to a firm, which motivates Sean to leave and go to work for a practice in Los Angeles (but Christian ultimately follows). In another particularly key episode, 412, "Diana Lubey," the potential of homosexual love between the men is explored explicitly and sincerely and both disregard it.
48. Sean has been treating a child removed from a Romanian orphanage who is given up because of imperfections. Sean is to take the child back to the orphanage and then assist medical philanthropists there.
49. Jennifer Stoy, "Brighter Discontent: Sean McNamera, His Mid-life Crisis, and the Failure of the Individualist Transformation," in *Nip/Tuck: Television That Gets under Your Skin*, edited by Roz Kaveny and Jennifer Stoy, 172–93 (London: Tauris, 2011), 187.
50. On a few occasions other characters are privileged as voiceover narrator for the episode, but most all is presented through JD's eyes.

51. Episode 606, "My Musical."
52. Episode 109, "My Day Off."
53. Simpson, "The Straight Men of Comedy," 140.
54. See also 108, "My Fifteen Minutes"; 109, "My Day Off"; 201, "My Overkill"; and 302, "My Journey."
55. Becker, "Guy Love," 132.
56. Some might excuse this as a function of genre, but I don't find this a compelling justification. *Scrubs* can take dramatic turns. More so than most primarily comedic series, it offers nonsaccharine lessons about life and all types of relationships alongside its hijinks, often explored through JD's voiceovers.
57. Episode 401, "The Agony and the 'Ex'-tasy."
58. Alan Shore joins *The Practice* during its final season after nearly all the original cast is fired due to budgetary reasons. He is presented as an old friend of Ellenor's who is a top antitrust attorney but was recently fired for embezzlement. After he is fired from Young, Frutt, and Berlutti, he hires Crane, Poole, and Schmidt to represent him for wrongful dismissal and he is represented by Denny Crane.
59. Episode 309, "On the Ledge." Becker, "Guy Love," 132.
60. Kelli Marshall, "Bromance and the Boys of *Boston Legal*," *FlowTV*, 28 Jan. 2011, http://flowtv.org/2011/01/bromance-and-boston-legal (accessed 24 May 2012).
61. Episode 513, "Last Call."
62. Biden to interviewer David Gregory, *Meet the Press*, 6 May 2012, NBC.
63. See, for example, Kathy Battles and Wendy Hilton-Morrow, "Gay Characters in Conventional Spaces: *Will and Grace* and the Situation Comedy Genre," *Critical Studies in Media Communication* 19, no. 1 (2002): 87–105; Helen A. Shugart, "Reinventing Privilege: The New (Gay) Man in Contemporary Popular Media," *Critical Studies in Media Communication* 20, no. 1 (2003): 67–91; E. Cooper, "Decoding *Will and Grace*: Mass Audience Reception of a Popular Network's Situation Comedy," *Sociological Perspectives* 46, no. 1 (2003): 513–33; T. J. Linneman, "How Do You Solve a Problem Like Will Truman? The Feminization of Gay Masculinities on *Will and Grace*," *Men and Masculinities* 10, no. 5 (2008): 583–603; G. Avila-Saavedra, "Nothing Queer about Queer Television: Televised Construction of Gay Masculinities," *Media, Culture, and Society* 31, no. 1 (2009): 5–21; C. Castiglia and C. Reed, "'Ah Yes, I Remember It Well': Memory and Queer Culture in *Will and Grace*," *Cultural Critique* 56 (2004): 158–88. E. Schiappa, P. B. Gregg, and D. E. Hewes, "Can One TV Show Make a Difference? *Will and Grace* and the Parasocial Contact Hypothesis," *Journal of Homosexuality* 51, no. 1(2006): 15–37.
64. Kimmel, cited in Spangler, "Buddies and Pals," 93.

CONCLUSION

1. Hanna Rosin, "Primetime's Looming Male Identity Crisis," *Atlantic*, 8 Sept. 2011, http://www.theatlantic.com/entertainment/archive/2011/09/primetimes-looming-male-identity-crisis/244692 (accessed 13 Sept. 2011).

2. Amy Chozick, "A New Generation of TV Wimps," *Wall Street Journal*, 10 June 2011, http://online.wsj.com/article/SB100014240527023044323045763715536820170000.html (accessed 21 June 2011).

3. Alessandra Stanley, "Downsized and Downtrodden, Men Are the New Women on TV," *New York Times*, 11 Oct. 2011, http://tv.nytimes.com/2011/10/11/arts/television/last-man-standing-and-man-up-on-abc-review.html (accessed 15 May 2012).

4. At least in the first season. Season two finds the *Ava Show* canceled and Regan learning how to be a stay-at-home mom.

5. Robert Hanke, "The 'Mock-Macho' Situation Comedy: Hegemonic Masculinity and Its Reiteration," *Western Journal of Communication* 62, no. 1 (1998): 74–93, 75.

6. The show lost its showrunner just as it began shooting because of a personal tragedy, which unquestionably impacted its first season. The show retooled in its second season by recasting the oldest daughter and "aging" the grandson Boyd from age two to age five. Kyle's role as Mike's millennial male foil was also shifted to Boyd's father, who was recast and added as a regular cast member. Rather than the contrast of a dimwit character (Kyle), Boyd's father, Ryan, is depicted as a liberal foil to the increasingly explicitly conservative Mike.

7. Significantly, Allen, born in 1953, is firmly a Boomer. His character seems a bit younger, but is not suggested to be a member of Generation X.

8. Episode 213, "Opening Night."

9. Many of those who embodied the earlier post-second-wave contestation of patriarchal masculinities—such as *thirtysomething*'s Michael Steadman (Ken Olin)—continued television careers, but mainly behind the camera, while *Hill Street Blue*'s Frank Furillo (Daniel J. Travanti) had few roles after.

10. Amanda Marcotte, "How to Make a Critically Acclaimed TV Show about Masculinity," 6 Sept. 2011, *Good Men Project.com*, http://goodmenproject.com/arts/how-to-make-a-critically-acclaimed-tv-show-about-masculinity (accessed 8 Sept. 2011).

11. Brian McGreevy, "Pimpin' Ain't Easy: Television's Ubiquitous Alpha Males," *GQ.com*, 31 May 2012, http://www.gq.com/entertainment/tv/blogs/the-stream/2012/05/mad-men-breaking-bad-similarities-golden-age-tv.html (accessed 12 June 2012).

12. Donald N. S. Unger, *Men Can: The Changing Image and Reality of Fatherhood in America* (Philadelphia; Temple University Press, 2010).

13. Herskovitz and Zwick, Pilot Commentatary. *thirtysomething* season 1 DVD (Shout Factory, 2009). Though they thought they were providing a narrative that dealt with the feelings of ambivalence women experience in negotiating the decision to work or stay home with young children, they soon found that having Hope choose to stay home unintentionally staked a position for the series in this contentious cultural debate.

14. Albert Auster and Leonard Quart, *thirtysomething: Television, Women, Men, and Work* (Lanham, MD: Lexington Books, 2008), 38.

15. Notably, there is evidence of change within the period of study. Tony Soprano's philandering is not quite glorified, but it also isn't presented as the character flaw that develops subsequently.

16. Neil Rattigan and Thomas P. McManus, "Fathers, Sons, Brothers: Patriarchy and Guilt in 1980s American Cinema," *Journal of Popular Film and Television* 20, no. 1 (Spring 1992): 15–23, 17.

17. Notably, *thirtysomething*'s Elliot does harbor anger, but it is anger over his father's walking out on the family. Tom Schatz identifies a thematic of guilt over not knowing the father among men in *St. Elsewhere*, see Thomas Schatz, "*St. Elsewhere* and the Evolution of the Ensemble Series," in *Television: The Critical View*, 4th ed., edited by Horace Newcomb, 85–100 (New York: Oxford University Press, 1987).

18. Susan Jeffords, *Hard Bodies: Hollywood Masculinity in the Reagan Era* (New Brunswick, NJ: Rutgers University Press, 1994); David Greven, *Manhood in Hollywood from Bush to Bush* (Austin: University of Texas Press, 2009); Brenton Malin, *American Masculinity under Clinton: Popular Media and the Nineties "Crisis of Masculinity"* (New York: Peter Lang, 2008).

19. David Brooks, "The ESPN Man," *New York Times*, 14 May 2012, http://www.nytimes.com/2012/05/15/opinion/brooks-the-espn-man.html (accessed 26 June 2012). Notably, Brooks's column was widely syndicated and appeared in my local newspaper with the title "The Preboomer, Postboomer Man."

20. Michael Kimmel, *Guyland: The Perilous World Where Boys Become Men* (New York: Harper, 2009).

21. Marcotte, "How to Make."

22. Indeed, popular discussion about *The Killing*'s Sarah Linden (Mireille Enos) as a failed mother suggests the continued difficulty of reading complicated characters simply as individuals and not as indictments of feminist gain. See "Is Sarah Linden a Bad Parent?" 11 June 2011, http://tvtree.blogspot.com/2012/06/is-sarah-linden-bad-parent.html (accessed 3 Jan. 2013) or her inclusion at the top of the list of the "Ten Worst Moms on TV," http://tv.yahoo.com/photos/mothers-day-the-10–worst-moms-on-tv-this-season-slideshow/sarah-linden-mireille-enos--photo-1336762710.html (accessed 3 Jan. 2013).

23. Michael S. Kimmel, *Manhood in America: A Cultural History*, 3rd ed. (New York: Oxford University Press, 2012), 294.

Alilunas, Peter. "Male Masculinity as the Celebration of Failure: The Frat Pack, Women, and the Trauma of Victimization in the 'Dude Flick.'" *Mediascape*, 2008. Accessed June 22, 2012. http://www.tft.ucla.edu/mediascape/Spring08_MaleMasculinity.html.

Allen, Dennis W. "Making Over Masculinity: A Queer 'I' for the Straight Guy." *Genders* 44 (2006). Accessed March 19, 2009. www.genders.org/g44/g44_allen.html.

Althusser, Louis. "Ideology and Ideological State Apparatuses." In *Lenin and Philosophy and Other Essays*, translated by Ben Brewster. London: Monthly Review Press, 1971.

"anti-hero." *Answers.com*, 2012. http://www.answers.com/topic/anti-hero.

Aumann, Kerstin, Ellen Galinsky, and Kenneth Matos. "The New Male Mystique." Families and Work Institute: National Study of the Changing Workforce, 2009. Accessed December 5, 2012. familiesandwork.org/site/research/reports/main.html, 1.

Auster, Albert, and Leonard Quart. *thirtysomething: Television, Women, Men, and Work*. Lanham, MD: Lexington Books, 2008.

Avila-Saavedra, G. "Nothing Queer about Queer Television: Televized Construction of Gay Masculinities." *Media, Culture, and Society* 31, no. 1 (2009): 5–21.

Barker, David. "Television Production Techniques as Communication." *Critical Studies in Mass Communication*, September 1985: 234–46.

Battles, Kathleen. "Low Stakes TV: The Basic Cable Original Series." *Flow*, 2008. Accessed July 10, 2011. http://flowtv.org/2008/06/low-stakes-tv-%E2%80%93-the-basic-cable-original-serieskathleen-battlesoakland-university.

Battles, Kathy, and Wendy Hilton-Morrow. "Gay Characters in Conventional Spaces: *Will and Grace* and the Situation Comedy Genre." *Critical Studies in Media Communication* 19, no. 1 (2002): 87–105.

Becker, Ron. "Becoming Bromosexual: Straight Men, Gay Men, and Male Bonding on U.S. TV." In *Rad Bromance: Male Homosociality in Film and Television*, edited by Michael DeAngelis (Detroit, MI: Wayne State University Press, forthcoming).

———. *Gay TV and Straight America*. New Brunswick, NJ: Rutgers University Press, 2006.

———. "Guy Love: A Queer Straight Masculinity for a Post-Closet Era?" In *Queer TV: Theories, Histories, Politics*, edited by Glyn Davis and Gary Needham, 121–40. New York: Routledge, 2009.

Bellafante, Ginia. "Thomas Jane on *Hung*, Symbol of the Recession." *New York Times*, August 10, 2010. Accessed August 18, 2010. http://www.nytimes.com/2010/08/06/arts/television/06hung.htm.

Biden, Joe. "Interview." Interview by David Gregory. *Meet the Press*. NBC. May 6, 2012.

Boycott, Rosie. "Feminism Has Turned Men into Second-Class Citizens, but Have Women's Victories Come at a Price?" *Daily Mail*, 2008. Accessed April 26, 2012. http://www.dailymail.co.uk/femail/article-512550/Feminism-turned-men-second-class-citizens-womens-victories-come-price.html.

Boyer, Peter J. "TV Turns to the Hard-Boiled Male." *New York Times*, February 16, 1986. Accessed June 10, 2009. http://www.nytimes.com/1986/02/16/arts/tv-turns-to-the-hard-boiled-male.html?sec=&spon=&&scp=1&sq=TV%20turns%20to%20the%20hard-boiled%20male&st=cse.

Brooks, David. "The ESPN Man." *New York Times*, May 14, 2012. Accessed June 26, 2012. http://www.nytimes.com/2012/05/15/opinion/brooks-the-espn-man.html.

Brooks, Tim, and Earle Marsh. *The Complete Directory to Prime Time Network and Cable TV Shows 1946–Present*. 9th ed. New York: Ballantine, 2007.

Brown, H. G. "How to Outfox TV's New Breed of Macho Man." *TV Guide* 34, no. 31 (1986): 10–12.

Bruzzi, Stella. *Bringing Up Daddy: Fatherhood and Masculinity in Post War Hollywood*. London: British Film Institute, 2005.

Butler, Judith. *Bodies That Matter: On the Discursive Limits of "Sex."* New York: Routledge, 1993.

———. *Gender Trouble: Feminism and the Subversion of Identity*. New York: Routledge, 1990.

Carroll, Hamilton. *Affirmative Reaction: New Formations of White Masculinity*. Durham, NC: Duke University Press, 2011.

———. "Men's Soaps: Automotive Television Programming and Contemporary Working-Class Masculinities." *Television & New Media* 9, no. 4 (2008): 263–83.

Castiglia, C., and C. Reed. "'Ah Yes, I Remember It Well': Memory and Queer Culture in *Will and Grace*." *Cultural Critique* 56 (2004): 158–88.

Chozick, Amy. "A New Generation of TV Wimps." *Wall Street Journal*, June 10, 2011. Accessed June 21, 2011. http://online.wsj.com/article/SB10001424052702304432304576371553682017000.html.

Coates, Jennifer. *Men Talk: Stories in the Making of Masculinities*. Malden, MA: Blackwell, 2003.

Cobley, Paul. "'Who Loves Ya, Baby?': *Kojak*, Action, and the Great Society." In *Action TV: Tough Guys, Smooth Operators, and Foxy Chicks*, edited by Bill Osgerby and Anna Gough-Yates, 53–68. London: Routledge, 2001.

Cohan, Steve. "Queer Eye for the Straight Guise: Camp, Postfeminism, and the Fab Five's Makeovers of Masculinity." In *Interrogating Postfeminism: Gender and the Politics of Popular Culture*, edited by Yvonne Tasker and Diane Negra, 176–200. Durham, NC: Duke University Press, 2007.

Cohan, Steve, and Ina Rae Hark, eds. *Screening the Male: Exploring Masculinities in the Hollywood Cinema.* New York: Routledge, 1993.

Connell, R. W. "An Iron Man: The Body and Some Contradictions of Hegemonic Masculinity." In *Sport, Men, and the Gender Order: Critical Feminist Perspectives,* edited by Michael Messner and Don Sabo, 83–95. Champaign, IL: Human Kinetics Books, 1990.

———. *Masculinities.* 2nd ed. Berkeley: University of California Press, 2005.

Connell, R. W., and James W. Messerschmidt. "Hegemonic Masculinity: Rethinking the Concept," *Gender & Society* 19, no. 6 (December 2005): 829–59.

Consoli, John. "What Are Men Watching Other Than Sports in Broadcast TV Prime-time?" *Broadcasting & Cable,* December 14, 2012. Accessed December 20, 2012. http://www.broadcastingcable.com/article/490878–What_Are_Men_Watching_ Other _Than_Sports_in_Broadcast_TV_Primetime_.php?rssid=20065.

Coontz, Stephanie. "Sharing the Load." In *The Shriver Report: A Woman's Nation,* edited by Heather Boushey and Ann O'Leary. New York: Free Press, 2009.

———. "The Myth of Male Decline." *New York Times,* September 29, 2012. Accessed October 2, 2012. http://www.nytimes.com/2012/09/30/opinion/sunday/the-myth-of-male-decline.html?pagewanted=3&_r=0&ref=general&src=me&pagewanted=p rint.

Cooper, Evan. "Decoding *Will and Grace*: Mass Audience Reception of a Popular Network's Situation Comedy." *Sociological Perspectives* 46, no. 1 (2003): 513–33.

Dawson, Max. "Network Television's 'Lost Boys': TV, New Media, and the 'Elusive' Male Viewer." Society of Cinema and Media Studies. Philadelphia, PA, March 2008.

Desjardins, Mary. "Lucy and Desi: Sexuality, Ethnicity, and TV's First Family." In *Television, History, and American Culture: Feminist Critical Essays,* edited by Mary Beth and Lauren Rabinovitz, 56–73. Durham, NC: Duke University Press, 1999.

Donalson, Melvin. *Masculinity in the Interracial Buddy Film.* Jefferson, NC: McFarland, 2006.

Doty, Alexander. "Introduction: What Makes Queerness Most?" In *Making Things Perfectly Queer: Interpreting Mass Culture,* xi-xix. Minneapolis: University of Minnesota Press, 1993.

Douglas, Susan. *Where the Girls Are: Growing Up Female with the Mass Media.* New York: Times Books, 1994.

Draper, Jimmy, and Amanda D. Lotz. "Making Sense of Homophobia in *Rescue Me*: Working Through as Ideological Intervention." *Television & New Media* 13, no. 6 (2012): 520–34.

"Educational Attainment." *United States Census Bureau.* 2008. Accessed May 10, 2011. http://www.census.gov/compendia/statab/cats/education/educational_attainment. html.

Ehrenreich, Barbara. *Hearts of Men: American Dreams and the Flight from Commitment.* Garden City, NY: Anchor Press, 1983.

Etzioni, Amitai. "Nice Guys Finish First." *Public Opinion* 7, no. 14 (1984): 16–18.

Faludi, Susan. *Backlash: The Undeclared War against American Women*. New York: Crown, 1991.

———. *Stiffed: The Betrayal of the American Man*. New York: Morrow, 1999.

———. *The Terror Dream: Myth and Misogyny in an Insecure America*. New York: Picador, 2008.

Fejes, Fred. "Images of Men in Media Research." *Critical Studies in Mass Communication*, June 1989: 215–21.

"Fictional Characters That Inspire: TV's Jack Bauer." Narrated by Robert Siegel. *All Things Considered*. NPR, January 28, 2008. Accessed July 17, 2011. http://www.npr.org/templates/story/story.php?storyId=18491526.

Fiske, John. *Television Culture*. London: Routledge, 1987.

Friedan, Betty. *The Feminine Mystique*. New York: Norton, 1963.

Fuchs, Cynthia J. "The Buddy Politic." In *Screening the Male: Exploring Masculinities in Hollywood Cinema*, edited by Steven Cohan and Ina Rae Hark, 194–210. New York: Routledge, 1993.

Gilbert, James. "The Ozzie Show: Learning Companionate Fatherhood." In *Men in the Middle: Searching for Masculinity in the 1950s*, 135–63. Chicago: University of Chicago Press, 2005.

Gilbert, Matthew. "Killer Serial." *Slate*, December 2008. Accessed July 20, 2011. http://www.slate.com/id/2206519.

Gilligan, Vince. "Interview: *Breaking Bad* Creator Vince Gilligan Post-Mortems Season 4." Interview by Alan Sipinwall. *Hitfix*, October 10, 2011. Accessed January 3, 2012. http://www.hitfix.com/blogs/whats-alan-watching/posts/interview-breaking-bad-creator-vince-gilligan-post-mortems-season-4.

———. "Vince Gilligan Walks Us through *Breaking Bad*'s Fourth Season (Part 1 of 4)." Interview by Todd VanDerWerff. *The AV Club*, October 10, 2011. Accessed May 31, 2012. http://www.avclub.com/articles/vince-gilligan-walks-us-through-season-four-of-bre,63013.

———. "Vince Gilligan Walks Us through *Breaking Bad*'s Fourth Season (Part 2 of 4)." Interview by Todd VanDerWerff. *The AV Club*, October 11, 2011. Accessed May 31, 2012. http://www.avclub.com/articles/vince-gilligan-walks-us-through-breaking-bads-4th,63113.

———. "Vince Gilligan Walks Us through *Breaking Bad*'s Fourth Season (Part 4 of 4)." Interview by Todd VanDerWerff. *The AV Club*, October 13, 2011. Accessed May 31, 2012. http://www.avclub.com/articles/vince-gilligan-walks-us-through-breaking-bads-four,63288.

Goodman, Tim. "They Steal, They Cheat, They Lie, and We Wouldn't Have it Any Other Way: The Timeless Appeal of the Anti-Hero." *San Francisco Chronicle*, June 22, 2005: E1.

Gray, Jonathan, Jeffrey P. Jones, and Ethan Thompson. *Satire TV: Politics and Comedy in the Post-Network Era*. New York: New York University Press, 2009.

Greven, David. "Dude, Where's My Gender? Contemporary Teen Comedies and New Forms of American Masculinity." *Cineaste* 27, no. 23 (June 2002): 14–21.

———. "Fears of Millennial Masculinity: *Scream*'s Queer Killers." In *Rad Bromance: Male Homosociality in Film and Television*, edited by Michael DeAngelis (Detroit, MI: Wayne State University Press, forthcoming).

———. *Manhood in Hollywood from Bush to Bush*. Austin: University of Texas Press, 2009.

Grose, Jessica. "Omega Males and the Women Who Hate Them." *Slate*, March 18, 2010. Accessed July 18, 2011. http://www.slate.com/id/2248156.

Gross, Robert F. "Driving in Circles: *The Rockford Files*." In *Considering David Chase: Essays on* The Rockford Files, Northern Exposure, *and* The Sopranos, edited by Thomas Fahy, 29–45. Jefferson, NC: McFarland, 2008.

Guerrero, Ed. "The Black Image in Protective Custody: Hollywood's Biracial Buddy Films of the Eighties." In *Black American Cinema*, edited by Manthia Diawara, 237–46. New York: Routledge, 1993.

Halberstam, J. Jack. *Gaga Feminism: Sex, Gender, and the End of Normal*. Boston: Beacon, 2012.

Halberstam, Judith. *Female Masculinity*. Durham, NC: Duke University Press, 1998.

Hamamoto, Darrell. *Nervous Laughter: Television Situation Comedy and Liberal Democratic Ideology*. New York: Praeger, 1989.

Hanke, Robert. "Hegemonic Masculinity in *thirtysomething*." *Critical Studies in Mass Communication* 7 (1990): 231–48.

———. "On Masculinity: Theorizing Masculinity with/in the Media." *Communication Theory* 8, no. 2 (1998): 183–203.

———. "The 'Mock-Macho' Situation Comedy: Hegemonic Masculinity and Its Reiteration." *Western Journal of Communication* 6, no. 1 (1998): 74–93.

Hart, Kylo-Patrick. "Representing Gay Men on American Television." *Journal of Men's Studies* 9, no. 1 (2000): 59–79.

Havrilesky, Heather. "In Defense of the Aging Frat Boy." *Salon.com*, October 29, 2009. Accessed January 9, 2010. http://www.salon.com/ent/tv/iltw/2009/10/28/aging_frat_boy_the_league_men_of_a_certain_age/print.html.

———. "*Men of a Certain Age, Community*: The Meek Inherit Your TV." *Salon.com*, December 20, 2009. Accessed January 9, 2010. http://www.salon.com/ent/tv/iltw/2009/10/28/aging_frat_boy_the_league_men_of_a_certain_age/print.html.

Henson, Lori, and Radhika E. Parameswaran. "Getting Real with 'Tell It Like It Is' Talk Therapy: Hegemonic Masculinity and the *Dr. Phil Show*." *Communication, Culture & Critique* 1 (2008): 287–310.

Herskovitz, Marshall, and Edward Zwick. "Pilot Commentaries." *Thirtysomething*. DVD. Directed by Marshall Herskovitz, 1987. Los Angeles: Shout Factory, 2009.

Hochschild, Arlie. *The Second Shift: Working Parents and the Revolution at Home*. New York: Viking, 1989.

Holloway, Diane. "Tortured Souls Are the New Breed of Antihero." *Cox News Service*, October 2006. Accessed July 20, 2011. http://www.thestar.com/entertainment/article/107075--cold-blooded-villains-now-tv-heroes.

Hollows, Joanne. "Oliver's Twist: Leisure, Labour, and Domestic Masculinity in *The Naked Chef*." *International Journal of Cultural Studies* 6, no. 2 (2003): 229–48.

hooks, bell. *Ain't I a Woman: Black Women and Feminism*. New York: South End Press, 1981.

Howard, Douglas L. "An Interview with *Dexter* Writer and Developer James Manos, Jr." In *Dexter: Investigating Cutting Edge Television*, 14–26. London: Tauris, 2010.

Hymowitz, Kay. *Manning Up: How the Rise of Women Has Turned Men into Boys*. New York: Basic Books, 2011.

Jeffords, Susan. *Hard Bodies: Hollywood Masculinity in the Reagan Era*. New Brunswick, NJ: Rutgers University Press, 1994.

Johnson, Derek. "That Other Jack." *Antenna*, May 2010. Accessed August 25, 2010. http://blog.commarts.wisc.edu/2010/05/25/that-other-jack.

Kellner, Douglas. *Media Culture: Cultural Studies, Identity, and Politics between the Modern and the Postmodern*. London: Routledge, 1995.

Kiesling, Scott F. "Men's Identities and Sociolinguistic Variation: The Case of Fraternity Men." *Journal of Sociolinguistics* 2, no. 1 (1998): 69–100.

Kimbrell, Andrew. *The Masculine Mystique: The Politics of Masculinity*. New York: Ballantine, 1995.

Kimmel, Michael. *Guyland: The Perilous World Where Boys Become Men*. New York: Harper, 2009.

———. *Manhood in America: A Cultural History*. 2nd ed. New York: Oxford University Press, 2006.

———. *Manhood in America: A Cultural History*. 3rd ed. New York: Oxford University Press, 2012.

King, Andrew. "The Politics of 'Dirt' in *Dirty Jobs*." *Flow* 13, no. 1 (2010). Accessed July 20, 2011. http://flowtv.org/2010/10/the-politics-of-%E2%80%98dirt%E2%80%99-in-dirty-jobs.

King, Scott Benjamin. "Sonny's Virtues: The Gender Negotiations of *Miami Vice*." *Screen* 31, no. 3 (1990): 281–95.

Klinenberg, Eric. *Going Solo: The Extraordinary Rise and Surprising Appeal of Living Alone*. New York: Penguin, 2012.

Leary, Denis. "Interview: 20 Questions with Denis Leary." Interview by Kristopher Tapley. *Incontention.com*. Accessed June 24, 2010. http://www.incontention.com/?p=9546.

Lee, Nancy. "'Let's Hug It Out, Bitch!': The Negotiation of Hegemony and Homosociality through Speech in HBO's *Entourage*." *Culture, Society & Masculinity* 2, no. 2 (2010): 181–98.

Lehman, Peter, ed. *Masculinity: Bodies, Movies, Culture*. New York: Routledge, 2001.

Linneman, T. J. "How Do You Solve a Problem Like Will Truman? The Feminization of Gay Masculinities on *Will and Grace*." *Men and Masculinities* 10, no. 5 (2008): 583–603.

Lipsitz, George. "The Meaning of Memory: Family, Class, and Ethnicity in Early Network Television Programs." In *Private Screenings: Television and the Female Consumer*, edited by Lynn Spigel and Denise Mann, 71–108. Minneapolis: University of Minnesota Press, 1992.

Littlejohn, Janice Rhoshalle. "Sensitive Men Take TV by Storm." *Florida Today*, August 22, 2007.

Lockett, Christopher. "Masculinity and Authenticity: Reality TV's Real Men." *Flow* 13, no. 1 (2010). Accessed July 20, 2011. http://flowtv.org/2010/10/masculinity-and-authenticity/.

Lotz, Amanda D. "If It's Not TV, What Is It? The Case of U.S. Subscription Television." In *Cable Visions: Television beyond Broadcasting*, edited by Sarah Banet-Weiser, Cynthia Chris, and Anthony Freitas, 85–102. New York: New York University Press, 2007.

———. *Redesigning Women: Television after the Network Era*. Urbana-Champaign: University of Illinois Press, 2006.

———. *The Television Will Be Revolutionized*. New York: New York University Press, 2007.

Malin, Brenton. *American Masculinity under Clinton: Popular Media and the Nineties "Crisis of Masculinity."* New York: Peter Lang, 2008.

Marcotte, Amanda. "How to Make a Critically Acclaimed TV Show about Masculinity." *GoodMenProject.com*, September 6, 2011. Accessed September 8, 2011. http://goodmen project.com/arts/how-to-make-a-critically-acclaimed-tv-show-about-masculinity.

Marshall, Kelli. "Bromance and the Boys of *Boston Legal*." *FlowTV*, January 28, 2011. Accessed May 24, 2012. http://flowtv.org/2011/01/bromance-and-boston-legal.

McGreevy, Brian. "'Pimpin' Ain't Easy': Television's Ubiquitous Alpha Males." *GQ.com*, May 31, 2012. Accessed June 12, 2012. http://www.gq.com/entertainment/tv/blogs/the-stream/2012/05/mad-men-breaking-bad-similarities-golden-age-tv.html.

Mellencamp, Patricia. "Situation Comedy, Feminism, and Freud: Discourses of Gracie and Lucy." In *Studies of Entertainment: Critical Approaches to Mass Culture*, edited by Tania Modleski, 80–95. Bloomington: Indiana University Press, 1986.

Miller, Margo. "Masculinity and Male Intimacy in Nineties Sitcoms: *Seinfeld* and the Ironic Dismissal." In *The New Queer Aesthetic on Television*, edited by James R. Keller and Leslie Stratyner, 147–59. Jefferson, NC: McFarland, 2006.

Mills, Brett. *The Sitcom*. Edinburgh, Scotland: Edinburgh University Press, 2009.

Mittell, Jason. "Serial Characterization and Inferred Interiority." *In Media Res*, 2011. Accessed January 3, 2012. http://mediacommons.futureofthebook.org/imr/2011/12/14/serial-characterization-and-inferred-interiority.

Moody, Nickianne. "'A Lone Crusader in the Dangerous World': Heroics of Science and Technology in Knight Rider." In *Action TV: Tough Guys, Smooth Operators, and Foxy Chicks*, edited by Bill Osgerby and Anna Gough-Yates, 69–80. London: Routledge, 2001.

Moseley, Rachel. "'Real Lads Do Cook . . . But Some Things Are Still Hard to Talk About': The Gendering of 8–9." *European Journal of Cultural Studies* 4, no. 1 (2001): 32–39.

Murphy, Ryan. "Interview." Interview by Terry Gross. *Fresh Air with Terry Gross*. NPR, May 18, 2009.

Murray, Susan. "Lessons from Uncle Miltie." In *Hitch Your Antenna to the Stars: Early Television and Broadcast Stardom*, 65–92. New York: Routledge, 2005.

Newcomb, Horace. "Magnum: The Champagne of TV." *Channels of Communication* 5, no. 1 (1985): 23–26.

Newcomb, Horace, and Paul Hirsh. "Television as a Cultural Forum." In *Television: The Critical View*, edited by Horace Newcomb, 505–13. New York: Oxford University Press, 1994.

Osgerby, Bill. "'So You're the Famous Simon Templar': The Saint, Masculinity, and Consumption in the Early 1960s." In *Action TV: Tough Guys, Smooth Operators, and Foxy Chicks*, edited by Bill Osgerby and Anna Gough-Yates, 32–52. London: Routledge, 2001.

Paley Festival. "*Breaking Bad*: Aaron Paul Almost Got Killed Off (Paley Interview)." *YouTube* video. 3:45, June 21, 2012. http://www.youtube.com/watch?v=YqnoJ1oHqP0.

———. "*Nip/Tuck*: Part 2/7." *YouTube* video. 9:47, March 22, 2010. http://www.youtube.com/watch?v=RrqTCB1tlow.

Paterson, Peter. "Television Mail: Oldest Sinners in Town." *Daily Mail*, February 20, 2002: 61.

Pearson, Roberta. "Anatomizing Gilbert Grissom: The Structure and Function of the Televisual Character." In *Reading CSI: Crime TV under the Microscope,*, edited by Michael Allen, 39–56. London: Tauris, 2007.

Penley, Constance, and Sharon Willis, eds. *Male Trouble.* Minneapolis: University of Minnesota Press, 1993.

Pennicott, Elaine. "'Who's the Cat That Won't Cop Out?': Black Masculinity in American Action Series of the Sixties and Seventies." In *Action TV: Tough Guys, Smooth Operators, and Foxy Chicks*, edited by Bill Osgerby and Anna Gough-Yates, 100–114. London: Routledge, 2001.

Pomerance, Murray. "The Bromance Stunt in *House*." In *Rad Bromance: Male Homosociality in Film and Television*, edited by Michael DeAngelis (Detroit, MI: Wayne State University Press, forthcoming).

Pomerance, Murray, and Frances Gateward, eds. *Where the Boys Are: Cinemas of Masculinity and Youth.* Detroit, MI: Wayne State University Press, 2005.

Pumphrey, Martin. "The Games We Play(ed): TV Westerns, Memory, and Masculinity." In *Action TV: Tough Guys, Smooth Operators, and Foxy Chicks*, edited by Bill Osgerby and Anna Gough-Yates, 145–58. London: Routledge, 2001.

Rattigan, Neil, and Thomas P. McManus. "Fathers, Sons, Brothers: Patriarchy and Guilt in 1980s American Cinema." *Journal of Popular Film and Television* 20, no. 1 (Spring 1992): 15–23.

Ray, Robert B. *A Certain Tendency of the Hollywood Cinema, 1930–1980.* Oxford: Oxford University Press, 1985.

Rollins, Peter C., and John E. O'Connor, eds. The West Wing: *The American Presidency as Television Drama.* Syracuse, NY: Syracuse University Press, 2003.

Rosin, Hanna. "Primetime's Looming Male Identity Crisis." *Atlantic*, September 8, 2011. Accessed September 13, 2011. http://www.theatlantic.com/entertainment/archive/2011/09/primetimes-looming-male-identity-crisis/244692.

———. "The End of Men." *Atlantic*, July/August 2010. Accessed November 3, 2010. http://www.theatlantic.com/magazine/archive/2010/07/the-end-of-men/8135.

———. *The End of Men: And the Rise of Women*. New York: Riverhead Books, 2012.

Ross, Andrew. "Masculinity and *Miami Vice*: Selling In." *Oxford Literary Review* 8 (1986): 143–54.

Ryan, Maureen. "The Watcher: Serial Dramas, Anti-Heroes under Scrutiny." *Chicago Tribune*, July 16, 2006. Accessed July 20, 2011. http://articles.chicagotribune.com/2006-07-17/features/0607170160_1_tommy-gavin-heroes-serialized.

Sandell, Jillian. "Reinventing Masculinity: The Spectacle of Male Intimacy in the Films of John Woo." *Film Quarterly* 49, no. 4 (1996): 23–34.

Sandoval, Chela. "U.S. Third World Feminism: The Theory and Method of Oppositional Consciousness in a Postmodern World." *Genders* 10 (1991): 1–24.

Sax, Leonard. *Boys Adrift*. New York: Basic Books, 2009.

Schatz, Thomas. "*St. Elsewhere* and the Evolution of the Ensemble Series." In *Television: The Critical View*, edited by Horace Newcomb, 85–100. New York: Oxford University Press, 1987.

Schiappa, Edward, Peter B. Gregg, and Dean E. Hewes. "Can One TV Show Make a Difference? *Will and Grace* and the Parasocial Contact Hypothesis." *Journal of Homosexuality* 51, no. 1 (2006): 15–37.

Sconce, Jeffrey. "What If? Charting Television's New Textual Boundaries." In *Television after TV*, edited by Lynn Spigel and Jan Olsson, 93–112. Durham, NC: Duke University Press, 2004.

Scott, James C. *Domination and the Arts of Resistance: Hidden Transcripts*. New Haven, CT: Yale University Press, 1990.

Sedgwick, Eve Kosofsky. *Epistemology of the Closet*. Berkeley: University of California Press, 1990.

Segal, David. "The Dark Art of *Breaking Bad*." *New York Times*, July 6, 2011. Accessed June 21, 2012. http://www.nytimes.com/2011/07/10/magazine/the-dark-art-of-breaking-bad.html?pagewanted=all.

Sepinwall, Alan. *The Revolution Was Televised: The Cops, Crooks, Slingers, and Slayers Who Changed TV Drama Forever*. Self-published by Alan Sepinwall, 2012.

Shales, Tom. "The Tough Guy Makes a Comeback." *Washington Post*, January 29, 1984: C1, C9.

Shimizu, Celine Parrenas. *Straightjacket Sexualities: Unbinding Asian American Manhoods in the Movies*. Palo Alto, CA: Stanford University Press, 2012.

Shugart, Helen A. "Reinventing Privilege: The New (Gay) Man in Contemporary Popular Media." *Critical Studies in Media Communication* 20, no. 1 (2003): 67–91.

Simpson, Mark. "The Straight Men of Comedy." In *Because I Tell a Joke or Two: Comedy, Politics, and Social Difference*, edited by Stephen Wagg, 137–45. London: Routledge, 1998.

Smith, Lynn. "TV's Role: Produce Male Leads; Shows Shift Attention to More Mature Complex Characters." *Ann Arbor News*, December 19, 2007: C5.

Spangler, Lynn C. "Buddies and Pals: A History of Male Friendships on Prime-Time Television." In *Men, Masculinity, and the Media*, edited by Steve Craig, 93–110. Newbury Park, CA: Sage, 1992.

Spigel, Lynn. *Make Room for TV: Television and the Family Ideal in Post-War America.* Chicago: University of Chicago Press, 1992.

Stanley, Alessandra. "Downsized and Downtrodden, Men are the New Women on TV." *New York Times*, October 11, 2011. Accessed May 15, 2011. http://tv.nytimes. com/2011/10/11/arts/television/last-man-standing-and-man-up-on-abc-review.html.

———. "Men with a Message: Help Wanted." *New York Times*, January 3, 2010. Accessed July 20, 2011. http://www.nytimes.com/2010/01/03/arts/television/03alpha. html?sq=men%20with%20a%20message&st=nyt&adxnnl=1&scp=1&adxn nlx=1311185095-yTx3XZY/Yr7y7fBD4Q2ddg.

Stoy, Jennifer. "Brighter Discontent: Sean McNamera, His Mid-life Crisis, and the Failure of the Individualist Transformation." In *Nip/Tuck: Television That Gets under Your Skin*, edited by Roz Kaveny and Jennifer Stoy, 172–93,187. London: Tauris, 2011.

Sutter, Kurt. "Sons of Anarchy: Kurt Sutter Q&A." Interview by Alan Sepinwall. *What Is Alan Watching,* November 26, 2008. Accessed September 8, 2011. http://sepinwall. blogspot.com/2008/11/sons-of-anarchy-kurt-sutter-q.html.

Tankle, Jonathan David, and Barbara Jane Banks. *The Boys of Prime Time: An Analysis of "New" Male Roles in Television.* Vol. 4 in *Studies in Communication*, edited by Sari Thomas, 285–90. Norwood, NJ: Ablex, 1986.

Tasker, Yvonne. "Kung-Fu: Re-Orienting the Television Western." In *Action TV: Tough Guys, Smooth Operators, and Foxy Chicks*, edited by Bill Osgerby and Anna Gough-Yates, 115–26. London: Routledge, 2001.

Thomas, June. "Television's First Great Brocedural." *Slate*, June 13, 2012. Accessed June 14, 2012. http://www.slate.com/blogs/browbeat/2012/06/13/brocedural_franklin_ bash_on_tnt_is_tv_s_first_great_brocedural_.html.

Thornton, Davi Johnson. "*Psych's* Comedic Tale of Black-White Friendship and the Lighthearted Affect of 'Post-Race' America." *Critical Studies in Media Communication* 28, no. 5 (2011): 424–49, 427.

Torres, Sasha. "Melodrama, Masculinity, and the Family: *thirtysomething* as Therapy." *Camera Obscura* 19 (1989): 86–107.

transcendenza. "Psych: At the Gay Bar." *Live Journal,* January 19, 2010. Accessed April 4, 2012. http://trascendenza.livejournal.com/377798.html.

Trujillo, Nick. "Hegemonic Masculinity on the Mound: Media Representations of Nolan Ryan and American Sports Culture." *Critical Studies in Mass Communication* 8 (1994): 290–308, 291–92.

Tuchman, Gaye, Arlene Kaplan Daniels, and James Benet, eds. *Hearth and Home: Images of Women in the Mass Media.* New York: Oxford University Press, 1978.

Tueth, Michael V. "Breaking and Entering: Transgressive Comedy on Television." In *The Sitcom Reader: America Viewed and Skewed*, edited by Mary M. Dalton and Laura R. Linder, 25–34. Albany: State University of New York Press, 2005.

Unger, Donald N. S. *Men Can: The Changing Image and Reality of Fatherhood in America*. Philadelphia: Temple University Press, 2010.

Vavrus, Mary Douglas. "Domesticating Patriarchy: Hegemonic Masculinity and Television's 'Mr. Mom.'" *Critical Studies in Media Communication* 19, no. 3 (2002): 352–75.

Warner, Michael. "Introduction." In *Fear of a Queer Planet: Queer Politics and Social Theory*, edited by Michael Warner, vii-xxxi. Minneapolis: University of Minnesota Press, 1993.

Warren, Elizabeth, and Amelia Warren Tyagi. *The Two-Income Trap: Why Middle-Class Mothers and Fathers Are Going Broke*. New York: Basic Books, 2003.

Weber, Brenda R. "What Makes the Man: Masculinity and the Self-Made (Over) Man." In *Makeover TV: Selfhood, Citizenship, and Celebrity*, 171–212. Durham, NC: Duke University Press, 2009.

Whittier, Nancy. *Feminist Generations: The Persistence of the Radical Women's Movement*. Philadelphia: Temple University Press, 1995.

Williams, Raymond. "Base and Superstructure in Marxist Cultural Theory." *New Left Review* 82 (1973): 3–16.

Wood, Robin. *Hollywood from Vietnam to Reagan*. New York: Columbia University Press, 1986.

Amanda D. Lotz is Associate Professor of Communication Studies at the University of Michigan. She is the author of *The Television Will Be Revolutionized* and *Redesigning Women: Television after the Network Era*; coauthor of *Understanding Media Industries* and *Television Studies*; and editor of *Beyond Prime Time: Television Programming in the Post-Network Era*.